A Da Capo Press Reprint Series

FRANKLIN D. ROOSEVELT
AND THE ERA OF THE NEW DEAL
GENERAL EDITOR : FRANK FREIDEL
*Harvard University*

———————

# SIX RURAL PROBLEM AREAS:
# RELIEF - RESOURCES -
# REHABILITATION

# Division of Research
## Work Projects Administration

# Research Monographs

Works Progress Administration
Division of Social Research
Research Monograph I

# SIX RURAL PROBLEM AREAS: RELIEF — RESOURCES — REHABILITATION

*An Analysis of the Human and Material Resources in
Six Rural Areas with High Relief Rates*

By P.G. Beck and M.C. Forster

DA CAPO PRESS • NEW YORK • 1971

A Da Capo Press Reprint Edition

This Da Capo Press edition of *Six Rural Problem Areas: Relief — Resources — Rehabilitation* is an unabridged republication of the first edition published in Washington, D.C., in 1935. It is reprinted by permission from a copy of the original edition owned by the Harvard College Library.

Library of Congress Catalog Card Number 71-165679
ISBN 0-306-70333-5

Published by Da Capo Press, Inc.
A Subsidiary of Plenum Publishing Corporation
227 West 17th Street, New York, N.Y. 10011
All Rights Reserved

Manufactured in the United States of America

# SIX RURAL PROBLEM AREAS: RELIEF - RESOURCES - REHABILITATION

FEDERAL EMERGENCY RELIEF ADMINISTRATION
DIVISION OF RESEARCH, STATISTICS AND FINANCE
RESEARCH SECTION

# SIX RURAL PROBLEM AREAS
# RELIEF - RESOURCES - REHABILITATION

An Analysis of the Human and Material Resources in
Six Rural Areas with High Relief Rates

BY

### P. G. BECK
AND
### M. C. FORSTER
OF THE RURAL RESEARCH UNIT

## RESEARCH MONOGRAPH

## I

WASHINGTON
1935

FEDERAL EMERGENCY RELIEF ADMINISTRATION

HARRY L. HOPKINS, *Administrator*

*Division of Research, Statistics and Finance*
CORRINGTON GILL

*Research Section*
HOWARD B. MYERS

# LETTER OF TRANSMITTAL

## FEDERAL EMERGENCY RELIEF ADMINISTRATION

Washington, D. C., September 20, 1935.

Sir: I have the honor to transmit herewith a report dealing with relief, resources, and rehabilitation in six rural high relief rate areas. The nature of the problems involved in these areas indicates the necessity for a fundamental readjustment of people and natural resources if the factors responsible for the relief situation are to be mitigated.

The survey was made during the summer of 1934 under the direction of Dwight Sanderson, Coördinator of Rural Research, June 1934—December 1934; E. D. Tetreau, Research Analyst; J. O. Babcock, Associate Research Analyst; and P. G. Beck, Associate Research Analyst.

The field work was carried out by the following area directors:

*Dr. E. L. Kirkpatrick*, Professor of Rural Sociology, University of Wisconsin, Madison, Wisconsin—Lake States Cut-Over Area.

*Dr. Paul H. Landis*, Assistant Professor of Sociology, South Dakota State College, Brookings, South Dakota—Spring Wheat Area.

*Professor B. F. Coen*, Professor of Sociology, Colorado State College, Fort Collins, Colorado—Winter Wheat Area.

*Dr. T. G. Standing*, Associate Professor of Sociology, University of Iowa, Iowa City, Iowa—Appalachian-Ozark Area.

*Dr. Harold C. Hoffsommer*, Associate Professor of Sociology, Alabama Polytechnic Institute, Auburn, Alabama—Eastern Cotton Belt.

*Dr. Z. B. Wallin*, Professor of Economics, Oklahoma State College, Stillwater, Oklahoma—Western Cotton Area.

This report was prepared by P. G. Beck and M. C. Forster. Both the survey and the preparation of the report were under the general direction of Howard B. Myers, Assistant Director in charge of research. Acknowledgement is due J. H. Kolb, Coordinator of Rural Research, March 1935 to September 1935, for constructive criticism during the preparation of this report. Acknowledgement is also made of the many other departments and individuals contributing to the survey.

CORRINGTON GILL,
*Assistant Administrator*
*Division of Research, Statistics and Finance.*

Hon. HARRY L. HOPKINS,
*Federal Emergency Relief Administrator.*

## CONTENTS

## TEXT TABLES

## FIGURES

CONTENTS                                         VII

## SUPPLEMENTARY FIGURES
### (Appendix B)

# SUMMARY

1.  The 65 counties surveyed are representative of six areas
which include approximately one-half of the rural families receiving relief in the United States. These areas included 36
percent of the rural population and 43 percent of the farmers
(about one-third of the farm owners, almost one-half of the farm
tenants and more than four-fifths of the farm croppers) of the
United States in 1930. More than three-fourths of all Negro
farmers were in the two Cotton Areas.

2.  Within each of these Problem Areas there are large amounts
of poor farm land which form one of the chief factors responsible
for the more or less permanent nature of the relief problem,
although this is less true of the Western Cotton Area than of the
other areas.

3.  Although two-thirds of the families receiving relief in the
counties surveyed lived in the open country, and 55 percent of
the heads of families were usually engaged in agriculture, the
problem of assisting these families to become self-supporting
is by no means wholly an agricultural one. Except in the Spring
Wheat Area where drought was the chief factor, 32 to 70 percent
of the heads of families were usually engaged in non-agricultural
occupations and many of the farmers were receiving relief because
of the loss of supplementary employment.

4.  The causes underlying the necessity for relief and consequently the methods necessary for permanent rehabilitation are
essentially different for the various areas.

   a.  In the Appalachian-Ozark Area the relief households have
       largely depended upon subsistence farming with supple-
       mentary employment for cash income. Better methods of
       farming on better land with new sources of supplementary
       employment will be necessary. The reasons assigned for
       families receiving relief in this area were in the main
       reasons which indicated loss of supplementary employment.
       This area is also suffering from over-population which
       will be alleviated only through emigration, education,
       and the development of a higher standard of living.

   b.  In the Lake States Cut-Over Area the problem is mainly one
       of loss of employment in mining and lumbering, combined

1

with a too rapid development of small farming on marginal
land. The most promising solution for the latter condition is wide adoption of the zoning regulations now being
set up by counties in Wisconsin, and the reforestation
of large areas.  Stranded mining populations will have
to be moved or new kinds of industrial employment developed. Further development of recreational resources will
also provide seasonal employment for a small proportion
of the population.

c.  In the Short-Grass Wheat Areas the major cause of relief
has been the unusual drought, but it must be recognized
that periodically recurring dry years are the rule in the
short-grass territory and that much land has been put
under the plow which should have remained in grass. Here,
again, some method of land classification and zoning which
will limit the attempt to cultivate land where normal
rainfall is so small as to make farming too hazardous a
gamble will be necessary, and some of the present surplus
population on this type of land will be forced to emigrate.

d.  In the Cotton Areas, particularly in the Eastern Cotton
Belt, the relief problem is complicated by the gradual
breaking down of the share-cropper and "furnishing" system
which has dominated the South since the period of reconstruction after the Civil War, and the consequent need for
public relief by aged Negroes and female Negroes - widowed,
divorced or separated - with young children. The agricultural system of the South is slowly shifting from the
patriarchal system inherited from the days of slavery to
one of independent tenancy and cash wages, a transition
which has been hastened by the present depression.  The
primary economic problem is a readjustment of the system
of farm management whereby greater security will be af-
forded farm tenants and laborers. The primary social
problem is one of education looking toward an improved
standard of living. Much of the relief problem in the
South is a result of the inability of an unschooled, almost illiterate group to adjust itself to changing economic conditions.

5.  The lack of schooling of a large proportion of the heads
of relief families appears to be one reason for their being on
relief, inasmuch as the least trained tend to be the first to

be dropped and the last to be employed whether for wages in industry or as farm tenants or laborers. In all but the two Wheat
Areas over 30 percent of the heads of families had less than 5
years schooling, and in the Eastern Cotton Belt 51 percent of
the Negro heads and 20 percent of the white heads of families
had had no formal schooling. As long as so large a proportion
of the poorer classes lack sufficient education to manage intel-
ligently their own affairs there will be need of public relief
and social case work. It would seem a good investment of funds
to maintain adequate school facilities, with federal aid  if
necessary, as partial insurance against federal relief in the
future.

6. About one-fourth of the heads of households were persons
65 years of age or over and females – widowed, divorced or separated – with children. Not all of these may be qualified for
old-age or mothers' pensions, but these two forms of social insurance would undoubtedly care for at least a fifth of the cases
now receiving relief in the counties studied.

7. The depression in agriculture has undoubtedly uncovered
many cases now reckoned permanently incapable of self-support
who in years past had achieved a meager livelihood or had been
supported from local funds. Thus but 2 percent of the cases
studied had ever received relief prior to 1930, these presumably
being those least able to support themselves, while about 20
percent of the cases were judged (in June 1934) to require continuous financial aid and supervision and to be incapable of rehabilitation. (Among the Negroes in the Eastern and Western Cotton
Areas this rose to 39 and 23 percent, respectively.) It seems
fairly clear that the cases involved in this difference had not,
for the most part, received relief heretofore but that most of
them will have to be cared for from public funds in the future.

# INTRODUCTION

As records of the number of families receiving unemployment relief became available on a nation-wide scale in 1933, it was evident that most of the areas with exceptionally high relief rates were rural regions in which the majority of the people lived in the open country, or villages and towns of fewer than 5,000 inhabitants. Study of county relief rates for several consecutive months revealed well-defined rural areas in which many counties reported 20 to 30 percent or more of their families receiving relief (Fig. 1).[1] It was tentatively concluded that the causes of such a condition were to be found in certain fundamental maladjustments between human and material resources and that the economic depression had simply brought many families on relief who were hardly able to maintain their independence under normal conditions. Further study made it possible to outline six homogeneous areas for special study (Fig. 2). They were the Appalachian-Ozark, the Lake States Cut-Over, the Short-Grass Spring Wheat, the Short-Grass Winter Wheat, the Western Cotton and the Eastern Cotton Areas. In each one a specific combination of factors appeared to be associated with high relief rates.

Although one-fifth of the population of the United States lived in the six areas in 1930, they included less than one-fourteenth of the population living in cities of 5,000 or more inhabitants. However, the areas contained over one-fourth of the population living in towns of 2,500 to 5,000 inhabitants. (Appendix Table I) On the other hand, more than two-fifths of the farmers of the United States lived in them in 1930. The two Cotton Areas alone included 77 percent of the farm croppers and 36 percent of all other farm tenants. (Appendix Table II) Moreover, two-thirds of the Negro farmers of the United States were in the Eastern Cotton Belt in 1930 (Appendix Table III); the two Cotton Areas taken together included 77 percent of all Negro farmers (52 percent of the owners, 87 percent of the croppers and 80 percent of other tenants) in the United States in 1930.

The predominance of rural and of farm populations in most of

---

[1]Tables and figures in the text have Arabic numerals.
Roman numerals denote tables and figures in Appendices.

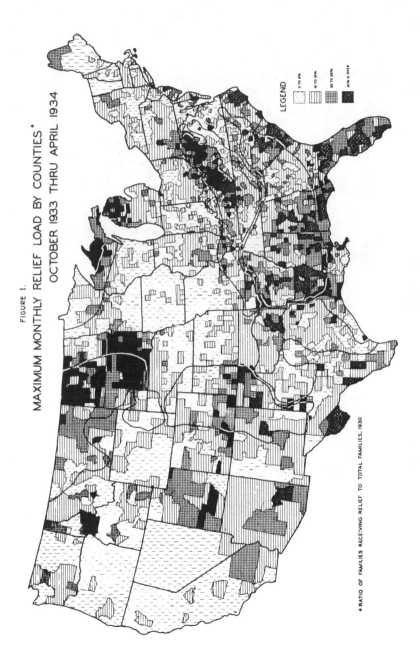

FIGURE 1.

MAXIMUM MONTHLY RELIEF LOAD BY COUNTIES *

OCTOBER 1933 THRU APRIL 1934

LEGEND

0 TO 9%

10 TO 19%

20 TO 29%

30% & OVER

* RATIO OF FAMILIES RECEIVING RELIEF TO TOTAL FAMILIES, 1930

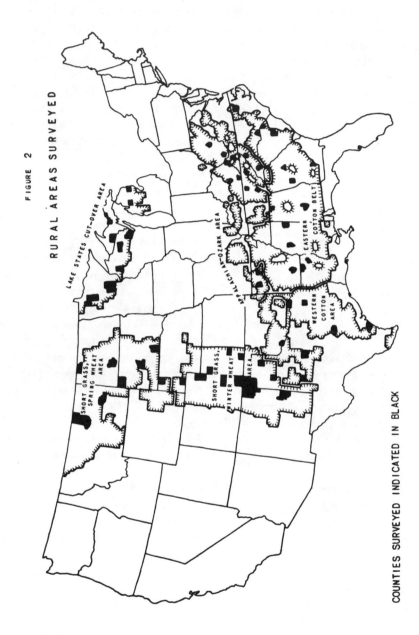

FIGURE 2

RURAL AREAS SURVEYED

COUNTIES SURVEYED INDICATED IN BLACK

the counties of these areas is indicated graphically in Figure 3.
Note the light area extending southward through the Great Plains
and eastward through the Appalachians and the Cotton Belt.

Although crop failure, speculative expansion, absentee ownership, and depressed price levels were among the factors which
precipitated the relief situation in the six rural problem areas,
the roots of the trouble obviously lay deeper. The frontier
philosophy which assumed that the individual, if given complete
freedom, would pursue an economic course that was to the best
interests of society, led to the present dilemma of stranded
communities, bankrupt farmers and widespread unemployment. The
rapid and heedless exploitation of the human and natural resources in these areas bears tragic witness to the fruits of such
a philosophy. In the Lake States Cut-Over and Appalachian-Ozark
Areas the destruction of the forests is a prime example of the
social consequences of our lack of national policy with respect
to the utilization of natural resources. In both areas commercial companies cut the marketable timber, destroying small growth
as they went, thus delaying the day when the area might again
yield a timber crop. When the timber was exhausted, the communities created during the period of exploitation were left
stranded. Yet under a planned system of timber utilization
these communities could have supported their populations over a
long period of years without the misery and suffering entailed
by the exploitation of their resources for immediate profits.

The philosophy which condoned the destruction of the forests
for private gain is not confined to any one area as the relief
situation in the Short Grass region aptly illustrates. In the
period of high wheat prices following the World War, large acreages of virgin sod were broken and planted to wheat. Because of
the chances for quick profits farmers rushed into wheat production on a large scale with little thought of whether the farm
economy which they were setting up could weather the vicissi-
tudes of a series of dry years such as had occurred with disturb-
ing regularity in the past. Neither did they consider the effects of removing all of the vegetation from large areas in which
erosion by wind was common. The present relief situation is
patently a result of the philosophy of making a "killing" and
letting the future take care of itself. Not only the farmers,
but the state governments pursued a policy which could only lead
to economic disaster. Specific discussions of each area will
clarify these generalizations.

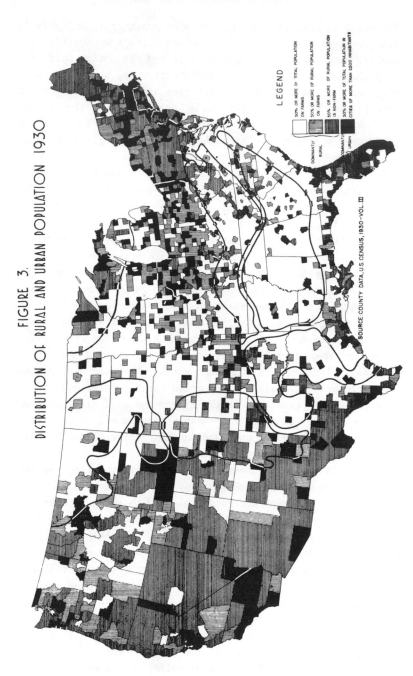

FIGURE 3.
DISTRIBUTION OF RURAL AND URBAN POPULATION 1930

LEGEND

50% OR MORE OF TOTAL POPULATION ON FARMS

50% OR MORE OF RURAL POPULATION ON FARMS

50% OR MORE OF RURAL POPULATION IS NON-FARM

50% OR MORE OF TOTAL POPULATION IN CITIES OF MORE THAN 2500 INHABITANTS

DOMINANTLY RURAL

DOMINANTLY URBAN

SOURCE: COUNTY DATA, U.S. CENSUS, 1930-VOL. III

# I. THE PROBLEM AREAS DEFINED

Because the central interest of this study was in the nature and situation of the groups receiving relief in the several areas, and the prospects of rehabilitating them, it was necessary to assemble and analyze data on the areas as wholes. The families receiving relief were obviously casualties of the economic system under which they lived. As a necessary preliminary to the extensive discussion of the types of families receiving relief, these data may profitably be presented in very summary fashion at this point. From such a review it should be possible to conclude what points about the families and their situation will have validity in all areas. These established, the method followed in assembling the data about them will be presented and the stage set for a detailed discussion of the populations which were actually receiving relief in June 1934. These groups may reasonably be taken as characteristic of the casualties in the several areas at any time before the necessary corrective measures have been taken or some important change in the general economic situation has come about. No such change occurred between the making of the survey and the composition of this final report. Rather the unfavorable conditions were intensified in several of the areas and the families on relief increased in number.

## A. The Appalachian-Ozark Area

As the name implies, this area consists of the Appalachian Highlands, its ridges, valleys and plateaus, extending from Pennsylvania, Maryland and Virginia, south and west through West Virginia, Kentucky, North Carolina and Tennessee and also the Ozark Mountain country of Arkansas, Missouri, and eastern Oklahoma. The early westward migrations from the Shenandoah Valley and the Virginia coastal plain flowed through this area, and the pioneers first occupied the more fertile valley and bottom lands, but later the less productive highlands were taken up. With the extension of the western frontier in the 1830's and after, particularly following the, building of the western railroads, migration into the area practically ceased and in its isolation it developed a distinctive mountaineer, agrarian cul-

9

ture.  Increases in population led to the clearing of more and
more land on the hillsides since the arable bottom land was of
limited area, and erosion early became an acute problem.  In fact
the highland plains and the hilly regions are submarginal for
intensive farming.  Rainfall throughout the area is quite adequate, ranging between 40 and 50 inches per year.[1]  Even today
but 17 percent of the area is in crop land with 60 percent in
forest land, largely second growth (15, p. 16).[2]  The area as
outlined in Figure 2 includes all the counties in the region in
which 15 percent or more of all farms were, in 1929, classified
as self-sufficing.[3]  The population, almost wholly native white,
and primarily of English and Scotch-Irish stock, has a rate of
natural increase in excess of that of any group of white people
of comparable size in the United States.  The population definitely presses on the means of subsistence and is an important
influence in keeping the standard of living low.

The period of isolation lasted until about 1880 when commercial lumbering was first attempted in the region, followed later
by mining.  With an increase in the demand for lumber, the virgin
timber lands were stripped in utter disregard for the needs of
the resident population.  Moreover, the introduction of a higher
wage rate than was customary in these backwoods areas disrupted
the old self-sufficient culture and introduced a way of life
for which the inhabitants were entirely unprepared.  Today it is
apparent that even had they been prepared, insufficient time
was allowed for the process, for the resources on which the new
economic system was based disappeared with great rapidity.  The
result was that many thousands of the inhabitants were suspended
mid-way between two disparate systems and their insecurity was
intensified by this fact when the depression came.

The cycle of exploitation followed a fairly uniform pattern.
With the beginning of operations, the high wages of the mining
or mill communities attracted workers from the hills and employed
them in exploiting the area's natural resources.  Employment
was very unstable and when the profitable timber was depleted
or when the mining operations became unprofitable, the mill operators moved on and the mines closed leaving the communities
which they had created without their usual means of support.

---

[1]For rainfall and native vegetation maps showing all areas surveyed, see Figure I,
Appendix B.
[2]Refers to list of references on page 165.
[3]Farms for which the value of the farm products used by the family was 50 percent
or more of the total value of all products.

In Jackson County, Kentucky, for example, the timber industry was centered in two companies. They existed between 1914 and 1929. When the first company closed in 1924 most of the employees found work with the second, but when it closed in 1929 approximately 300 families were left stranded. In a survey of nine counties in northern West Virginia, 91 stranded communities were uncovered; 62 of these had been dependent upon coal mining and 29 upon lumbering (*20*, p. 84). While the families of these communities comprised only 11 percent of the families in these nine counties, they represented over 50 percent of the relief load and although many of them attempted farming, their inexperience, the poor soil and the adverse crop conditions in 1930 and 1931 resulted in no improvement of their economic position.

Bank failures and tax delinquency had only an indirect effect upon the relief families as the farmers receiving relief were on the smaller and poorer farms. They had influence, however, through the contraction of supplementary private and public employment.

### B. The Lake States Cut-Over Area

The northern limits of this area are the Great Lakes and the Canadian border, and the southern boundary is set by the length of the growing season and soil type. Because of the short growing season (90 to 120 days) and the prevalence of poor, stony soil, the plow has not been successful in following the ax as in states to the south where many of the settlers originated. The area therefore presents the spectacle of decadent lumber, woodworking and mining industries in a region where recourse to agricultural pursuits is unprofitable because of climatic and soil conditions. The population is predominantly native white, a considerable proportion of the people are of Scandinavian origin, and the area includes important American Indian populations. The area is dotted with lakes and most of the land is covered with stumps, reminders of the days when the entire region was covered with virgin forest. Today the timber resources are almost entirely exhausted except in the Upper Peninsula of Michigan. Subsurface resources are iron and copper ore.

Long latent social and economic maladjustments are at the roots of the relief problem. They have been a malignant growth resulting from the three waves of economic exploitation which have swept through the area since it was opened to occupancy.

The first phase occurred with the development of copper mining and later, of iron mining, the second during the mushroom growth and rapid decline of the lumber industry which left, in its wake, unused railroads, depleted timber resources and stranded towns. This decline led to a third, an over-emphasis on agriculture brought about by the colonization schemes of states and large land-holders who induced families to settle on unfavorable soils and under poor climatic conditions.

The topography varies from level to very rough. Over most of the area gravelly and stony loams predominate. In particular areas marsh and swamp lands and sandy soils, low in moisture holding capacity, are prominent. The soils are characteristic of timber lands and are deficient in humus though normal in content of potential mineral plant food.

Rainfall varies from 20 to 40 inches. Such light rainfall on light soils is a serious handicap to successful crop production. For most of the Cut-Over region, the frost-free season is between 100 and 130 days, though in certain inland regions this period drops to less than 60 days. Soil erosion—wind or rainfall, sheet or gully—is not a particularly important factor.

Copper mining began in the Upper Peninsula of Michigan in 1847 and this area led in copper production until 1887 when it was displaced by the opening of the mines in Montana. A sharp decrease in the demand and the opening of rich deposits in Africa where cheap labor made it possible to deliver the product in London for less than five cents per pound depressed the domestic price below the cost of producing Michigan copper (12.5 cents per pound in 1930). The present prospect of the mines reopening is not particularly hopeful. Iron ore mining has been a principal industry since 1854 when production began in Michigan. Minnesota definitely displaced Michigan as the leading producer of iron ore about 1900 with the opening of the Mesabi Range followed in 1905-1906 by the Cuyuna Range. The depression affected both ranges equally and operations have been contracted. Although the data indicate an apparent recovery and show an increase in the tonnage of ore shipped, it is not an accurate barometer of employment conditions as much of the current increase represents a reduction of mined surpluses.

Logging and lumbering enterprises developed rapidly soon after the area was opened. Lumber mills, shipping centers and wood-working industries opened, grew and were prosperous, and

along with their growth, villages and towns were incorporated
and flourished, only to decline after the lumbering industry had
exhausted the virgin timber and left a wake of cut-over land
covered with debris, brush and unmarketable second growth timber.
The present situation is summarized by Zon (*12*, p. 5):

> "Two significant facts with regard to forests and
> forest lands in Michigan, Wisconsin, and Minnesota
> stand out clearly. First, that the area of the re-
> maining old merchantable timber is small (17.7 per-
> cent of the total forest land) as compared with the
> large area of oncoming second growth (46.4 percent)
> and the vast area of non-restocking and unproductive
> cut-over land (35.9 percent); second, that most of
> the forest land (95 percent) is owned by private
> individuals and corporations."

The history of agriculture is that of the speculative land
boom. The development described by the committee on Land Utilization in Minnesota (*4*, p. 56) is characteristic of the whole
area:

> "In the settlement of both southern and northern
> Minnesota, public policies encouraged the transfer
> of all kinds of public lands to private ownership
> and permitted the uncontrolled exploitation of the
> natural resources. These policies, which were so
> successful in the development of the agricultural
> lands of the southern part of the state, had entirely
> different results when applied in the north. In a
> large measure the unfortunate situation now prevail-
> ing in the cut-over counties can be attributed to
> the public policies of the past.

> "The great forests of pine and spruce which were
> once the pride of northern Minnesota are now prac-
> tically gone. The early lumberman assumed that the
> forests were practically inexhaustible, and it was
> the common belief that substantially all the cut-
> over land was suitable and would ultimately be need-
> ed for agricultural settlement.

> "The cutting of the timber was followed by an at-
> tempt, fostered by land promoters, to settle the
> cut-over lands. The state, the railroad and logging
> companies, and other large landholders for years
> engaged in extensive advertising and selling cam-
> paigns to dispose of their lands. In one way or
> another all asserted that for the man of small means
> who wished to become independent, the cut-over lands
> offered excellent agricultural opportunities. Farm-
> ers and city dwellers, both native and foreign-born,
> heard the call of the land salesmen and bought land
> in the cut-over region. Today the evidence of their
> heroic efforts to clear and till the land is every-

> where to be seen. Some of them found good land, of
> course, but many others located upon sandy, swampy,
> and stony land unsuitable for cultivation."

The economic depression, therefore, precipitated from the social economy of the Lake States Cut-Over Area a series of immediate problems which forced families of this area on the relief rolls. The depressed price level increased tax delinquency, made the farm debt structure top heavy, brought on bank failures, contracted part-time employment, and made farming unprofitable. From 1920 to 1930 tax rates increased until some farmers were paying about one-third of their net income to the county treasurer. Data from a preliminary and scattered survey on debt structures of farmers in this area "show that the indebtedness of individual farmers ranged from 85 to 150 percent of their total assessed value of all property. In some instances the indebtedness was as high as 600 percent" (7, p. 46). This probably is a biased sample as only 53 percent of the farm owners on relief reported real estate mortgages, but it does indicate the presence of this problem among the factors which forced families onto relief rolls.

Part-time farmers, lumbermen, and mine workers and the more frugal families who had laid aside funds for old age were forced onto the relief rolls by the failure of the banks. Commercial and public funds of the locality were frozen, throwing out of employment those men who were dependent upon such funds for part-time work to supplement earnings at their usual occupation.

The conditions surrounding the families usually dependent on mine operations for employment can be illustrated by the situation in Crow Wing County, Minnesota. Two movements, technological improvements in mining methods and the consolidation of mines, are particularly relevant. For example, by electrification and other technological developments one mine which formerly employed 325 men now produces twice as much ore with 125 men. On the other hand, consolidations in the last few years have resulted in five operating companies instead of fifteen, and two of the five are small. One social disadvantage of the larger companies is that they operate the more profitable mines, leaving the others and their dependent communities idle until needed.

The lumbering, wood-working and paper industries have never been interested in developing a stable population and those companies owned by outside agencies have, on the contrary, encour-

aged migratory labor and caused great unemployment, the expense
of which has now had to be shouldered by the local communities
and industries. Technological changes in the wood products industry have also increased unemployment. The introduction of a
process of tanning that does not require hemlock bark threw 200
men out of employment in one county. Decreased mine operations
had a concomitant effect upon the forest lands of the mining
companies, for men usually engaged in cutting mine props were
laid off. Low prices caused shut-downs by timber operators as
well as by lumber jobbers who not only employed a large number
of men in the woods, but bought logs, tie and pulpwood cuttings
from the small farmers to whom this type of lumbering was a
supplementary occupation.

Many of the farm families settling in this area depended upon
supplementary employment for income to keep going while clearing their fields. With the decline in wage levels more and more
time was required off the farm to insure a living income, and
when employment utterly failed, many farmers found that their
cleared ground had gone to brush. Families living in the open
country were discovered having farms of 40, 60, and 80 acres
with but 2 to 10 acres cleared, certainly not enough land to
insure them self-support.

Other farm families specialized in commercial agriculture but
failed to clear enough land to make profitable operations possible except under extraordinarily favorable conditions. In
the case of overstocked dairy and stock farms they resorted to
the purchasing of feed as long as this was a profitable proce-
dure—as long as dairy and stock prices were high. However,
when farm prices were depressed, it was impossible for them to
keep out of debt as they had insufficient cleared land available
for crop production and hay.

## C. The Short Grass Wheat Areas:  General Observations

The short grass country is found between the 100th meridian
on the East and the Rocky Mountains on the West. The eastern
boundary marks the line where the tall grass of the Eastern
Great Plains gives way to the wiry short grass because of type
of soil and scanty moisture; it follows the 18-inch precipitation line from northwestern North Dakota southward to the 24-
inch line in Texas where, because the rate of evaporation is
higher, the growing conditions are comparable in spite of the

higher average rainfall. The Short Grass Area is conventionally
divided into two parts, the Spring Wheat and the Winter Wheat
Areas. In both, the available moisture is so low that dry land
farming methods are followed. Only one crop in two years can
be produced on any given piece of land, since it must, in alternate years, lie fallow to accumulate sub-soil moisture. The
Black Hills country of South Dakota and other well watered sections are, for the most part, excluded from the area as here
defined.

1. *The Spring Wheat Area.* The northern half of the Short Grass
region, known as the Spring Wheat Area, is geologically new and
in many counties the soil is shallow and unsuitable for arable
agriculture. The topography of the region is generally rolling
and, in some sections, dotted with buttes. It lies to the west
of the glaciated area and exhibits the usual characteristics of
shales and sandstones which have weathered under dry land conditions. The soils are lighter in color than those to the East
and they are generally called the "Dark Brown Belt" or "Chest-
nut Earths". This lighter color is largely due to a light rainfall and consequently to a less vigorous plant growth and to a
lower content of organic matter than in soils of deeper color.
Much of the area has been cut up into small holdings occupied
by homesteaders; the native sod has been plowed up and planted
to spring wheat, other small grains and flax. Small farms, thin
soils, and the unreliable moisture conditions in the area, com-
bine to make crop production a precarious business. The average annual precipitation ranges from 15 to 20 inches, but marked
annual deviations from normal precipitation result in periodi-
cal crop failures. (See Figure II.) Except for gold and other
minerals in the Black Hills, the most important subsurface resources are stone, clay and lignite coal, the latter being
available in large quantities in the Western Dakotas and Eastern
Montana. This area is sparsely populated, containing only ten
cities of 5,000 or more inhabitants outside the Black Hills region. The population contains a large number of people of Scandinavian and German origin.

Previous to the opening of this area by the railroads in 1900,
which marked the beginning of a colonization program by the
states and the railroads, ranching was the primary industry.
The range was free and plentiful which permitted much feed to
be cured while standing and cattle could feed off the open range

the year round.  Since 1900 the population of the area has increased rapidly as has the acreage of land in farms and the
acreage of land sown to small grain (primarily wheat). With the
breaking of sod and the beginning of intensive dry land farming,
this area was thrown open to wind and sheet erosion which has
continued until at present it constitutes a serious problem
(Fig. III). A normal drought frequency dovetailed with low crop
prices and with a change from ranching to a more intensive dry
land type of agriculture is basic in the relief problems of
the area.

Tax delinquency in the counties surveyed ranged between $42
and $390 per family and bank failures have been frequent, the
average loss per family ranging up to $140. Since in this area
a ruling existed that a family's resources should either be exhausted or mortgaged before relief was granted, the relief rolls
contained those families whose resources were practically depleted. This ruling when combined with the high relief rate of
the area (28 percent) clearly indicates that the mortgage load
throughout the area was exceedingly heavy. There is no question but that the loss, potential or real, of assets played a
considerable role in bringing many families to the relief rolls.
2.  *The Winter Wheat Area.* The southern part of the Short Grass
region is known by its principal crop, winter wheat. Its soils
are generally brown with calcareous subsoils, and are easily pul-
verized. The growing season is longer than in the Spring Wheat
Area and a greater diversity of crops is possible. In addition
to wheat and other small grains, cotton, the sorghums, and corn
are important crops. The normal precipitation is from 15 to 25
inches.  Dry land farming has been greatly extended during the
past 15 years by the introduction of the tractor and the com-
bine. Although the population has also been increasing rapidly
during the present century, the area is still sparsely settled
and contains only four cities of 5,000 or more inhabitants.
Old American stock predominates, with a considerable number of
Spanish-Americans, and many Mexicans in some counties of New
Mexico and Colorado.  Extensive oil fields in the vicinity of
Amarillo, Texas, tap the only important sub-surface resource
other than stone, gravel and clay.

The area, as it was settled in the westward migration, was
devoted to cattle grazing, but the level prairies were inviting
to the establishment of small homesteads and to the extension

of dry land farming. With the building of railroads, the development of farm machinery for extensive farming—gang plows, tractors and combines—and a market price for wheat favorable to dry land wheat farming, immigration increased and the area shifted from an extensive pastoral economy to a wheat growing economy. In some of the counties this shift did not occur until 1926 and 1927. In Baca County, Colorado, where the extension of a railroad in 1927 facilitated the shift, about 60 percent of the sod had been turned for wheat by 1931.

An example of the complex factors underlying the relief problem in the Winter Wheat Area is furnished by data from Western Kansas. The Winter Wheat Area includes the western third of the state. The land is gently rolling in a fashion typical of prairie land. It lies in the 15 to 24 inch rainfall belt and before the sod was broken the natural cover was buffalo grass. Since 1913 the acreage sown to wheat has increased threefold. This expansion was facilitated by the production of a wheat suitable to the soil and climatic conditions of the area, and by the introduction and increased use of tractors and combines which made extensive farming practical. Since 1915 the number of tractors in the area has increased eight-fold and since 1923 the number of combines has increased three-fold (Table IV).

If for a number of years the deviations from normal rainfall between May and August are distributed, between one-fifth and one-sixth of the years are found to have less than two-thirds of the normal precipitation (Fig. II). Generalizing, it might be said that a deficient rainfall during the growing season is to be expected periodically. A deficient rainfall is not the sole agent responsible for crop failure, however, but its correlation with the seasons, with temperature conditions, with prevalence of grasshoppers, rust, etc., produces a rather striking cycle of crop successes and failures. Wheat sown in the fall may not weather the winter or it may have adverse growing conditions during the spring and a proportion of the acreage sown is not harvested. An examination of the data on crop abandonment in this area since 1911 shows quite an unusual picture of crop successes. In Figure 4 the cycle of crop failure and crop successes shows a five year period. The regularity of the cycles is significant and emphasizes the need for long time crop planning and crop control, if a similar fluctuation in farm in-

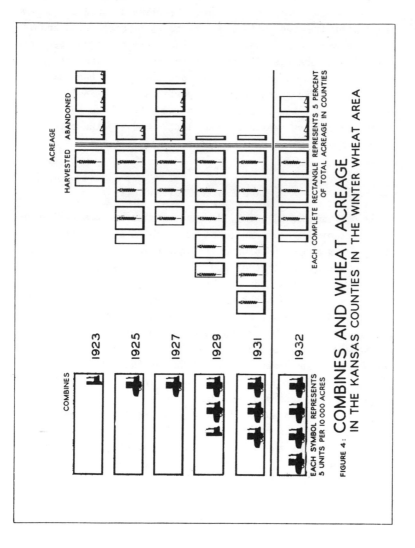

FIGURE 4: COMBINES AND WHEAT ACREAGE
IN THE KANSAS COUNTIES IN THE WINTER WHEAT AREA

come is to be eliminated and a stable economy established.
The present adverse farming conditions in Kansas were precipitated by conditions not previously suffered. The current crop
failure has as antecedents successive years of deficient rainfall and an excess of temperature. The climatic conditions have
dehydrated the top soils and with no cover crops wind erosion
has been more serious than usual. Furthermore, it has been estimated that between 10 and 20 percent of the farm acreage in
Kansas had been destroyed by water erosion before the summer of
1935 (16, p. 75). With larger proportions of grazing lands devoted to wheat, the existing range lands have been over-grazed
under the abnormal weather conditions. However, the cattle men
are less severely hit by the present conditions than the dry land
farmers.

## D.  The Eastern Cotton Belt

As outlined in Figure 2, this area includes almost all counties east of Oklahoma and Texas in which 40 percent or more of
the land in crops was planted to cotton in 1929. Its northern
limit is set by the line of 200 frost-free days of growing season, a line determined by the configuration of the country.
The Ozark Highlands push the line southward in northeastern Arkansas, and the Appalachian Highlands turn it southward across
eastern Tennessee, from which point it runs eastward across northern Georgia and then continues in a north-easterly direction
through western North Carolina. The southern limit is set by
precipitation, for more than 10 to 11 inches of autumnal rain
delays cotton picking and damages the lint.

The most common soils of the region are the yellowish sandy
and silt loams, the reddish sandy and clay loams and the allu-
vial deposits in the delta regions. The soils of the coastal
plains, the clay hills and the rolling uplands in Mississippi,
Alabama (the Black Belt), southwestern Arkansas and Louisiana
are normally very fertile. In the more hilly regions in the
northern portion of the area, particularly the Old Piedmont region, the soils are stony, less fertile and seriously eroded.
Annual precipitation varies from 40 to 50 inches and water erosion has been extensive in the rolling uplands which have been
in constant cotton production and without a cover crop for a
number of years. The original cover was timber. At the present time about 60 percent of the land is in farms and 40 per-

cent under intensive cultivation. Over half of the harvested
area is in cotton which contributes a large proportion to the
total products sold (*19*, p. 41). Corn is next in importance,
but it is largely a maintenance crop for the work stock and human population. From 70 to 80 percent of all gainful workers
are employed in agriculture and five percent in closely allied
industries. Although the Cotton Belt ranked second to the Corn
Belt in total value of agricultural products (1929), the average value of farm products per person was about 60 percent lower
(*19*, p. 41). Thus a problem closely allied to that of adequate
farm living conditions is one of parity in income of farm operators. Any maladjustment in the cotton business affects over
three-quarters of the gainful workers in the area. Many cotton
textile mills are located in the smaller cities and villages of
the Piedmont country of the Carolinas, Georgia, and Alabama.
Four cities of 100,000 or more inhabitants serve as major assembling and distributing centers.

The population increased most rapidly prior to the Civil War
when cotton culture and the plantation system, which were later
to be so influential in the area's maladjustment, became established. On the plantations that had withstood the reconstruction period following the Civil War, the cropper system displaced the old slave system. For a satisfactory share of the
harvest, the landlord would agree to "furnish" the cropper while
he cultivated the crop. The "furnish" consisted of living quarters, foodstuff and equipment. The cropper and his family furnished the labor, and the family with a large number of workers
was always more satisfactory as a tenant. After the harvest
the cropper would be paid for his portion of the crop less the
value of his "furnish." In the "Black Belt", as for example in
Dallas County, Alabama, cotton raising became less profitable
following the dissolution of the slave system and many of the
owners moved from the plantations to the towns, and rented their
land. This divorcement of the owner from the immediate cultivation of the land was one of the central characteristics of the
economic situation in the "Black Belt." In the counties surveyed in the Eastern Cotton Belt, 78 percent of the farm operators were either croppers or tenants (*23*) and 69 percent of
these were Negroes. Under absentee ownership the depletion of
soil fertility was rapid through constant cotton culture, soil
erosion and inefficient management. While the cropper system

offered ample opportunity for the landlords to be fair, and some
croppers may have profited under the system (9, Sec. II), in
general, the cropper's independence was only nominal. Obviously, the system was merely a variation of the old slave relationship and kept the cropper on the margin of economic existence.
This marginal existence, with its pseudo-economic freedom along
with the owner's spirit of the landed aristocracy, emphasized
whatever deficiencies appeared in the cropper class, fostered
an attitude of dependence and suppressed initiative.

Before and during the World War the price of cotton was favorable to the development of a one crop agricultural system,
but in the post-war depression two factors appeared which led
inexorably to the present relief situation. The first was a
depressed market price. Under a high price level the marginal
and submarginal lands could be extensively fertilized, thus partially restoring the plant food of the soil and insuring a profitable crop, but with low prices this undertaking led to bankruptcy. At about the same time the boll weevil spread into the
Eastern Cotton Belt from Mexico. In 1910 it was noticeably present in Mississippi, in 1914 in Alabama, and in 1921 in Georgia.
The severity and quickness of its onslaught is indicated in the
following data on the number of bales of cotton ginned in Morgan
County, Georgia, from 1916 to 1933 (21, p. XIV):

| Years | Bales (IN 000's) | Years | Bales (IN 000's) |
|---|---|---|---|
| 1916 | 23 | 1925 | 6 |
| 1917 | 26 | 1926 | 10 |
| 1918 | 35 | 1927 | 10 |
| 1919 | 36 | 1928 | 12 |
| 1920 | 30 | 1929 | 13 |
| 1921 | 7 | 1930 | 16 |
| 1922 | 2 | 1931 | 14 |
| 1923 | 2 | 1932 | 10 |
| 1924 | 5 | 1933 | 11 |

Although the boll weevil is under partial control, this county
has never equaled its former production of cotton. The disas-
trous effect of the boll weevil, coupled with a depressed market
price, reduced not only the owner's profits but also the tenant's standard of living. Until the owners refused to re-engage
all of their croppers and offered "furnish" to selected families only, or to the able workers within a family, this low

THE PROBLEM AREAS DEFINED

standard of living was masked. When the unemployed members were forced onto relief, the conditions came to light as an acute social problem. In this manner the contraction of credit and the depletion of owners' reserves precipitated the social and racial problem of the Eastern Cotton Belt. The cropper problem has received rather extensive treatment in various places, but the story is the same for the tenant and the farm laborer, whether white or Negro, as there is little distinction between these tenure classes.

## E. The Western Cotton Area

This area includes those parts of Oklahoma and Texas where cotton farms predominate, the western limit being the 20 inch precipitation line. (Cotton growing without irrigation requires about 20 inches of rainfall.) The eastern portion was originally covered with timber. Average annual precipitation decreases from 50 inches in the east to 15 inches in the west as the timber lands give way to the short grass of the Great Plains. In the eastern portion, the soil is a continuation of the fertile land of the Eastern Cotton Belt, but in the western and more arid sections the brown and less fertile soils of the wheat areas are prevalent.

In the period following the World War the acreage under cultivation increased at a rapid rate in response to a high market price and to physiographic conditions of the western part of this area which were favorable to cotton growing but unfavorable to the boll weevil. The increase continued up to 1929 and during this development over nine million acres were opened to cotton cultivation in Texas and Oklahoma. Although this increase represented only four percent of the total acreage, it was 17 percent of all land under cultivation in 1930 and over 40 percent of the acreage devoted to cotton in 1930.

Such an expansion of a one crop agricultural system created its own labor problems as its seasonal work demanded heavy peak loads of labor. As a consequence there are large tenant, cropper and farm laboring groups with extremely low annual incomes. In some cases the laborers have been described as being under a more intolerable slave system than that which existed in the Eastern Cotton Belt before the Civil War. Approximately half (49 percent) of the heads of families on relief in this area were either tenants, croppers, or farm laborers.

Tax delinquency, the debt structure, and bank failures had an effect upon the relief rolls insofar as they operated to contract employment and to reduce wage rates.

The recent drought brought about the present crisis. On the average, this area has a marked deficiency in precipitation about every fifth year. When the cotton crop is destroyed by drought, the soil is generally so dry that no other crop could have been produced. Both of these factors indicate the great need for a long-range agricultural program in the more arid parts of the area so that the production of the more prosperous years can tide the farmers over the inevitable lean years. However, this point of view is not frequently found among pioneer farmers.

### F.   The Problems Common to All Areas and How the Data on Them Were Assembled

From the foregoing review it is apparent that in each of the six areas the factors which appear to be associated with high relief rates are such that the problem of helping the families to become self-supporting and to maintain themselves at a socially desirable standard of living involves more fundamental measures than the granting of relief over a short period of time. They are areas in which unemployment relief will need to be given continuously or at periodic intervals in the future unless drastic measures are taken to remove the causes of the economic insecurity. Yet each of the areas presents a distinctive set of social and economic problems which must be taken into consideration in planning a program of rehabilitation. Nevertheless, reduced to its elements, each such set of conditions involves:

1. The types of families receiving relief and the capacity of each to become self-supporting under specified economic and social conditions.

2. The social and economic resources of the areas in which these families live and their availability for the rehabilitation of the families receiving relief.

3. The relationships of the types of families receiving relief to the social and economic resources of the areas in which they live.

4. The role of relief policies and practices in each area in determining the number and types of families receiving relief, i.e., consideration

of the validity of the relief rates as a mea-
sure of the degree and types of socio-economic
maladjustment in each area.

Each of these points is specifically analyzed in subsequent
chapters and a tentative solution of the problems involved is
suggested.  Data on the families receiving relief were secured
through intensive study in 65 counties, chosen, with the advice
of State Agricultural Colleges and State Emergency Relief Administrations, to represent as nearly as possible the range of
social and economic conditions found in each area. The 65 counties included (in 1930) 298,523 families that resided in rural
territory and in towns of less than 5,000 population, or five
percent of all such families in the six areas (Table V).   The
proportion surveyed varied from but 4 percent in the Eastern
Cotton Belt to 15 percent in the Lake States Cut-Over Area.
While it was impossible to include all local variations of the
relief situation in the sample, the homogeneity of each area,
with respect to the fundamental factors responsible for the relief loads insures that the samples chosen rather adequately
portray the area situations.

From the standpoint of the relative proportions of the farm
families of each tenure group and of the non-farm families, the
counties surveyed are representative of the areas (Table VI).
However, families living in towns of 2,500-5,000 population were
over-represented in the counties surveyed except in the  Appalachian-Ozark Area (Table V), but as this bias—which was una-
voidable because of the small number of counties surveyed—was
not accompanied by a corresponding bias in the proportion of farm
and non-farm families represented, the sample counties appear
to portray reliably the occupational antecedents of the relief
situation. In the selection of the counties, those with important rural non-agricultural industries were included roughly in
proportion to their frequency (in terms of the number of gainful
workers in each industry in 1930) in each area.

Direct comparison of the relief rates of the populations under study in the counties with the relief rates of the comparable populations of the areas as a whole was impossible, as the
official relief reports give only total county figures.   However, the relief rates in the counties surveyed in the Appalachian-Ozark and the two Cotton Areas were very close to those
for all counties in the respective areas (Table 1); but in the
Spring and Winter Wheat Areas, the percentage of all families

receiving relief in the counties surveyed was almost 20 percent
greater than for the areas as a whole. Most of this difference
was due to the inclusion of a greater proportion of city families in the total area computation and in these drought areas
rural relief rates were higher than city rates.  The wide difference between the area and the sample county relief rates in
the Lake States Cut-Over Area appears to be due to an error in
the number of relief cases reported by the states concerned, for
the investigators of this survey reported a rate almost identical with that for the area as a whole.

    In each of the counties selected for study all, or a random
sample of the families living in the open country, or in villages and towns of less than 5,000 population and receiving unemployment relief during June 1934, were studied.  The data on
the types of families receiving relief were secured from the
case records and through interviews with local relief workers.[1]

---

[1] See Appendix E for schedule used.

## II.  THE RELIEF SITUATION:  GENERAL CONSIDERATIONS

It is difficult to evaluate the relief situation of these areas in terms of the proportion of the total number of families receiving relief because of the variation from area to area in the items included as "relief".  In the states affected by the drought of 1933 and 1934 work relief was granted to farmers in order that they might procure feed for their livestock as well as subsistence for themselves.  Parts of the drought area are included in the Spring and Winter Wheat and Western Cotton Areas. In the other areas most of the relief granted was "human" relief only, although an occasional mule or ox given to a cropper in the Eastern Cotton Belt was reported as direct relief.

### A.  Relief Rates in the Areas

The percentage of all families receiving relief (including city families) in the six areas in June 1934 was about 15, almost identical with the percentage for the United States for the same month.  Nevertheless, the relief rates in all except the two Cotton Areas were 27 to 87 percent above the United States average (Table 1) and there the relief rates were below the national average.  However, because of the prevalent low standard of living among the unskilled worker class in these two areas, relief rates are a poor index of comparison between the socio-economic condition of families in these and other areas. The A.A.A. crop adjustment program has undoubtedly been of some assistance in improving general economic conditions in

TABLE 1. PERCENTAGE OF FAMILIES RECEIVING RELIEF[a] IN JUNE 1934

|  | TOTAL ALL AREAS | APPA- LACHIAN OZARK | LAKE STATES CUT- OVER | SHORT GRASS | | WESTERN COTTON | EASTERN COTTON |
|---|---|---|---|---|---|---|---|
|  |  |  |  | SPRING WHEAT | WINTER WHEAT |  |  |
| TOTAL FAMILIES IN AREA.............. | 15 | 19 | 22 | 28 | 19 | 12 | 12 |
| TOTAL FAMILIES IN COUNTIES SURVEYED | 18 | 22 | 32 | 33 | 23 | 11 | 11 |
| RURAL AND TOWN FAMILIES......... | 17 | 22 | 25 | 33 | 23 | 10 | 9 |
| RURAL FAMILIES............... | 16 | 22 | 25 | 33 | 22 | 9 | 8 |
| TOWN FAMILIES............... | 21 | 16 | 22 | 28 | 28 | 17 | 16 |

[a]TOTAL RESIDENT RELIEF CASES IN JUNE 1934 PER 100 FAMILIES, U. S. CENSUS 1930.

the South and thus has indirectly affected relief rates. The
Rural Rehabilitation Program of the Federal Emergency Relief
Administration had taken a few families off relief by June 1934.
In spite of the relatively low relief rate, the Cotton Areas are
definitely "problem" areas because of the precarious economic
position of a large proportion of their families under the one-
crop, share cropper system of farm tenure and the dependence of
those not engaged in agricultural pursuits upon the same crop,
cotton, or upon a decadent lumbering industry.

### B.  Obligations Incurred for Unemployment Relief in the Areas

About 203 millions of dollars were spent for unemployment
relief in the six areas, by federal, state and local governmental agencies during the 19 month period from April 1, 1933
through October 1934. The amount of the obligations incurred
during this period for relief purposes in all counties, and the
average per family, was as follows:

| AREA | OBLIGATION IN DOLLARS[a] APRIL 1, 1933 TO NOVEMBER 1, 1934 | | |
| --- | --- | --- | --- |
| | TOTAL | PER FAMILY | PER FAMILY RECEIVING RELIEF (APPROXIMATE) |
| ALL AREAS........................... | $202,797,000 | $37 | $220 |
| APPALACHIAN-OZARK.............. | 46,010,000 | 41 | 190 |
| LAKE STATES CUT-OVER........... | 26,178,000 | 86 | 390 |
| SPRING WHEAT................... | 15,172,000 | 77 | 310 |
| WINTER WHEAT................... | 15,428,000 | 53 | 310 |
| WESTERN COTTON................. | 25,264,000 | 24 | 180 |
| EASTERN COTTON................. | 74,745,000 | 29 | 240 |

PRELIMINARY DATA.

The average obligation incurred for relief during the 19
month period per family receiving relief varied from about $400
in the Lake States Cut-Over Area to less than $200 in the West-
ern Cotton and Appalachian-Ozark Areas. It should be recalled
that the Lake States Cut-Over Area contains a larger proportion
of city families (about one-third) than any of the other areas
and that the majority of the rural and town families receiving
relief were the families of unemployed non-agricultural workers.
Because of greater budgetary deficiencies or as a result of more
liberal relief policies the average obligations per family receiving relief were greater than in the Short-Grass Wheat Areas
where, as stated before, a considerable amount of the relief
money went for livestock feed. In contrast, in the Cotton
Areas and the Appalachian-Ozark Area, where less than 25 percent of the families live in cities, the expenditures per family
were relatively low.

## C.  Trends in Relief Rates

The percentage of families receiving relief in the counties surveyed[1] increased sharply during 1934 in all except the Appalachian-Ozark and Eastern Cotton Areas. In the Spring Wheat Area (which because of drought had the highest relief rate of all the areas by June 1934) the proportion of families receiving relief increased steadily from 7 percent in July 1933 to almost 40 percent in November 1934 and remained at about that level through May 1935.[2] For the same reason, the relief rate in the Winter Wheat Area increased from about 6 percent in January 1934 to 32 percent in August 1934 after which it declined slightly, to again increase during the early months of 1935. The Western Cotton Area relief rate showed a trend similar to that in the Wheat Areas but the increase was not as great nor did it reach so high a figure, for only part of the area was affected by the drought. (See Fig. 5.)

The percentage of families receiving relief in the Eastern Cotton Belt counties increased from 9 percent in October 1933 to about 18 percent in February 1934. After February the rates declined steadily with minor fluctuations to 8 percent in December 1934 after which they remained fairly constant with only a slight increase in January and February 1935. The low relief rates in this area in recent months were a result of two factors: more stringent rules as to who should receive relief and the transfer of families to the rural rehabilitation rolls. The rural rehabilitation program removed more families from the relief rolls during 1934 in this than in other areas.

The proportion of families receiving relief in the Lake States Cut-Over Area increased from about 11 percent in February 1934 to about 25 percent in July, remained about constant at that figure through October, increased sharply through January 1935 and declined slightly during the early months of 1935. Due to unemployment in the industries of this area and the precariousness of farming due to poor soil and the short growing season, little reduction in relief rates in the near future can be expected.

The proportion of families receiving relief in the Appalachian-Ozark counties has fluctuated around 20 percent for most of

[1]These percentages are for all families including those in cities; no monthly data are available for rural families alone.
[2]The percentages cited are the actual monthly data. Figure 5 is based on a three months moving average.

FIGURE 5

COMPARISON OF TRENDS IN RELIEF RATES*
BETWEEN THE
COUNTIES SURVEYED AND THE UNITED STATES**

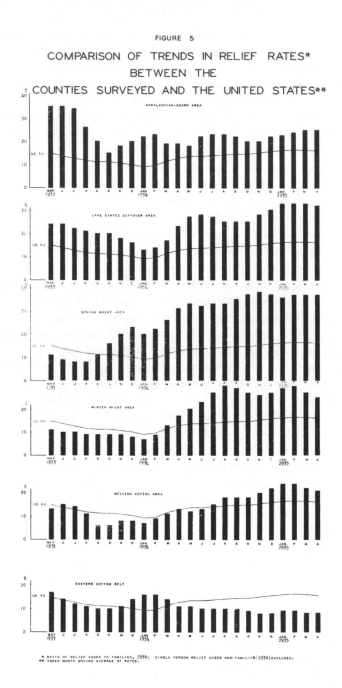

* RATIO OF RELIEF CASES TO FAMILIES, 1930; SINGLE PERSON RELIEF CASES AND FAMILIES (1930) EXCLUDED.
** THREE-MONTH MOVING AVERAGE OF RATES.

the period for which records are available. Although the record
covers only two winters, the relief rate appears to have a distinct seasonal variation, tending to increase in the winter
months. From October 1934 to January 1935 the proportion of
families receiving relief increased from 19 to 24 percent; in
1933 and 1934 the increase between these two months was from
16 to 22 percent. It appears likely that the relief rate for
this area will continue to increase gradually unless employment
is found for the increasing population. Due to the abandonment
of mines, the cessation of lumbering operations in much of the
area, and the lack of industrial employment elsewhere which
formerly drew off some of the excess population, unemployment of
persons of working age is steadily increasing. About one-sixth
of the families containing able-bodied workers who were receiving relief in June 1934 in the counties surveyed had been receiving relief for four or more years. Most of these families
are trying to farm but are unable to wrest a living from the
poor soil so prevalent in this area. Living standards are low
and relief giving seems to have become standardized near the
level of subsistence, the number of families receiving relief
increasing in the winter when clothing, food and fuel must be
bought and decreasing in the summer when needs are less pressing.

### D.  Relief Rates of Rural and Town Families

In general, high relief rates in the counties surveyed were
the result of the large percentage of rural families receiving
relief; the relief rates for town families were lower than those
for open country and village families in all the high relief
rate areas except the Winter Wheat Area. As will be demonstrat-
ed below, the higher town relief rate in the latter area was
due to the considerable immigration of unemployed agricultural
workers. In the Cotton Areas, where relief rates were much lower than in the other four areas, the rates for towns were almost twice those in rural territory (Table 1). As indicated
below the proportion of tenant and cropper families on relief
in the Cotton Areas was very small. White farm families were
receiving relief in more instances than were Negro farm families
but Negro families living in villages and towns appeared to be
receiving relief at about the same, or possibly a higher, rate
than white families.

### E.  The Type and Value of Relief Received

The proportion of families in the 65 counties receiving only
direct relief was not correlated with the percentage of such
families with gainful workers. The type of relief received depended more upon state and local relief policies than upon the
presence of persons willing and able to work. Some counties
had work projects adequate to give employment to all able-bodied
workers, others had no work projects. Of all the states in the
Appalachian-Ozark Area, Kentucky, with its policy of giving
largely direct relief, was having more difficulty with relief
clients than any other state. The investigators were told many
tales of favoritism and complaint. So far as could be learned,
these were without foundation, but the enforced idleness of relief clients led to a great deal of discontent which was fostered by local public officials in some counties, making the
job of administering relief extremely difficult. Nine of the
thirteen counties in the Appalachian-Ozark Area granted work
relief to less than 25 percent of the families, two granted it
to over 75 percent of the families receiving relief and two
granted no work relief at all. The averages for the area were
67 percent direct relief only, 28 percent work relief only and
5 percent both work and direct relief (Table VII).

The practice of giving direct relief was also widespread in
the Lake States Cut-Over Area; 65 percent of the families received only direct relief, 18 percent both direct and work relief and only 17 percent work relief alone. Although there were
fewer families containing gainful workers in this than in the
Appalachian-Ozark Area, there were more families in which no
member had any employment in June 1934 (Tables 6 and XIV-A).

The use of work relief was more consistent in the Winter
Wheat than in any other area; each county studied granted such
relief to 50 percent or more of the families receiving relief,
six granted it to 50 to 74 percent and seven to 75 percent or
more. Only 21 percent of all families in this area received
only direct relief; 62 percent received only work relief and
the remaining 17 percent both work and direct relief. In the
Spring Wheat Area also, more of the families were receiving work
relief than in any except the Winter Wheat Area.

In the Cotton Areas, whites were receiving work relief to a
much greater extent than Negroes. In the Western Cotton Area,
69 percent of the whites were receiving only direct relief,

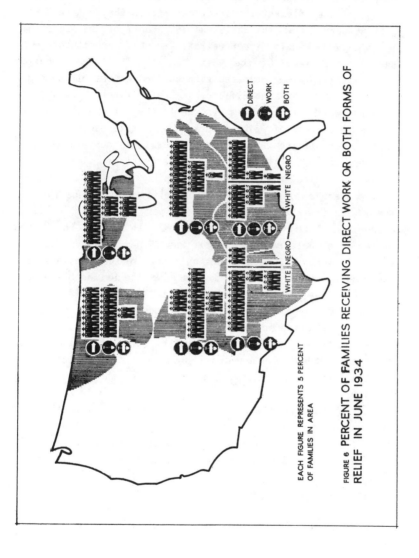

EACH FIGURE REPRESENTS 5 PERCENT OF FAMILIES IN AREA

FIGURE 6 PERCENT OF FAMILIES RECEIVING DIRECT WORK OR BOTH FORMS OF RELIEF IN JUNE 1934

another 20 percent direct and work relief making a total of 89
percent receiving direct relief.  The comparable figure for
Negroes was 99 percent, for they seldom received work relief
except as a supplement to direct relief. In the Eastern Cotton
Belt 56 percent of the white and 75 percent of the Negro families received only direct relief, 9 and 7 percent both work
and direct relief.  Of the white families 35 percent received
work relief only as compared with but 18 percent of the Negro
families.  Some of the difference in the types of relief received by whites and Negroes was due to the large number of Negro families without gainful workers but this factor does not
account for all the variation. Negro families containing workers were not given work relief to as great an extent as were
comparable white families (Table VII).

The average value of the relief received during June 1934 by
the 10,771 families studied was $13 per family (Table VIII).
Comparison of the average relief benefit with that for the United
States as a whole reveals that it was 75 percent less than the
national average, less than one-half that of the principal cities, and about 40 percent less than for the United States exclusive of the principal cities (Table IX).  Comparison of the
counties surveyed in each area with the states in which the
areas lie indicates interesting differences. In practically all
areas the state averages are higher than for the rural counties
surveyed, probably because of the greater cost of relief in urban than in rural territory. The averages for the Cotton Areas,
however, were almost identical.  Only in the Winter Wheat Area
was the average for the counties surveyed greater than that for
the states as a whole.  There is strong suspicion that a good
part of this difference was due to county work relief expenditures not reported to the Federal Emergency Relief Administration but reported in this survey and to the inclusion in some
of the counties surveyed of surplus commodities as a part of
relief benefits. In some counties in this area the local relief
offices had estimated their value and included them as relief
granted.

For those receiving direct relief only, in the counties surveyed, the average was but $8, for those receiving work relief
only, $19, and for those receiving both forms of relief $21.
Families receiving work relief therefore received approximately
twice as much as those receiving direct relief in each of the

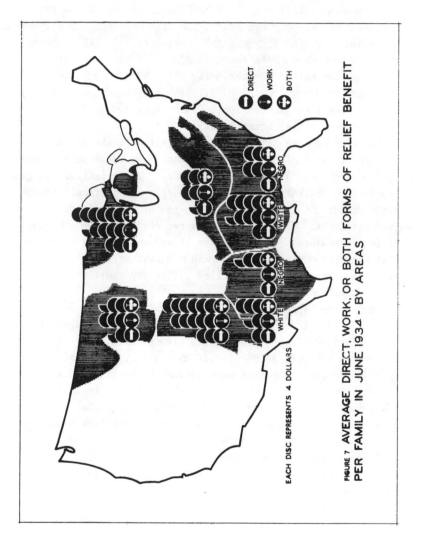

EACH DISC REPRESENTS 4 DOLLARS

FIGURE 7 AVERAGE DIRECT, WORK, OR BOTH FORMS OF RELIEF BENEFIT PER FAMILY IN JUNE 1934 - BY AREAS

areas. The largest relief benefits were granted in the Winter
Wheat and Lake States Cut-Over Areas: families receiving direct
relief only averaged $12 apiece in both areas and those re-
ceiving work relief only, $25 in the Winter Wheat and $23 in
the Lake States Cut-Over Area. Families receiving both types
of relief averaged $28 and $27, respectively. Relief grants
in the Spring Wheat Area averaged $14 and grants to white fam-
ilies in the Eastern Cotton Belt, $13. Work relief benefits
in these two areas averaged $17, the slightly higher average
for all families in the Spring Wheat Area being due to the
larger direct relief benefits paid.

Larger relief benefits were to be expected in the Wheat Areas
because of the inclusion of items other than human subsistence
in the families' budgetary allowances. The relatively large
benefits in the Lake States Cut-Over Area are difficult to explain except in terms of the influence of urbanization on relief standards. The investigators reported a number of cases
of former residents of Milwaukee living in the area whose relief benefits were still being paid by Milwaukee and at a higher
rate than that of the local relief office for families in similar circumstances.

Only among Negroes in the Cotton Areas were the average relief benefits lower than in the Appalachian-Ozark Area where
work relief benefits averaged $12, direct relief only $6, with
an average of only $8 per family for all types. Most of the
Appalachian-Ozark families were living on the land and most of
them had never known anything other than a very simple standard
of living so the average relief benefit of $8 probably repre-
sented as much actual cash as many of the families have ever
had to spend in any one month.

Negroes not only received work relief in fewer instances
but also received smaller average benefits than whites in the
same area regardless of whether they were receiving work relief,
direct relief or both work and direct relief. Since the rural
Negro family group appears to be unable to care for its aged
members under the present economic system in the South, there
has been a definite selection of aged families for the relief
rolls. These older, smaller families are able to subsist on
less than larger families containing children. This factor accounts in part for the smaller direct relief benefits paid to
Negroes. The lower work relief benefits, however, were obviously

evidence of the lower scale of living of the Negro accepted by relief officials as the basis for determining budgetary deficiencies.

## III. THE FAMILIES RECEIVING RELIEF

In assessing the human resources of the population receiving relief in the 65 counties surveyed—a necessary preliminary to any discussion of the *material* resources—consideration must be given to a number of points of a statistical nature difficult to translate into qualitative terms without risking inaccuracy. Nevertheless, it may clarify the detailed discussion that follows to begin with the statement that the majority of the families receiving relief in five of the six areas (the exception being the Lake States Cut-Over as will emerge later) were families of farmers and farm laborers and were "normal" in the sense that they usually consisted of husband and wife or husband, wife and children. About four-fifths of the families included one or more gainful workers and almost 90 percent of these families included one or more *male* gainful workers 16 years of age and older.[1] In none of the areas, except among Negro families in the Cotton Areas, was the proportion with at least one gainful worker, either male or female, less than 86 percent and with less than one *male* gainful worker, less than 77 percent. Refinement and qualification of these broad findings is undertaken in the pages which follow. The text contains information on such matters as family size, composition, age and sex of the members, occupations of those usually gainfully employed together with further data of an occupational nature, and ends with an evaluation of the capacity of the families to become self-supporting in the light of the human resources they represent. Interpretative material appears where it is relevant.

### A. Types of Families Receiving Relief

The types of families receiving relief are a good indication of the kind of relief and rehabilitation problems presented in each area. Normal families[2] predominated among the families receiving relief in the 65 counties. Nearly three-fourths were families of this type and 55 percent of the families were normal families with children under 16 years of age (Table 2).

[1] A "gainful worker" as used throughout this report, is any person 16 years of age or older who had worked previously (at other than a work relief job) and who was working or seeking work at the time of this survey (June 1934). Housewives who had done only housework in their own homes were not classified as gainful workers.
[2] Family, as used here, includes all persons receiving relief as one relief case.

In the Appalachian-Ozark Area and the Short Grass Areas 83 and 79 percent of the families, respectively, were normal families. In the Cotton Areas about three-fourths of the white families were normal families. Among the whites the variation from area to area in the percentage of normal families receiving relief was due to variation in the proportion of families with children under 16 years of age: the percentage of "husband-wife" and "husband-wife-children 16 years of age and over only" families was almost identical in all areas. In other words, areas having a large proportion of normal families had a high proportion of relatively young families on relief. In the Appalachian-Ozark Area, where 83 percent of the families receiving relief were normal families, almost two-thirds were families with children under 16 years of age. The proportion of normal families was smallest among the Negro families in the Cotton Areas, less than 50 percent of the families in Eastern Cotton Belt falling in this class.

Broken families including children occurred most frequently in the Cotton Areas, particularly among Negroes (22 percent in the Eastern Cotton Belt) and least frequently in the Wheat Areas (9 and 10 percent). Practically all this variation was due to differences in the proportion of families consisting of women and children.

Only 3 percent of the families receiving relief in the Appalachian-Ozark Area were one-person families, less than one-half the number in any other area. In contrast, among the Negro families, 13 percent in the Western Cotton Area and 22 percent in the Eastern Cotton Belt were one-person families, with lone women predominating.

In the Lake States Cut-Over Area, 17 percent of the families receiving relief were one-person families, 15 percent being lone males, and only 69 percent normal families. The families in this area are, for the most part, immigrants from other states. Many of those receiving relief came into this area to work in the lumbering and mining industries. They separated from their kinship groups in moving into the area and many of them, especially those men who formerly worked in the lumber camps, when unable to work or unable to find work, had no relatives nearby to support them.

The types of families receiving relief in the two Wheat Areas were similar except that the families in the Spring Wheat Area

Table 2. Percentage Distribution of Types of Families Receiving Relief in the Counties Surveyed

| | Total All Areas | Appalachian Ozark | Lake States Cut-Over | Short Grass | | Western Cotton | | Eastern Cotton | |
|---|---|---|---|---|---|---|---|---|---|
| | | | | Spring Wheat | Winter Wheat | White | Negro | White | Negro |
| Total Families.................................. | 100.0 | 100.0 | 100.0 | 100.0 | 100.0 | 100.0 | 100.0 | 100.0 | 100.0 |
| Normal Families[a]............................... | 73.5 | 82.6 | 68.8 | 79.3 | 79.0 | 76.6 | 65.3 | 74.2 | 47.0 |
| Husband-Wife.................................... | 12.3 | 11.5 | 12.3 | 11.4 | 12.4 | 11.6 | 21.9 | 11.4 | 14.7 |
| Husband-Wife, Children under 16 years only..... | 37.2 | 42.3 | 33.9 | 39.4 | 42.0 | 39.1 | 28.7 | 39.7 | 19.8 |
| Husband-Wife, Children under 16 years and over. | 18.2 | 23.2 | 16.3 | 21.5 | 18.9 | 20.0 | 11.0 | 16.3 | 9.3 |
| Husband-Wife, Children 16 years and over only.. | 5.8 | 5.6 | 6.3 | 7.0 | 5.7 | 5.9 | 3.7 | 6.8 | 3.2 |
| Broken Families with Children[a]................ | 12.8 | 11.7 | 12.2 | 8.7 | 9.5 | 13.1 | 14.6 | 15.1 | 22.3 |
| Woman-Children under 16 years only............. | 3.6 | 3.4 | 2.1 | 1.5 | 2.3 | 4.5 | 5.0 | 4.1 | 9.5 |
| Woman-Children under 16 and 16 years and over.. | 3.5 | 3.7 | 3.4 | 1.8 | 2.0 | 3.5 | 3.0 | 4.4 | 5.3 |
| Woman-Children 16 years and over only.......... | 2.7 | 2.0 | 3.3 | 1.8 | 1.6 | 1.8 | 3.0 | 3.5 | 4.8 |
| Man-Children under 16 years only............... | 0.9 | 0.6 | 0.9 | 0.8 | 0.9 | 0.3 | 0.6 | 1.0 | 0.8 |
| Man-Children under 16 and 16 years and over.... | 1.1 | 1.0 | 1.0 | 1.1 | 1.5 | 2.5 | --- | 1.0 | 1.1 |
| Man-Children 16 years and over only............ | 1.2 | 1.0 | 1.5 | 1.7 | | 0.5 | | | 1.0 |
| One-Person Families............................ | 9.9 | 2.8 | 17.5 | 8.4 | 8.1 | 6.3 | 12.8 | 6.3 | 21.9 |
| One Man........................................ | 6.2 | 1.4 | 15.0 | 6.0 | 6.6 | 4.8 | 6.1 | 2.6 | 6.7 |
| One Woman...................................... | 3.6 | 1.4 | 2.3 | 2.4 | .5 | 1.5 | 6.7 | 3.7 | 15.2 |
| All Other Combinations......................... | 3.9 | 2.9 | 1.7 | 3.6 | 3.4 | 4.0 | 7.3 | 4.4 | 8.8 |

[a] WITH OR WITHOUT OTHER PERSONS.

were "older" i.e., a larger proportion were families which included children 16 years of age and older. Most of the families
in these two areas were normal in type although 8 percent were
one-person families, the majority of which were probably migratory laborers, stranded because of old age or unemployment.

The large proportion of one-person families among the Negro
families receiving relief, especially in the Eastern Cotton Belt
where the plantation system of agriculture is more common, and
the large numbers of persons 65 years of age and older among
Negroes receiving relief, is illustrative of the types of social
and economic organization in the area. As in the Appalachian-
Ozark Area, the Eastern Cotton Belt population is indigenous to
the area. In both areas, the social organization is that of
an agricultural people. In the former, nearly all of the population is native white, the family is the important social
group, the independent family farm the economic unit, and the
old people are cared for by their families. In the latter,
however, from 40 to 50 percent of the population is Negro, and
the important social and economic functions, so far as the rural
Negro is concerned, are associated with the plantation or some
variation of it. The family is the labor unit, but it in turn
is dependent upon the plantation owner or the landlord for its
existence as a group. When economic conditions in the cotton-
growing industry became adverse, the landlord in many cases de-
creed that aged croppers and non-productive adults in cropper
families should be supported by public relief. As the cropper
is dependent upon, and often subservient to, his landlord, the
relatively low relief load in June 1934 and the large proportion
of persons 65 years of age and older receiving relief undoubtedly reflect the relief policies of the landlord group.

### B.  Size of Families Receiving Relief

Families receiving relief tend to be relatively large. The
largest families surveyed were in the Appalachian-Ozark Area
where one-half included 5 or more persons, one-fifth 8 or more
persons; and the smallest white families were in the Lake States
Cut-Over Area where more than one-half included fewer than 4
persons and almost one-third fewer than 3 persons (Table 9).
The average (median) size of Negro families was about 3.5 persons in the Western Cotton Area and 3.1 persons in the Eastern
Cotton Belt. These comparatively low averages were a result of

the large number of one and two-person families, for one-third of the Negro families in the Western Cotton Area and 41 percent of those in the Eastern Cotton Belt included fewer than three persons. In the Eastern Cotton Belt one-person Negro families[1] occurred more frequently (22 percent) than families of any other size while in the Western Cotton Area two-person Negro families were most common (21 percent) followed by three, four and one-person families in the order named. These two to four person families were largely young families and appeared to be a group of recent migrants into the area. It does not follow that there were no large Negro families on the relief rolls, however. As a matter of fact, in the Western Cotton Area 30 percent, and in the Eastern Cotton Belt 25 percent, of the families included 6 or more persons.

TABLE 3.  SIZE OF FAMILIES RECEIVING RELIEF

| NUMBER OF PERSONS | TOTAL ALL AREAS | APPA- LACHIAN OZARK | LAKE STATES CUT- OVER | SHORT GRASS | | WESTERN COTTON | | EASTERN COTTON | |
|---|---|---|---|---|---|---|---|---|---|
| | | | | SPRING WHEAT | WINTER WHEAT | WHITE | NEGRO | WHITE | NEGRO |
| *Number* | | | | | | | | | |
| ALL FAMILIES............ | 10,771 | 2,167 | 1,738 | 1 311 | 2,007 | 800 | 164 | 1,347 | 1,237 |
| 1.................. | 1,062 | 61 | 301 | 110 | 163 | 50 | 21 | 85 | 271 |
| 2.................. | 1,514 | 232 | 260 | 172 | 295 | 98 | 34 | 183 | 240 |
| 3.................. | 1,721 | 318 | 259 | 202 | 357 | 125 | 27 | 253 | 180 |
| 4.................. | 1,672 | 317 | 260 | 219 | 378 | 126 | 23 | 221 | 128 |
| 5.................. | 1,426 | 294 | 243 | 183 | 284 | 115 | 10 | 187 | 110 |
| 6.................. | 1,108 | 294 | 131 | 141 | 191 | 105 | 17 | 126 | 103 |
| 7.................. | 822 | 228 | 101 | 95 | 129 | 72 | 9 | 121 | 67 |
| 8.................. | 604 | 173 | 72 | 70 | 86 | 50 | 8 | 86 | 59 |
| 9.................. | 374 | 117 | 49 | 42 | 63 | 27 | 5 | 43 | 33 |
| 10 OR MORE........... | 468 | 138 | 62 | 77 | 61 | 32 | 10 | 42 | 46 |
| *Percent* | | | | | | | | | |
| ALL FAMILIES............ | 100.0 | 100.0 | 100.0 | 100.0 | 100.0 | 100.0 | 100.0 | 100.0 | 100.0 |
| 1.................. | 9.9 | 2.8 | 17.3 | 8.4 | 8.1 | 6.2 | 12.8 | 6.3 | 21.9 |
| 2.................. | 14.1 | 10.7 | 15.0 | 13.1 | 14.7 | 12.3 | 20.7 | 13.6 | 19.4 |
| 3.................. | 16.0 | 14.6 | 14.9 | 15.4 | 17.8 | 15.6 | 16.5 | 18.8 | 14.6 |
| 4.................. | 15.5 | 14.6 | 15.0 | 16.7 | 18.9 | 15.7 | 14.0 | 16.4 | 10.3 |
| 5.................. | 13.2 | 13.6 | 14.0 | 14.0 | 14.2 | 14.4 | 6.1 | 13.9 | 8.9 |
| 6.................. | 10.3 | 13.6 | 7.5 | 10.8 | 9.5 | 13.1 | 10.4 | 9.3 | 8.3 |
| 7.................. | 7.6 | 10.5 | 5.8 | 7.2 | 6.4 | 9.0 | 5.5 | 9.0 | 5.4 |
| 8.................. | 5.6 | 8.0 | 4.1 | 5.3 | 4.3 | 6.3 | 4.9 | 6.4 | 4.8 |
| 9.................. | 3.5 | 5.2 | 2.8 | 3.2 | 3.1 | 3.4 | 3.0 | 3.2 | 2.7 |
| 10 OR MORE........... | 4.3 | 6.4 | 3.6 | 5.9 | 3.0 | 4.0 | 6.1 | 3.1 | 3.7 |
| MEDIAN SIZE............ | 4.2 | 5.0 | 3.7 | 4.3 | 4.0 | 4.5 | 3.5 | 4.2 | 3.1 |

Further evidence that more mature families were receiving relief in the Spring Wheat than in the Winter Wheat Area is the difference in family size in the two areas. Although families of four occurred most frequently in both areas, the Spring Wheat Area had more families of each size from six up to ten or more persons. In the Western Cotton Area the white families receiving relief were similar in size to those in the Spring Wheat

[1]As indicated above, some of these one-person families were not *bona fide* families, but aged persons living with families not receiving relief, who were reported by the relief agencies as one-person cases.

Area but there was a considerably higher percentage of families
of from six to eight persons and fewer one-person families.

Among white families in the Eastern Cotton Belt, families of
three persons appeared most frequently (19 percent) followed by
families of four, five and two persons in the order named. The
contrast between the types of white and Negro families receiving relief in this area was striking and illustrates the difference between the socio-economic position of the two groups.
The white families were largely normal in type, almost one-half
of them consisting of husband and wife with one to four children. The number of one-person families receiving relief among
the whites was less than one-third of that for Negroes and the
number of two-person families 6 percent less. Aged women, wid-
ows with children and extremely large families made up the bulk
of the Negro families receiving relief, while among the whites
the majority of the families were normal families containing
able-bodied workers. Whether Negro families containing male
workers found it easier to get employment or whether they found
it necessary to take jobs which the whites refused was not evident.

The contrast between the size of the families receiving relief in the Lake States Cut-Over and Appalachian-Ozark Areas is
indicative of the differences in their socio-economic organization. There were six times as many families consisting of
one-person and 4 percent more two-person families in the Lake
States Cut-Over Area. The proportion of families of three to
five persons was almost identical, but there were 20 percent
more families of six or more persons in the Appalachian-Ozark
Area. This difference was due to the larger number of families
of child-producing age and the greater tendency to "double up"
in the Appalachian-Ozark Area where aged persons usually found
sanctuary in the homes of relatives and seldom appeared on the
relief rolls except as members of the household of a son or
daughter.

Although direct comparisons cannot be made, contrast of the
average (median) size of family receiving relief with that of
all rural farm and rural non-farm families of typical states of
each area in 1930 (Table X) reveals definite differences among
the areas. The families receiving relief in the Appalachian-
Ozark, Spring Wheat and Winter Wheat Areas and the white families in the Western Cotton Area were larger than the average

for the area. It was in these areas that the highest percentages of normal families occurred among those receiving relief
(Table X).

Families receiving relief appeared to be of about average
size for the area in the Lake States Cut-Over Area, among the
Western Cotton Area Negroes and the Eastern Cotton Belt whites.
The Negro families receiving relief in the Eastern Cotton Belt
were smaller than average. This was partially due to the fact
that aged persons, receiving relief, while living in families
not on relief, were often reported as one-person families. However, the number of *bona fide* families on relief which consisted of one woman, or of a mother with young children, was large
among Negroes in this area.

## C. Age Composition of the Families

The age composition of the families illustrates in a rough
way the probable number of dependent persons in them, dependency
being interpreted as a consequence of *age* and *youth*. It is of
the first importance, therefore, that less than one-fifth of the
families receiving relief in the 65 counties surveyed included
persons 65 years of age or older and only 4.4 percent contained
more than one person of this age group (Table 4). About three-
quarters of the persons 65 years of age or older, were the heads
of families, and in the majority of the cases the only person
of this age in the family i.e., the families consisted of one
person 65 years of age or older, alone or with other persons of
younger age. The percentage of persons 65 years of age or older
who were heads of families was largest among Negroes in the
Cotton Areas (82 and 85 percent), and among the families in the
Lake States Cut-Over Area (81 percent). In contrast, among the
whites in the Eastern Cotton Belt, about 59 percent of the persons of this age were family heads. For the three remaining
area groups, the percentage was, Appalachian-Ozark Area and
Western Cotton Area whites  67 percent, Spring Wheat Area 68 percent, and Winter Wheat Area 71 percent.

Each ten families receiving relief included an average of two
persons 65 years of age and older, but in the Spring Wheat Area
the average number was about one in ten families, in the Lake
States Cut-Over Area three in ten, and among the Negroes in the
Eastern Cotton Belt, four in each ten families. The average

number of persons 65 years and older in families containing persons in this age group was twelve per each ten families.

TABLE 4.   AGE COMPOSITION OF FAMILIES RECEIVING RELIEF

| NUMBER OF PERSONS 65 YEARS OF AGE AND OLDER | TOTAL ALL AREAS | APPA- LACHIAN OZARK | LAKE STATES CUT- OVER | SHORT GRASS | | WESTERN COTTON | | EASTERN COTTON | |
|---|---|---|---|---|---|---|---|---|---|
| | | | | SPRING WHEAT | WINTER WHEAT | WHITE | NEGRO | WHITE | NEGRO |
| | | | | *Percent of Families* | | | | | |
| ALL FAMILIES............ | 100.0 | 100.0 | 100.0 | 100.0 | 100.0 | 100.0 | 100.0 | 100.0 | 100.0 |
| 0..................... | 81.4 | 83.4 | 79.4 | 85.3 | 86.4 | 85.0 | 77.8 | 83.2 | 65.1 |
| 1..................... | 14.2 | 11.9 | 15.7 | 11.5 | 10.0 | 11.5 | 14.2 | 12.4 | 29.3 |
| 2..................... | 4.3 | 4.7 | 4.9 | 3.1 | 3.5 | 3.5 | 7.4 | 4.2 | 5.3 |
| 3 OR MORE............. | 0.1 | * | ----- | 0.1 | 0.1 | ----- | 0.6 | 0.2 | 0.3 |
| NUMBER OF PERSONS UNDER 16 YEARS OF AGE[a] | | | | | | | | | |
| ALL FAMILIES............ | 100.0 | 100.0 | 100.0 | 100.0 | 100.0 | 100.0 | 100.0 | 100.0 | 100.0 |
| 0..................... | 31.3 | 20.8 | 41.0 | 32.0 | 29.9 | 25.8 | 38.9 | 28.8 | 43.9 |
| 1..................... | 16.9 | 15.8 | 15.2 | 18.0 | 19.2 | 16.7 | 14.8 | 18.4 | 14.8 |
| 2..................... | 16.0 | 15.2 | 15.1 | 15.1 | 18.6 | 18.9 | 14.2 | 17.5 | 12.0 |
| 3..................... | 12.6 | 15.4 | 11.5 | 12.5 | 12.3 | 13.1 | 10.5 | 13.2 | 8.9 |
| 4..................... | 9.6 | 13.6 | 6.8 | 7.9 | 9.2 | 11.5 | 8.7 | 9.1 | 8.5 |
| 5..................... | 6.2 | 9.9 | 4.4 | 6.3 | 4.8 | 6.5 | 3.7 | 6.1 | 4.4 |
| 6..................... | 4.3 | 5.5 | 3.4 | 4.2 | 3.3 | 4.9 | 4.3 | 5.0 | 4.0 |
| 7 OR MORE............. | 3.1 | 3.8 | 2.6 | 4.0 | 2.7 | 2.6 | 4.9 | 1.9 | 3.5 |
| DISTRIBUTION OF DEPENDENT AGE GROUPS | | | | | | | | | |
| ALL FAMILIES............ | 100.0 | 100.0 | 100.0 | 100.0 | 100.0 | 100.0 | 100.0 | 100.0 | 100.0 |
| FAMILIES HAVING: NO PERSONS UNDER 16 YRS. OR 65 AND OVER... | 18.8 | 12.3 | 24.4 | 21.0 | 20.3 | 15.4 | 25.3 | 18.1 | 19.5 |
| PERSONS UNDER 16 YRS. BUT NONE 65 AND OVER.. | 62.7 | 71.1 | 55.0 | 64.3 | 66.1 | 69.6 | 52.5 | 65.1 | 45.6 |
| PERSONS UNDER 16 YRS. AND 65 YEARS AND OVER. | 5.9 | 8.1 | 4.1 | 3.7 | 4.0 | 4.6 | 8.6 | 5.2 | 10.6 |
| PERSONS 65 YRS. AND OVER BUT NONE UNDER 16 | 12.6 | 8.5 | 16.5 | 11.0 | 9.6 | 10.4 | 13.6 | 10.6 | 24.3 |

*LESS THAN 0.05 PERCENT.
[a]THE NUMBER OF PERSONS UNDER 16 YEARS OF AGE INCLUDES PERSONS WHOSE STATUS IS NOT THAT OF DEPENDENT CHILDREN. THIS ACCOUNTS FOR THE APPARENT DISCREPANCY BETWEEN TABLES 2 AND 4.

As to young dependents, about 69 percent of the families receiving relief included persons under 16 years of age. The average number of children under 16 years of age per family including persons in this age group was highest in the Appalachian-Ozark Area (3.2) and lowest in the Winter Wheat Area (2.7); the other area averages ranged from 2.9 to 3.1 with the Western Cotton Negro families averaging highest and the Eastern Cotton whites and Lake States Cut-Over families the lowest. About one-fourth of all the families included four or more children under 16 years of age, the proportion varying from about one-third of the Appalachian-Ozark families and over one-fourth of the Western Cotton white families to 18 percent of the Lake States Cut-Over families (Table 4). Most of the variation among the areas in the average number of children was due to the variation in the number of families containing children rather than to the variation in the number per family with children.

Taking the old and the young together, it appears that about
81 percent of the families receiving relief in the 65 counties
contained one or more persons normally dependent upon others
for support (persons under 16 years of age and 65 years and
older).  Seven-eighths of the Appalachian-Ozark families included normally dependent persons, as compared with about three-
fourths of the Lake States Cut-Over and Western Cotton Negro
families, four-fifths of the Wheat Area and Eastern Cotton Negro
families and approximately five-sixths of the white families in
the Cotton Areas  (Table 4).  As in the case of children, the
differences between areas in the average number of normal dependents was largely a result of differences in the proportion
of families containing normally dependent persons.

Further light is thrown on the type of family receiving relief by an examination of the combinations of persons under 16
years of age and 65 years of age and over existing in each family.  Approximately 69 percent of the families contained children under 16 years, 63 percent of which included no persons 65
years of age and over, and 6 percent, both children under 16
years and persons 65 years and older. Aged persons and children
under 16 years in the same family occurred most frequently among
Negroes in the Western and Eastern Cotton Areas (9-11 percent
of all families), the families of the Appalachian-Ozark Area
(8 percent) and the white families of the Eastern Cotton Belt
(6 percent). In the remaining area groups, less than 5 percent
of the families were included in this combination of age groups.

Families containing persons 65 years of age and older but no
persons under 16 years were most common among the Eastern Cotton
Belt Negro families (24 percent), the Lake States Cut-Over Area
families (17 percent), and the Western Cotton Area Negro families (14 percent), and least frequent among the families receiving relief in the Appalachian-Ozark Area (9 percent) for the
reason given earlier (Tables XI and XII).

### D.  Incidence of Relief by Age

Children, young adults and persons 65 years of age and older
were receiving relief more  frequently  than persons 25 to 64
years of age in most of the areas. In all areas, children under
10 years of age appeared in the relief group in greater proportion than in the general population; in all except the two Wheat
Areas and the Western Cotton Area, white persons 65 years of age

and over were receiving relief out of proportion to their numbers in the general population in 1930. Adolescents and young
adults, 10 to 24 years of age, appeared on the relief rolls in
slightly greater proportion than their numbers in the total
white population of the same counties in 1930.

The relief population in the Appalachian-Ozark Area counties
was more nearly of the same age and sex composition as the general population than in any other area. The group receiving
relief was almost a cross-section of the total population except
for an excess of aged males. Despite the fact that children
under 10 years of age were not receiving relief in much greater
proportion than their numbers in the population, about one-third
of all persons receiving relief were under 10 years of age.

Although only about 27 percent of the persons receiving relief in the Lake States Cut-Over counties were under 10 years,
the proportion of all children of this age on the relief rolls
in the counties surveyed was approximately three out of every
10 (Table 5). Persons 65 years of age and older, both male and

TABLE 5. PERCENTAGE DISTRIBUTION BY AGE AND SEX OF PERSONS RECEIVING RELIEF

| SEX AND AGE GROUP | TOTAL ALL AREAS | APPA- LACHIAN OZARK | LAKE STATES CUT- OVER | SHORT GRASS | | WESTERN COTTON | | EASTERN COTTON | |
|---|---|---|---|---|---|---|---|---|---|
| | | | | SPRING WHEAT | WINTER WHEAT | WHITE | NEGRO | WHITE | NEGRO |
| MALES — TOTAL........... | 100.0 | 100.0 | 100.0 | 100.0 | 100.0 | 100.0 | 100.0 | 100.0 | 100.0 |
| UNDER 10 YEARS........ | 29.3 | 31.7 | 25.7 | 26.8 | 28.7 | 30.0 | 28.0 | 30.1 | 33.0 |
| 10 – 24.............. | 31.7 | 32.5 | 30.0 | 31.9 | 31.4 | 34.4 | 32.1 | 31.3 | 30.7 |
| 25 – 44.............. | 19.7 | 19.4 | 20.5 | 20.5 | 21.2 | 17.6 | 20.8 | 20.9 | 14.5 |
| 45 – 64.............. | 13.7 | 11.7 | 16.3 | 16.0 | 13.9 | 13.6 | 11.0 | 13.1 | 11.7 |
| 65 AND OVER.......... | 5.6 | 4.7 | 7.5 | 4.8 | 4.8 | 4.4 | 8.1 | 4.6 | 10.1 |
| FEMALES — TOTAL......... | 100.0 | 100.0 | 100.0 | 100.0 | 100.0 | 100.0 | 100.0 | 100.0 | 100.0 |
| UNDER 10 YEARS........ | 29.1 | 31.6 | 28.1 | 28.3 | 29.4 | 28.8 | 29.8 | 27.7 | 26.6 |
| 10 – 24.............. | 32.7 | 33.3 | 31.8 | 35.3 | 32.7 | 33.5 | 30.9 | 32.9 | 29.5 |
| 25 – 44.............. | 22.0 | 21.4 | 22.2 | 20.2 | 24.0 | 23.0 | 21.0 | 23.4 | 19.6 |
| 45 – 64.............. | 11.6 | 10.3 | 13.0 | 13.3 | 10.9 | 11.3 | 12.1 | 11.2 | 12.8 |
| 65 AND OVER.......... | 4.6 | 3.4 | 4.9 | 2.9 | 3.0 | 3.4 | 6.2 | 4.8 | 11.4 |

Female, made up a larger percentage of the relief population
than for whites in any other area. The percentage of males 45
to 64 years of age (16.3 percent) was higher than in any other
area for either whites or Negroes. The large number of persons
over 45 years of age on the relief rolls in this area is a reflection of the age distribution of the general population and
not due to an abnormally high relief rate for persons of ad-
vanced age.

The populations of the counties of the Wheat Areas and the white population of the Western Cotton Area were characterized by a relief rate higher than average for persons 10 to 24 years of age and lower than average for persons 25 years of age and over. In the Spring Wheat Area this was a result of the extreme drought situation which forced farmers with older children onto the relief rolls: 29 percent of all farm owners were receiving relief and many of them were men 45 to 64 years of age with completed families. In the other two areas the excess of persons 10 to 24 years of age receiving relief appears to consist largely of young adults who migrated into the areas in recent years in search of employment only to become stranded there when unable to find work. More than one-third of the persons receiving relief in these three areas were between the ages of 10 and 24 years.

The Negro population receiving relief in both Cotton Areas included more aged persons, especially aged women, than any other group. In the Western Cotton Area counties, persons 65 years of age and older were almost two and one-half times as numerous in the relief as in the general population. A similar situation was found in the Eastern Cotton Belt where women 65 years of age and older were almost 4 times (and men 3 times) as numerous in the relief population as in the general population. It is obvious from these data that an unduly large proportion of aged Negroes were on the unemployment relief rolls in the Cotton Areas. The fact that this was true *only among Negroes* points to the socio-economic system of the Cotton South as the causal factor. In the Appalachian-Ozark Area, in some parts of which the cropper system also exists, aged white persons were on the relief rolls in much greater numbers than in the general population, but the excess there was much smaller than among Negroes in the Cotton Areas. All information gathered in this study points to the fact that there has been considerable local effort to get aged Negroes on the unemployment relief rolls in the South.

### E.  Gainful Workers in the Families

The number of gainful workers—especially males—in these families has a direct relation to the prospect of the families sustaining themselves if given the economic opportunity. It is therefore indicative of the fact that the final solution of the

problem is more intricate than appears at first glance.
Although this survey included only families on the rolls of
governmental unemployment relief agencies, more than 11 percent
of the families receiving relief included no gainful workers 16
years of age or older and an additional 8 percent no male gainful workers (Table 6). In general, the areas with the lowest

TABLE 6. PERCENTAGE DISTRIBUTION BY NUMBER AND SEX OF GAINFUL WORKERS
IN FAMILIES RECEIVING RELIEF

| NUMBER AND SEX OF GAINFUL WORKERS[a] | TOTAL ALL AREAS | APPALACHIAN OZARK | LAKE STATES CUTOVER | SHORT GRASS | | WESTERN COTTON | | EASTERN COTTON | |
|---|---|---|---|---|---|---|---|---|---|
| | | | | SPRING WHEAT | WINTER WHEAT | WHITE | NEGRO | WHITE | NEGRO |
| ALL FAMILIES............. | 100.0 | 100.0 | 100.0 | 100.0 | 100.0 | 100.0 | 100.0 | 100.0 | 100.0 |
| NO GAINFUL WORKERS.... | 11.3 | 8.6 | 14.4 | 7.4 | 6.5 | 10.9 | 13.4 | 9.9 | 24.8 |
| 1 MALE................. | 51.5 | 56.9 | 62.8 | 62.1 | 71.1 | 47.6 | 26.2 | 30.1 | 12.8 |
| 1 FEMALE............... | 6.6 | 4.1 | 3.2 | 3.3 | 3.7 | 6.0 | 11.0 | 10.7 | 19.4 |
| 2 MALES................ | 9.0 | 12.7 | 8.6 | 11.4 | 11.9 | 8.9 | 4.3 | 4.5 | 1.0 |
| 2 FEMALES.............. | 1.1 | 0.9 | 0.3 | 0.4 | 0.4 | 1.2 | 3.7 | 1.6 | 3.6 |
| 1 MALE AND 1 FEMALE... | 10.6 | 7.6 | 5.2 | 3.6 | 1.9 | 11.9 | 27.4 | 28.2 | 22.9 |
| 3 MALES................ | 2.7 | 3.9 | 1.7 | 5.0 | 3.0 | 3.6 | 0.6 | 0.8 | 0.5 |
| 3 FEMALES.............. | 0.2 | 0.1 | 0.1 | ----- | ----- | ----- | ----- | 0.4 | 0.6 |
| 2 MALES AND 1 FEMALE.. | 2.2 | 2.1 | 1.4 | 2.4 | 0.5 | 4.1 | 6.7 | 3.0 | 3.2 |
| 2 FEMALES AND 1 MALE.. | 1.8 | 1.0 | 0.9 | 0.7 | 0.2 | 1.9 | 3.0 | 4.6 | 5.3 |
| 4 OR MORE............. | 3.0 | 2.1 | 1.4 | 3.7 | 0.8 | 3.9 | 3.7 | 6.1 | 5.9 |

[a] A "GAINFUL WORKER," AS USED THROUGHOUT THIS REPORT, IS ANY PERSON 16 YEARS OF AGE OR OLDER, WHO HAD
WORKED PREVIOUSLY (AT OTHER THAN A WORK RELIEF JOB) AND WHO WAS WORKING OR SEEKING WORK AT THE TIME
OF THIS SURVEY (JUNE 1934). HOUSEWIVES WHO HAD DONE ONLY HOUSEWORK IN THEIR OWN HOMES WERE NOT CLAS-
SIFIED AS GAINFUL WORKERS.

relief rates included the largest percentage of families with
no gainful workers. The Lake States Cut-Over was an exception
to this generalization, however, over 14 percent of the families containing no gainful workers; only among Negro families
in the Eastern Cotton Belt, where almost 25 percent contained
no gainful workers, was this percentage exceeded.

As most of the families which included only one female gainful worker were families consisting of a woman with young children, the majority of these families were not *bona fide* unemployment relief cases. It is therefore likely that had a program of aid for aged persons and dependent children been in op-
eration in these areas, the number of families on the unemployment relief rolls would have been from 10 to 33 percent lower.
For example, the evidence indicates that nearly one-half the
Negro families in the Eastern Cotton Belt and about one-fourth
of those in the Western Cotton Area would not have been on the
unemployment relief rolls if the states involved had made comprehensive provision for aid to mothers with children and the
aged. Moreover, about 21 percent of the white families receiving unemployment relief in the Eastern Cotton Belt included no
gainful workers or only one female gainful worker, and 17 percent of the white families in the Western Cotton Area and 18
percent of the families in the Lake States Cut-Over Area fell

into this class. In the Wheat Areas similar cases accounted
for about 11 percent of the families receiving relief; in the
Appalachian–Ozark Area, for about 13 percent.

However, the majority of the families receiving relief in
all six areas included at least one male gainful worker. The
proportion varied among the areas from 52 percent of the Eastern
Cotton Belt Negro families to 89 percent of the families in the
Wheat Areas. Only in the Eastern Cotton Belt and among Negro
families in the Western Cotton Area was the percentage of families containing at least one male gainful worker less than 80.
More than one–fifth of the families in the Appalachian–Ozark
and Spring Wheat Areas and of the white families in the Western
Cotton Area included 2 or more male gainful workers. Around 80
percent of the families containing one or more male gainful
workers included only one male worker.

The larger percentages of the families in the Cotton Areas
which reported one or more female gainful workers in combination with one or more males is illustrative of the fact that
the family is the labor unit in these areas. In the other areas
the wife and daughters usually do only the housework and incidental chores, leaving the farm work to the husband and sons.
Even among these families who were receiving relief only 13
percent in the Appalachian–Ozark, 10 percent in the Spring Wheat,
9 percent in the Lake States and fewer than 4 percent in the
Winter Wheat Area reported both male and female gainful workers
in the same family. In the Winter Wheat Area where farming is
most highly mechanized, the percentage of families with female
gainful workers was lowest, but in the Eastern Cotton Belt where
farming is largely hand work, 42 percent of the white families
and 37 percent of the Negro families reported both male and
female gainful workers. These differences will be an important
factor in determining the type of rehabilitation program to be
instituted in each area.

### F.  Usual Occupation of Heads of Families

1. *Relief Rates.*  Indicative of the relief situation in these
areas is the occupational background of the heads of families
on relief as shown by their usual occupation. In none of the
areas were farm owners' families on the relief rolls in proportion to their relative numbers at the time of the 1930 Census.
In all except the Cotton Areas the families of farm tenants and

croppers made up a larger percentage of the relief load in June
1934 than they did of rural and town families in the same counties in 1930 (Table VI). In the Eastern Cotton Belt, however,
white[1] cropper families were receiving relief in June 1934 out
of proportion to their numbers in 1930, and the relief rate for
croppers and tenants in this area (based on the 1930 Census)
was three times as high for whites as for Negroes (Table 7)

TABLE 7.  PERCENTAGE[a] OF FAMILIES RECEIVING RELIEF IN THE
COUNTIES SURVEYED BY TENURE STATUS OF HEADS OF FAMILIES

| OCCUPATION OF HEAD OF FAMILY | TOTAL ALL AREAS | APPA- LACHIAN OZARK | LAKE STATES CUT- OVER | SHORT GRASS | | WESTERN COTTON | | EASTERN COTTON | |
| | | | | SPRING WHEAT | WINTER WHEAT | WHITE | NEGRO | WHITE | NEGRO |
|---|---|---|---|---|---|---|---|---|---|
| ALL FAMILIES............ | 17 | 22 | 25 | 33 | 23 | 10 | 16 | 10 | 7 |
| FARM FAMILIES[b]........ | 13 | 24 | 10 | 40 | 21 | 7 | 9 | 7 | 4 |
| OWNERS.............. | 12 | 15 | 8 | 29 | 13 | 4 | 7 | 3 | 4 |
| TENANTS AND CROPPERS | 14 | 47 | 26 | 65 | 33 | 9 | 9 | 9 | 3 |
| NON-FARM FAMILIES[c].... | 22 | 19 | 36 | 22 | 26 | 13 | 23 | 17 | 19 |

[a]PERCENT FAMILIES RECEIVING RELIEF IN JUNE, 1934 IS OF FAMILIES IN EACH GROUP
IN 1930.

[b]NUMBER OF FARM FAMILIES ASSUMED TO BE THE SAME AS NUMBER OF FARMERS: NON-FARM
FAMILIES, 1930 SECURED BY SUBTRACTING TOTAL FARMERS FROM TOTAL FAMILIES.

[c]ALL FAMILIES OTHER THAN THE FAMILIES OF FARM OPERATORS: INCLUDES FARM LABORERS.

This large difference between white and Negro relief rates did
not hold for other occupational groups. The rate for Negro
non-farm families was greater than for whites. In the Lake
States Cut-Over Area, in the Winter Wheat Area and in the Cotton
Areas, a larger percentage of non-farm families (which included
farm laborer families) was receiving relief than farm families.[2]
The percentage of farm laborer families among the non-farm families receiving relief was highest (18 to 29 percent) in three
of the areas with high relief rates for non-farm families. Families of farm laborers, non-agricultural laborers and servants
and waiters made up 52 to 65 percent of the non-farm families
receiving relief.

In all of the areas, with the exception of Negro families in
the Eastern Cotton Belt, the relief rates for farm owners' families were lower than those for tenants and croppers. In fact
in every area, except for Negro families in the Cotton Areas,

[1]White, as used here, includes all non-Negro groups. In this area Mexicans are the
only other non-white group of any importance. Separate analysis of the small number of Mexicans.included did not indicate enough difference between their relief
rates and occupations and those of the whites to warrant treating them as a separate group.
[2]As it was impossible to secure data from the 1930 Census on the number of farm
laborer families, no rates could be computed for them separately.

the relief rate for tenants and croppers was more than twice
that for owners. The lower relief rate for Negroes in the Eastern Cotton Belt is especially striking and indicates that croppers and tenants found it difficult to get public relief during
the growing season, regardless of the permanence of the job or
the rate of remuneration. The lower relief rate for Negro than
for white tenants and croppers in the Eastern Cotton Belt indicates that the Negroes probably obtain public relief in this
area during the busy season to even a lesser degree than the
whites. That this difference in relief rates indicates less
need for relief among Negroes is questionable.

2. *Occupations Represented.*  Only in the Lake States Cut-Over
Area were the usual occupations of the heads of families receiving relief chiefly non-agricultural. In this area the largest single group on relief was non-agricultural laborers (25
percent); farm owners were second in number (14 percent) followed by mechanics (12 percent), miners (11 percent) and lumbermen, woodchoppers and raftsmen (6 percent) (Table XIII). The
remaining one-third of the family heads reported a variety of
occupations, farm tenants, factory and railway employees and
farm laborers accounting for one-half of the group. The majority of the families receiving relief were therefore on the relief rolls because of loss of employment in the mining, lumbering and wood-working industries of the area or because of the
loss of jobs in industry elsewhere: 21 percent of the families
had lived in the county in which they were receiving relief less
than five years.

From the standpoint of the usual occupations represented, the
relief problem in the Lake States Cut-Over Area in June 1934
was an agricultural one only in that many of those usually employed in non-agricultural industry had turned to agriculture
after losing the jobs which in normal times had furnished all
or the greater part of their incomes. There were relatively
few *bona fide* farmers on the relief rolls in June 1934. The
drought of 1934, however, resulted in an increase in the number
of farmers receiving relief.

In the Spring Wheat Area farm families made up three-fourths
of the relief load: 40 percent of the heads of families were
farm owners and 35 percent farm tenants. The next largest group
were non-agricultural laborers, 8 percent. Only 2 percent were
farm laborers, about one farm laborer family to each 45 farm

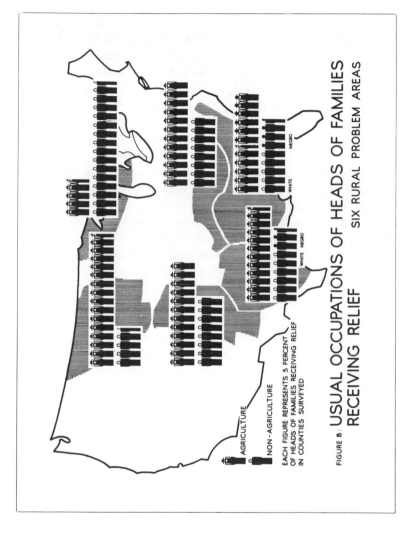

FIGURE 8: USUAL OCCUPATIONS OF HEADS OF FAMILIES
RECEIVING RELIEF    SIX RURAL PROBLEM AREAS

AGRICULTURE

NON-AGRICULTURE

EACH FIGURE REPRESENTS 5 PERCENT
OF HEADS OF FAMILIES RECEIVING RELIEF
IN COUNTIES SURVEYED

families receiving relief. Yet on April 1, 1930 there were 18 farm wage laborers per 45 farms in the counties surveyed. Although direct comparisons cannot be made between the two ratios (one deals with families and the other with persons per farm) it is obvious that the number of farm laborers' families receiving relief was very small in proportion to the number of such families which must have lived in these same counties in 1930. This points to the conclusion that the farm laborers had either moved to the cities or out of the area and the fact that much of the farm labor in this area has been performed in the past by migratory workers lends credence to this conclusion. Moreover, considerable numbers of farm laborers from this section have been reported in the transient camps of the F.E.R.A. In this area, as in none of the others, the relief problem was one for which agricultural conditions alone were almost solely responsible.

In the Winter Wheat Area farm tenant families were the largest single occupational group on relief, with the farm owner families next. These two groups made up 52 percent of the relief load and the farm laborer families another 9 percent. The relief rate for farmers (owners and tenants) in this area was only about one-half that for farmers in the Spring Wheat Area. The relief rate for tenants in both the Wheat Areas was more than twice that for owners. Non-agricultural laborers and mechanics (skilled and semi-skilled laborers) with 14 and 8 percent, respectively, were the only other individual occupational groups in the Winter Wheat Area making up more than 5 percent of the relief load. The usual occupations of the heads of the remaining 17 percent of the families were varied. Non-farm families made up a larger proportion of the rural and town families in this area (in 1930) than in the Spring Wheat Area and the relief rate for non-farm families exceeded that for farm families. Tenant families, however, were receiving relief at a higher rate than the non-farm group. The heads of more than one-fifth of the tenant families receiving relief in the Winter Wheat Area were unemployed in June 1934, as compared with less than 10 percent in the Spring Wheat Area (Table XIV). Crop failure due to successive dry years was a major cause of the high relief rates and about 46 percent of all families—90 percent of the farm families—were reported to be receiving relief because of crop failure. Unemployment of farmers (i.e., actual

displacement), of farm laborers, and of non-agricultural workers was responsible for almost twice as many families receiving
relief in this area as in the Spring Wheat Area.

In the Western Cotton Area 25 percent of those on relief were
tenants and approximately 7 percent each were farm owners  and
farm croppers, while farm laborers' families contributed 17 percent, bringing the total for those engaged in agriculture to 56
percent.  Of the remaining families, non-agricultural laborers
(16 percent), mechanics (8 percent), and servants and waiters
(6 percent) accounted for the majority. Unemployment and drought
were the two major reasons for families receiving relief. About
90 percent of the male heads of families who usually worked as
farm laborers and more than 90 percent of the male heads of all
other non-farm families were unemployed in June 1934. Of the
farm family heads, about 30 percent of the owners, 40 percent
of the tenants, and almost 60 percent of the croppers were unemployed.  Unemployed farm operators made up about 20 percent
of all the unemployed receiving relief. About 45 percent of the
farm operators were reported to be receiving relief because of
crop failure due to drought.

Cotton *acreage harvested* in Texas and Oklahoma in 1934 decreased about 7 percent from 1933 but the number of *bales of
cotton produced* in 1934 was less than one-half the 1933 figure.
The decrease in cotton acreage in this area[1] along with the introduction of machine methods in cotton farming has resulted in
the displacement of many farmers. Migration into this area
from other parts of 'the country (30 percent of families had
moved into the county in which they were receiving relief within
the past 5 years) which began in a period of expanding agriculture appears to have continued after there was a decreasing need
for labor, for many of the unemployed farmers and farm laborers
were migratory workers who came into the area for seasonal work
in the cotton fields and failing to find it were without sufficient resources to enable them to leave.

About 17 percent of the families receiving relief in the
Western Cotton Area were Negro families. The unskilled laborer
group (farm and non-agricultural laborers and servants and waiters), which included 62 percent of all Negro families receiving
relief, contained more than the average proportion of Negroes.

---
[1] Cotton acreage in Oklahoma and Texas had decreased in 1934 to 60 percent of the
1925 (maximum) acreage. Most of this decline occurred before the advent of the
A.A.A. program. This program prevented an increase in acreage harvested in 1933,
however.

Although the farm tenant families receiving relief included less than the average proportion of Negroes, the percentage of unemployed Negro tenants was less than for whites (Fig. 9).

The families receiving relief in the Eastern Cotton Belt were largely families of the wage-earning class, which depends upon others for its employment. Most of the heads of families were unskilled laborers (including farm croppers). As in no other area, families in occupations at the lower end of the socio-economic scale predominated among both whites and Negroes: croppers, farm laborers, non-agricultural laborers, and servants and waiters comprised 58 percent of all families receiving relief. Seventy-five percent of the Negro and 43 percent of the white heads of families receiving relief reported the above group of usual occupations.

Although the percentage of farm operators' families receiving relief in the Eastern Cotton Belt was identical (39 percent) with that of the Western Cotton Area, the percentage of croppers was greater and that of the tenants, smaller. The percentage of owners and tenants among both Negro and white families receiving relief was only one-half that of the latter area. Non-agricultural laborers, and servants and waiters accounted for 15 percent of the families receiving relief, and mechanics, and factory and railroad employees, another 15 percent. This latter group, consisting largely of skilled and semi-skilled workers, was larger in this area than any other except the Lake States Cut-Over where 19 percent of the family heads reported their usual occupations in this category. The introduction of cotton textile mills into the South during the present century has provided some industrial employment. Lumbering and the woodworking industry have also been important in some counties. As the condition of the cotton growing industry is reflected in employment in the cotton mills, the presence of a fairly large industrial group on relief was to be expected.

Of the families receiving relief, 48 percent were Negro and the highest proportions of Negroes were in the unskilled laborer classes. The servant and waiter group was 91 percent Negro, the non-agricultural labor group 65 percent, the farm laborer group 66 percent and the farm cropper group 49 percent. The low percentages of Negro families were in the skilled labor groups and among farm owners and tenants. In proportion to their numbers in the counties surveyed in 1930, almost one and one-half

FIGURE 9

USUAL OCCUPATION OF HEADS OF FAMILIES RECEIVING RELIEF IN COTTON AREAS, BY RACE

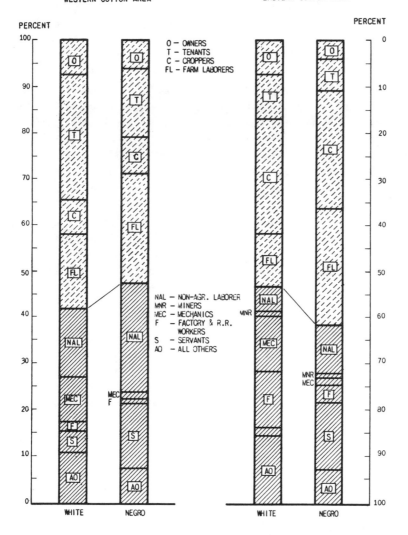

times as many white as Negro families were receiving relief in
this area. This difference in relief rates was primarily the
result of a low relief rate in June 1934 among Negro croppers.

The Appalachian-Ozark Area with almost as large a proportion
of its families on relief as the drought-stricken Winter Wheat
Area had a relief rate[1] among farm families which was exceeded
only by that in the Spring Wheat Area, where 40 percent of all
farmers were receiving relief. Almost one-fourth of the farm
families in the Appalachian-Ozark Area (15 percent of the owners
and 47 percent of the tenants and croppers) and about one-fifth
of all non-farm families were on the relief rolls in June 1934.

Of the heads of families receiving relief, 26 percent reported their usual occupation as farm owner, 10 percent as tenant,
23 percent as cropper, making a total of 59 percent for farm
families. An additional 2 percent were farm laborers. Of the
remaining 39 percent, 11 percent were non-agricultural laborers,
6 percent miners, 5 percent lumbermen, 3 percent mechanics, and
3 percent factory and railroad employees. The other 11 percent
reported varied occupations, about one-half of them (largely
female heads of families) reporting that they had no usual occupation.

As these occupation figures indicate, the relief problem in
the Appalachian-Ozark Area is both an agricultural and an industrial one. The large number of farmers on relief and the
high relief rate for farmers of all tenure groups in this area,
where economic conditions have not changed radically since 1930,
indicate the chronic nature of the problem and the presence of
a marginal type of agriculture.

To say that 59 percent of the families receiving relief were
farmers does not describe the occupational distribution of the
heads of families in this area. The farmers on relief practiced
part-time agriculture and depended upon the lumbering and mining and woodworking industries for supplementary income. In
this respect the farmer on relief was in much the same predic-
ament as his fellows in the Lake States Cut-Over Area. However,
the farmer of the Appalachian-Ozark Area is of an indigenous
stock and has always considered himself a farmer and his other
job a sideline. He has a simple standard of living and is never

---

[1]As these rates are based on the 1930 population, it is probably that they are
somewhat high; there has been some return of families to this area from cities.
The high rate of population increase in this area would also increase the number
of families and thus indicate a lower rate than the one given.

far from the bare subsistence level of living as measured by
modern standards.  Unlike the tenant, and particularly the cropper of the cotton fields, he has not been, in the past, subservient to a landlord class. He is willing to fend for himself
if given a chance, but is just a bit bewildered by his sudden
introduction in recent years to the complexities of our modern
industrial system and is often unable to cope with it.  This
area is a definite culture area as well as a geographic region
or type of farming area. The farmer of this area is "the man
with the hoe" who learned to depend on modern industry for partial support only to learn of its undependability when it was
too late to look elsewhere.

*3. Sex of Family Heads in Each Usual Occupation.*  Of the families receiving relief in the 65 counties surveyed, 14 percent
had female heads, the percentage for whites varying among the
six areas from 7 to 17 percent. For Negro families in the Western and Eastern Cotton Areas the percentages were 22 and 40,
respectively (Table XV). Outside the Cotton Areas, only in the
Appalachian-Ozark Area was the percentage of females among family heads who were usually farm owners greater than 6, and the
percentages of female heads among tenants and croppers was even
smaller. One of the lowest proportions of female heads of families (8 percent) was in the area with the highest relief rate
(Spring Wheat) and the largest proportion (40 percent) in the
area with the lowest relief rate: the Negro families of the
Eastern Cotton Belt. The majority of the families with female
heads were broken families, consisting of a woman and her children. As farming in the Cotton Areas is a family task, the loss
of a husband and father is not as much a handicap as in a more
complex economy where women seldom work in the fields. As a
result, farm families with female heads were more frequent.

Only in the Cotton Areas were farm families with female heads
on relief in greater numbers than their proportion of all heads
of families in the sample states indicated in 1930. Other data
at hand indicate that among Negroes many of these were aged
females no longer able to secure contracts as croppers nor to
live as members of another cropper family's household because
of the landlord's refusal to "furnish" any but the immediate
members of the cropper's family. In the absence of relief many
of these women would have been cared for by the landlord group.
Under a system which gives the cropper so little return that he

must depend upon his landlord to advance him enough food to enable him to make a crop, it is difficult for him to care for
elderly members of his household.  If the landlord refuses to
advance him enough food to support the extra person, he has no
choice except to allow his aged relative to apply for relief.
Comparisons of the percentages of farm families with female
heads (1930) in typical states in each area with the percentage
of female heads among farm families receiving relief in June
1934, in the counties surveyed in each area, appear below:

| AREA AND TYPICAL STATE | FARM FAMILIES WITH FEMALE HEADS | |
| --- | --- | --- |
| | 1930 | RELIEF FAMILIES IN COUNTIES SURVEYED IN AREA |
| APPALACHIAN–OZARK | | |
|    WEST VIRGINIA................................ | 7 | 7 |
| LAKE STATES CUT–OVER | | |
|    MICHIGAN................................... | 5 | 5 |
| SPRING WHEAT | | |
|    SOUTH DAKOTA............................... | 3 | 3 |
| WINTER WHEAT | | |
|    KANSAS.................................... | 4 | 3 |
|   WESTERN COTTON | | |
|    TEXAS | | |
|     WHITE............................ | 4 | 7 |
|     NEGRO............................ | 8 | 13 |
|  EASTERN COTTON | | |
|   MISSISSIPPI | | |
|     WHITE............................ | 5 | 5 |
|     NEGRO............................ | 11 | 27 |
|   GEORGIA | | |
|     WHITE............................ | 6 | -- |
|     NEGRO............................ | 12 | -- |

About 94 percent of the heads of families reported as having
no usual occupation were women who had no employment save that
of housework in their own homes. One-fourth of the female heads
of families receiving relief fell in this category. Most of the
385 female heads in this classification, in the 65 counties
surveyed, were in the Appalachian–Ozark and Lake States Cut–Over
Areas where 41 and 55 percent, respectively, reported that they
had no usual occupation.

The only usual occupation reported by many female heads was
that of servant or waitress (including all domestics) which
included 20 percent of all female heads. Of those reporting
this occupation, 84 percent were female and 16 percent male
heads of families. Other occupations including more than the
average percentage of female heads of families were "clerical
worker or salesman", the professional and proprietor group, and
farm laborers.

4. *Age of Heads of Families in Each Usual Occupation.* As almost
three-fourths of the families receiving relief in the 65 coun-

ties were normal families, the age of the family head is a use-
ful index of family composition. One-half the male heads of
families receiving relief in the 65 counties were under 44 years
of age and one-half of the female heads were under 50 years of
age. The average age of white male family heads ranged from 42
years in the Eastern Cotton Area to 47.5 years in the Lake States
Cut-Over Area; for Negroes from 43.5 years in the Western to
49.0 years in the Eastern Cotton Belt. In all except the white
family group in the Western Cotton Area, female heads of families were, on the average, 4 to 7 years older than the male
heads. Approximately 7 percent of all male and 5 percent of
all female heads were under 25 years of age and 13 percent of
the males and 23 percent of the females were 65 years of age or
older (Tables XVI and XVII).

In the Appalachian-Ozark Area, one-half of the farm owners
were under 48 years of age, one-half the croppers under 39 years,
and one-half of the non-agricultural laborers under 40 years.
The average age of male farm owners receiving relief in this
area was less than in any other area, and only for the Western
Cotton Area whites was the average age of both croppers and non-
agricultural laborers as low. This is partly due to the type
of family organization; aged persons instead of living as separate families were found living with the family of a son or
daughter. As a result fewer persons over 65 years of age were
receiving relief in this area, and the number of aged persons
per family receiving relief was smaller than, for example, among
Negro families in the Cotton Areas. The seriousness of the
unemployment problem in the Appalachian-Ozark Area lies in the
fact that such a large proportion of the unemployed were young
adults who had never had an opportunity to earn their own living. One-fourth of the male family heads receiving relief were
under 32 years of age and more than three-fourths under 51 years
of age. The younger family heads were usually croppers, tenants,
or unskilled laborers.

In the Lake States Cut-Over Area the average age ranged from
55.5 years for farm owners to 43.5 years for non-agricultural
laborers.[1] The youngest occupational group made up the largest
proportion of the relief load; the oldest group the second largest. Lumbermen, raftsmen and wood-choppers receiving relief

---

[1]Exclusive of farm laborers who averaged only 36 years of age but were a relatively
small group, accounting for only two percent of the families receiving relief.

averaged 54.5 years of age. This group and the aged farm owners
accounted for most of the unemployable males on the relief rolls.
Moreover, the average male family head receiving relief in this
area was older than the average white family head of any other
area.

In the Spring Wheat Area the average age of male farm owners
was 51 and of tenants 40.5 years. In the Winter Wheat Area the
average age of owners was 50 years and of tenants 39 years. As
relief rates for tenants in these two areas were more than twice
those for owners, it follows that young farmers were more frequently receiving relief than older and presumably better established ones. This fact is of considerable importance because of
the probable necessity for aiding families in these areas to
relocate in more favorable areas.

In the Western Cotton Area the average age of the male heads
of families receiving relief was 43.5 years, for both whites
and Negroes. However, the average Negro owner and cropper was
older than the white, but the average age of the Negro male family heads who were usually farm laborers was 37 years, 5.5 years
younger than for whites in this occupation. As in the Winter
Wheat Area the younger family heads receiving relief were largely unskilled laborers and these younger families were, to a
large extent, recent migrants into the area. Most of them were
unemployed in June 1934 and were living as squatters wherever
they could find a vacant shack to house themselves. In this
area there were more families literally stranded due to a failure to find employment in agriculture than in any other.

In the Eastern Cotton Belt the average age of white male
heads of families receiving relief was lower than in any other
area, except Winter Wheat, and that for Negroes higher than for
any other area among either whites or Negroes. Among male family heads the youngest were farm laborers or non-agricultural
workers. There was little difference in the average ages of
whites and Negroes usually employed in non-agricultural occupations, practically all of the variation in average age occur-
ring among those usually engaged in agriculture. This difference means that the families of young Negroes, who were usually
employed as farmers and farm laborers, were not on the relief
rolls to the same extent as the whites. The whites were a more
migratory group than the Negroes, and more of them were without
employment in June 1934. This may explain to some degree the

higher relief rates for white farm families but the differences
in the ages of the two groups suggest  that there was some dis-
crimination in favor of white families in the granting of relief.  This belief is supported by the difference in the relative amounts of relief given to the two groups (Table VIII).

## G. Occupational Shifts and Current Employment
## Status of Male Heads of Families

Actual unemployment as a "cause" for relief varied inversely
to the nearness of the families to the land. Although the farm
owners receiving relief were not unemployed in the same sense as
the wage workers, they were probably in just as dire need of
help. Because of their control over the capital and land which
they worked and the fact that they were not without some work,
they were much less a social problem than the laborer who depended entirely upon  others for an opportunity to work.  Only
48 percent of the  male heads of households receiving relief  were
unemployed  in  June 1934, i.e., they had no work (exclusive of
work relief) at any time during the month, farm operators being
considered employed if operating a farm even though drought made
it impossible to  grow a crop.  About 42  percent  of  all male
heads  were  employed at  their  usual occupation, 10 percent at
some occupation other  than  their usual one.  Farm owners were
most frequently employed at their usual occupation (86 percent),
followed by tenants, croppers, farm laborers and non-agricultural workers in descending order, only six percent of the latter
group being so employed (Table XVIII). Although the proportions
employed at their usual occupations varied widely from area to
area, the order indicated above held for all areas.

Only 10 percent of the male farm owners by usual occupation
were unemployed in June 1934, and only in the Cotton Areas was
there an indication of actual displacement of farm owners.  As
farm owners made up 7 percent or less of the relief loads in the
Cotton Areas, this displacement was a relatively minor factor
in the relief situation in all of the areas. On the other hand,
displacement of tenants and croppers was a major factor in some
of the areas. Twenty percent of all male family heads who were
usually employed as tenants were unemployed in June 1934.  In
the Western Cotton Area, where tenant families made up 25 percent of the relief load, 45 percent of the white and 23 percent
of the Negro male tenants were unemployed.  The majority of

these displaced tenants were still living in houses or shacks as
squatters, but were unable to secure work of any kind and were
without sufficient resources to move elsewhere. There were also
a considerable number of unemployed tenants receiving relief in
the Winter Wheat Area. Farm tenant families made up almost one-
third of those receiving relief and about 21 percent of the male
heads of families in the latter area who were usually farm tenants were without employment. Repeated crop failure, due to
drought, had forced many tenants into bankruptcy and off their
farms. Although a large percentage of the tenants receiving
relief in the Lake States Cut-Over and Eastern Cotton Areas were
unemployed, this did not represent the displacement of many
able-bodied families. In the former area less than 6 and in the
latter only 8 percent of the families receiving relief were usually tenants. Moreover, other data at hand indicate that more
than one-half of them were aged family heads no longer able to
work.

The most extensive displacement of farmers had occurred among
the croppers of the Eastern Cotton Belt. About 25 percent of
all family heads receiving relief were croppers and 57 percent
of the white and 49 percent of the Negro male heads of cropper
families were unemployed in June 1934. In addition, another 9
percent had become farm laborers and non-agricultural workers,
making a total of two-thirds of the whites and 58 percent of the
Negroes who had been displaced from their farms (Table XVIII).
About 75 percent of the whites and 50 percent of the Negroes
were the heads of families considered capable of self-support
by the local relief workers, indicating that at least 45 percent
of the white and one-third of the Negro cropper families receiving relief were families displaced from their farms for reasons
other than absence of persons in them able to work. A similar
situation existed in the Western Cotton Area, but cropper families made up only 7 percent of the relief load in that area
where most of the farmers on relief were tenants, many of whom
as indicated above also had been displaced from their farms.

Almost three-fourths of the male heads of families receiving
relief, who were usually farm laborers, were unemployed in June
1934. The proportion varied from a low of 41 to 43 percent in
the Appalachian-Ozark and Lake States Cut-Over Areas to a high
of 86 to 89 percent in the Spring and Winter Wheat and Western
Cotton Areas. In the Eastern Cotton Belt approximately two-

thirds were unemployed. Like the tenant and the cropper in the Winter Wheat and the Cotton Areas, the farm laborer, too, had lost his job because of drought and the adverse economic condition of agriculture, and the change to machine methods in some areas. In the Appalachian-Ozark and Lake States Cut-Over Areas, both poor land regions, 41 and 30 percent, respectively, of the farm laborers had become owners, tenants and croppers, and 19 and 26 percent were still employed as farm laborers. For no farm occupation group in any area was the number that had shifted to non-agricultural occupations as much as 4 percent of the total number of farmers and farm laborers receiving relief.

The shift from non-agricultural to agricultural employment, however, was quite pronounced in the Appalachian-Ozark and Lake States Cut-Over Areas. None of the other areas, except the Eastern Cotton Belt, showed any noteworthy shifts of this character. The shift to agriculture was most important in the Lake States Cut-Over, both from the standpoint of the number of families involved and the percentage increase in the number of farmers in the group: 17 percent of all the male heads of families receiving relief and usually employed in non-agricultural occupations were farming, and an additional one percent had become farm laborers. As the heads of almost 80 percent of the families receiving relief in this area were usually employed in non-agricultural occupations this means that approximately 15 percent of the heads of all families receiving relief had become agricultural workers in recent years, most of them because of unemployment in their usual jobs. Some of these families already owned land which was farmed by their families while the family head worked elsewhere. Since he had lost the job which was the chief source of family income, he was classified as a farmer. The "farm" which was formerly only an incidental source of income—a place to live, to grow a garden or truck patch and perhaps to pasture a cow or two and to raise a few chickens—became the family's sole source of income and subsistence. Some of the families did not own any land but were farming land belonging to others without the owner's knowledge or permission. Squatters, if they were farming, were classified occupationally as farm owners.

The Appalachian-Ozark shift to agriculture involved 41 percent of all male heads of households receiving relief and usually engaged in non-agricultural pursuits. As about 40 percent

of the family heads in this area were normally engaged in non-
agricultural pursuits, about 16 or 17 percent of all families
receiving relief were involved, but the ratio of families shifting into agriculture to those already there was smaller than in
the Lake States Cut-Over Area. Like the families of the latter
area, many of those who had recently become farmers made no
radical change either in their residence or their mode of living. Most of them were formerly employed in nearby mines, in
lumbering operations, or in small factories. A shift to agriculture was to the Appalachian-Ozark family simply a return to
agriculture—to the traditional mode of living on which the culture of this area is based—in a neighborhood in which the family was "kin" to most of the families living there. In this
latter respect the Appalachian-Ozark Area was sharply in contrast with the Lake States Cut-Over Area where there were few
family ties and many of the inhabitants past the age of 50 years
were immigrants from other sections of the country.

About 6 percent of both the white and the Negro male heads
of families in the Eastern Cotton Belt, who were usually in non-
agricultural occupations, had agricultural jobs in June 1934.
Most of the whites were tenants and croppers, most of the Negroes, croppers and farm laborers. The other areas had some
occupational shift toward agriculture but the number of families
involved was a relatively small part of the relief load.

### H. Relation of Occupational Changes to Shifts in Residence

The occupational shifts of the heads of families receiving
relief were accompanied by a movement of families between the
open country and villages and towns. In the Appalachian-Ozark
Area where the proportion of the heads of families who were
totally unemployed in June 1934 was relatively small, there was
little movement of families receiving relief, either to or from
the open country, between 1930 and 1934. Yet the proportion of
the male family heads that had shifted to agriculture by June
1934 (41 percent) was larger in this area than in any other.
The shift was obviously made by people already living in the
open country who had lost the jobs which had been their chief
source of income, or who had moved from an open country non-farm
residence onto a farm.

In the Lake States Cut-Over Area 18 percent of the male heads
of families had shifted to agricultural pursuits by June 1934.

In the same area 10 percent of the open country families receiving relief had moved there from towns and villages and 11 percent from cities since 1930 (Fig. 10). The net gain in the number of families receiving relief in the open country, due to migration between the open country and villages and towns, was only 7 percent because of some movement of families from the open country to villages and towns. As city families were not included in this survey, it was impossible to tell to what extent the families who had moved into the open country since 1930 were compensated for by families who had moved to cities during the same period. Probably about one-sixth of the open country relief load in the Lake States Cut-Over counties surveyed was a result of movement of families between the open country, villages, towns and cities, since 1930. Over 6 percent of the families receiving relief in villages and towns had migrated from cities since 1930.

In the remaining four areas the trend of migration was predominantly from the open country into villages and towns. This was especially true in the Winter Wheat and Western Cotton Areas where the net change in the open country relief load due to migration of families from the open country to villages and towns was equal to 10 and 14 percent respectively of the families receiving relief in the open country (Fig. 10). The movement was largely one of unemployed farm tenants and farm laborers. In neither of these areas had many of the families receiving relief migrated into the open country since 1930.

The open country relief population of the Spring Wheat and Eastern Cotton Areas also showed decreases due to the emigration of families receiving relief from the open country to villages and towns. As indicated above, this survey included no families living in cities of 5,000 or more inhabitants and as a result it is probable that a great many more families receiving relief have emigrated from the Short Grass and Cotton Areas than are indicated by the data given. The small number of farm laborers receiving relief in the Spring Wheat Area indicates that many such families who were living in this area in 1930 had emigrated. Likewise in the Eastern Cotton Belt the evidence points to a considerable migration of rural families into cities. The decline in the number of farmers in the Mississippi Delta region and the large number of rural Negroes receiving relief in cities such as Memphis, Tennessee, are undoubtedly related.

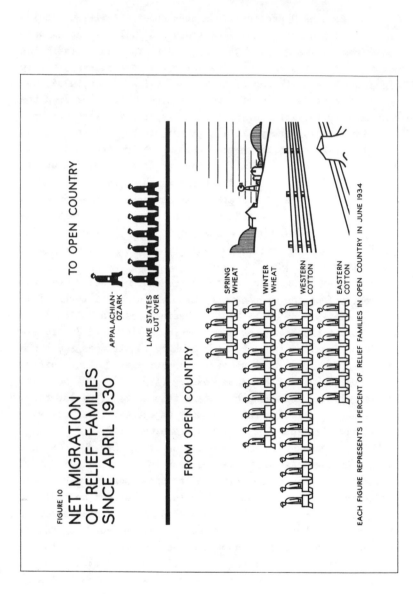

FIGURE 10

NET MIGRATION
OF RELIEF FAMILIES
SINCE APRIL 1930

TO OPEN COUNTRY

APPALACHIAN-OZARK

LAKE STATES CUT OVER

FROM OPEN COUNTRY

SPRING WHEAT

WINTER WHEAT

WESTERN COTTON

EASTERN COTTON

EACH FIGURE REPRESENTS 1 PERCENT OF RELIEF FAMILIES IN OPEN COUNTRY IN JUNE 1934

The unemployed relief clients tended to migrate into, or remain in, the towns and villages.  Figure 11 indicates for male
heads of households usually employed in agricultural and in non-
agricultural occupations (1) the percentage employed in June
1934 and, (2) the percentage of the employed and unemployed in
each group living in the open country or in villages and towns
in June 1934. In all except the Appalachian-Ozark Area the percentage of the unemployed living in villages and towns was considerably greater than for the employed, among male family heads
usually engaged in agriculture.  Most of the unemployed agricultural workers living in villages and towns in the Spring
Wheat and Lake States Cut-Over Areas were aged and retired farmers who had, in all likelihood, moved there before the effects
of the present adverse conditions in these areas made themselves
felt.  In the other three areas, and particularly in the Winter
Wheat and Western Cotton Areas the difference in residence of
employed and unemployed agricultural workers was a result of the
migration of displaced farm tenants, croppers and laborers into
population centers.  On the other hand, in the Eastern Cotton
Belt proportionately more of the displaced farmers and farm
laborers who were receiving relief in the counties surveyed in
June 1934 remained in the open country.
     Among male heads of families usually employed in non-agri-
cultural occupations, the proportion of the unemployed living
in the open country was largest in the areas which had the greatest normal employment in industries (other than agriculture)
located in the open country.  In these same areas—the Appalachian-Ozark, Lake States Cut-Over and Eastern Cotton—the proportion of non-agricultural workers that had shifted to agriculture was also greatest.  It is evident from this that the
shift from non-agricultural to agricultural occupations was almost entirely a matter of the proximity of the families to land
and particularly to cheap land. In other words, areas with industries which were located in the open country—such as mining,
lumbering, wood-working—and which in addition had unoccupied
poor land, had the greatest influx of the industrially unemployed
into agriculture. That the movement of families receiving relief
to the land was not an isolated phenomenon is vividly portrayed
by the striking increase in the total number of farmers in the
Appalachian-Ozark and Lake States Cut-Over Areas from 1930-1935
(Fig. 12).

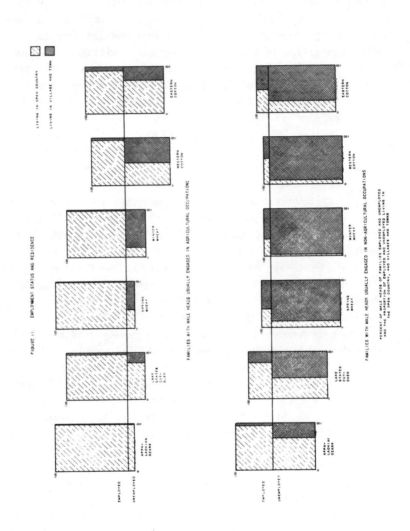

FIGURE 11. EMPLOYMENT STATUS AND RESIDENCE

FAMILIES WITH MALE HEADS USUALLY ENGAGED IN AGRICULTURAL OCCUPATIONS

FAMILIES WITH MALE HEADS USUALLY ENGAGED IN NON-AGRICULTURAL OCCUPATIONS

PERCENT OF MALE HEADS OF FAMILIES EMPLOYED AND UNEMPLOYED
AND THE PROPORTION OF EMPLOYED AND UNEMPLOYED LIVING IN
THE OPEN COUNTRY, AND VILLAGES AND TOWNS

In addition to the movement of the relief population between the open country and population centers, there had been a considerable movement from county to county within the previous 10 years. About 30 percent of the families in the 65 counties had lived less than 10 years in the county in which they were receiving relief. The most stable relief populations were those in the Appalachian-Ozark and Spring Wheat Areas and the Negroes of the Eastern Cotton Belt. In these areas, 84, 79, and 87 percent of the families receiving relief had lived 10 years or longer in the same county. Less than one-half of the white families receiving relief in the Western Cotton Area and only a few more than one-half of the Winter Wheat Area families had lived 10 years or more in the county in which they were receiving relief. In the former area one-third of the white families had moved into the counties during the past five years; in the latter, 23 percent, (Table XIX).

Much of the movement of families into these counties represented a change of residence without a change in occupation. The rapid expansion of wheat and cotton-growing in the Winter Wheat and Western Cotton Areas brought many farmers from other sections into these areas and the population increased steadily until about 1932. Since that time, a series of dry years has bankrupted many of the farm operators and forced them off their farms and into villages and towns, along with the farm laborers whom they formerly employed.

In the Eastern Cotton Belt, the 21 percent of the white families who had moved, during the previous five years, into the counties in which they were receiving relief, were apparently of two types: croppers who had moved from one county to another, and unemployed families who had moved from farms or cities to towns and villages. The white families on the relief rolls in this area were a much more mobile and a much younger group than the Negro families.

In the Lake States Cut-Over Area, the movement of families into the counties surveyed was definitely a part of the emigration of families from cities and the shift to agricultural occupations. The occupational shifts of family heads in this area resulted in many more changes in the place of residence than in the Appalachian-Ozark Area. In the latter, a change in occupation consisted, in most cases, in nothing more than attempting to farm the land on which the family already lived, or

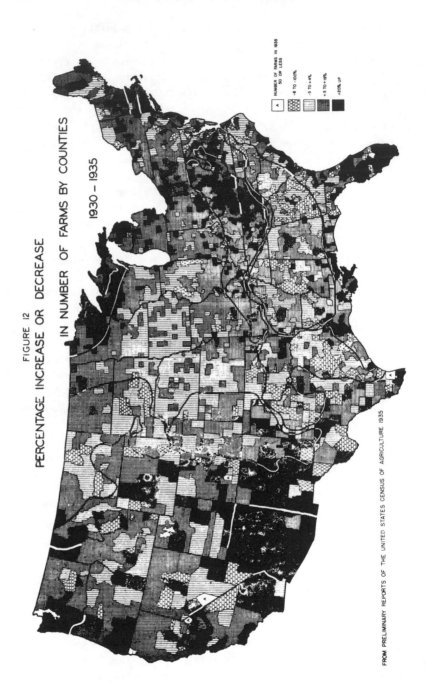

FIGURE 12

PERCENTAGE INCREASE OR DECREASE

IN NUMBER OF FARMS BY COUNTIES

1930 – 1935

FROM PRELIMINARY REPORTS OF THE UNITED STATES CENSUS OF AGRICULTURE 1935

a return to the "home" farm nearby; but in the former, the family more frequently had to move from a city or village in order to get on the land.

On the basis of the preliminary figures from the 1935 Census of Agriculture, it appears that the shift to agriculture of the families receiving relief in the Appalachian-Ozark and Lake States Cut-Over Areas was not an isolated phenomenon, but part of a general movement. The number of farms in the Appalachian-Ozark counties surveyed increased almost one-third, in the Lake States Cut-Over almost one-fourth. Although these figures are preliminary and later revision may reduce them, the increase is large enough to indicate a significant change in the number of farm units. The Spring Wheat and Western Cotton Area counties showed practically no change and the Eastern Cotton Belt counties show an actual decline in the number of farms. This may have been partially due to under-enumeration but general information of the conditions in these counties would indicate the probable accuracy of the Census figures. The increase in the Winter Wheat counties is probably a reflection of the increase in the number of farms which occurred in this area during the period 1930–1932. Information on conditions in this area indicates that there has been some decrease in the number of farms since 1932 as a result of the severe drought conditions of 1933 and 1934.

PERCENTAGE INCREASE OR DECREASE IN NUMBER OF FARMS IN THE COUNTIES SURVEYED, 1930–1935[a]

| AREA | PERCENT INCREASE (+) OR DECREASE (−) |
|---|---|
| ALL AREAS............................................................. | + 7.2 |
| APPALACHIAN-OZARK.................................................. | +32.2 |
| LAKE STATES CUT-OVER............................................. | +23.9 |
| SPRING WHEAT...................................................... | + 0.8 |
| WINTER WHEAT...................................................... | + 7.1 |
| WESTERN COTTON.................................................... | + 0.2 |
| EASTERN COTTON.................................................... | − 4.1 |

[a]SOURCE: U. S. CENSUS OF AGRICULTURE PRELIMINARY REPORTS, 1935

## I.  Residence of Families with Female Heads

Families with women heads were, as in the general population, living in villages and towns more frequently than in the open country. Of all relief families living in the open country, 12 percent had female heads as compared with 18 percent of village and 18 percent of town families (Table 8). Except in the Lake States Cut-Over Area, where only 10 percent of the family heads were women, and among the Eastern Cotton Belt Negro families of which 40 percent of the families had women heads, there was a

higher proportion of women heads of families in the villages
than in either towns or the open country. But among all groups,
except the Western Cotton Area white families, the proportion
of families with women heads was greater in the towns than in
the open country. The concentration of Negro families with
women heads who were receiving relief in the open country and

| | TOTAL ALL AREAS | APPA- LACHIAN OZARK | LAKE STATES CUT- OVER | SHORT GRASS | | WESTERN COTTON | | EASTERN COTTON | |
|---|---|---|---|---|---|---|---|---|---|
| TABLE 8. RESIDENCE OF FAMILIES RECEIVING RELIEF BY SEX OF HEAD | | | | SPRING WHEAT | WINTER WHEAT | WHITE | NEGRO | WHITE | NEGRO |
| ALL FAMILIES.. | | | | | | | | | |
| NUMBER.................. | 10,771 | 2,167 | 1,738 | 1,311 | 2,007 | 800 | 164 | 1,347 | 1,237 |
| PERCENT.................. | 100 | 100 | 100 | 100 | 100 | 100 | 100 | 100 | 100 |
| OPEN COUNTRY......... | 66 | 91 | 63 | 75 | 51 | 47 | 37 | 59 | 62 |
| VILLAGE.............. | 21 | 8 | 24 | 19 | 24 | 35 | 26 | 26 | 25 |
| TOWN................. | 13 | 1 | 13 | 6 | 25 | 18 | 37 | 15 | 13 |
| FAMILIES WITH MALE HEADS | | | | | | | | | |
| NUMBER.................. | 9,235 | 1,921 | 1,560 | 1,208 | 1,860 | 704 | 128 | 1,114, | 740 |
| PERCENT.................. | 100 | 100 | 100 | 100 | 100 | 100 | 100 | 100 | 100 |
| OPEN COUNTRY......... | 67 | 92 | 64 | 77 | 54 | 48 | 41 | 61 | 61 |
| VILLAGE.............. | 20 | 7 | 23 | 17 | 22 | 34 | 21 | 25 | 29 |
| TOWN................. | 13 | 1 | 13 | 6 | 24 | 18 | 38 | 14 | 10 |
| FAMILIES WITH FEMALE HEADS | | | | | | | | | |
| NUMBER.................. | 1,536 | 246 | 178 | 103 | 147 | 96 | 36 | 233 | 497 |
| PERCENT.................. | 100 | 100 | 100 | 100 | 100 | 100 | * | 100 | 100 |
| OPEN COUNTRY......... | 57 | 81 | 53 | 44 | 27 | 43 | * | 52 | 65 |
| VILLAGE.............. | 27 | 14 | 28 | 45 | 40 | 41 | * | 30 | 19 |
| TOWN................. | 16 | 5 | 19 | 11 | 33 | 16 | * | 18 | 16 |
| *Percentage of All Heads of Families, Females* | | | | | | | | | |
| ALL FAMILIES............ | 14 | 11 | 10 | 8 | 7 | 12 | 22 | 17 | 40 |
| OPEN COUNTRY......... | 12 | 10 | 9 | 5 | 4 | 11 | 15 | 15 | 42 |
| VILLAGE.............. | 18 | 20 | 12 | 19 | 12 | 14 | 36 | 20 | 31 |
| TOWN................. | 18 | * | 14 | 13 | 10 | 11 | 20 | 21 | 50 |

*PERCENTAGES NOT COMPUTED BECAUSE OF SMALL NUMBER OF CASES.

in the towns in the Eastern Cotton Belt is probably a result of
the life of the rural Negro, particularly in the plantation
areas, which has been centered around the plantation rather than
a village community. It is to this social unit that the Negro
has looked for sanctuary in his declining years rather than to
the local community centered in a village or small towns as does
the retired farmer of the Corn Belt. In the Appalachian-Ozark
Area, where a large proportion of the families with female heads
were found living in the open country, the life of the family
has been centered in the kinship group and in the neighborhood
which consists of the families that live on the same "branch".
In this case the widowed and the aged depend upon the kinship
group to care for them and the results are the same as in the
Cotton Belt. The fact that women can, and do, work on the farms
in these two areas also helps to account for the presence in the
open country of a large number of families with female heads.

At first glance the fact that one-half of the heads of Negro
families receiving relief and living in towns were women may

seem to refute the explanation offered above for their presence
in such large numbers in the open country. However, aside from
farm work, the chief opportunities for employment for Negro
women are as servants, waiters and domestics, and since the
larger towns make greater use of services of this type than do
villages, they have attracted more families seeking these types
of work than have the latter. As employment in such work fluc-
tuates widely with economic conditions, the servants and waiters
are forced to apply for relief in large numbers.

## IV. SOCIO-ECONOMIC RESOURCES OF FAMILIES RECEIVING RELIEF

In the foregoing chapter the "human resources" were analyzed and assessed. It is now in order to attempt an analysis of the "material resources" actually in the possession of the families receiving relief when this survey was made. Since unemployment relief was not, either by policy or accident, confined to the utterly destitute or the completely unemployed, but rather was granted to all those who could not, by their own efforts, achieve the minimum subsistence living standards deemed as adequate by the relief authorities of the area in question, such an analysis is possible. The nature of the resources, whether employment or property, naturally varies from area to area. For example, the amount of land in the possession of farm owners on relief is significant only when measured against the amount apparently necessary for economic sufficiency in the area in question. No national standard of acreage can be used. Similarly with livestock and poultry: area practices in farm economy decidedly influence the figures here given and are significant only in relation to the possessions of the non-relief farmers of the same area. Moreover, when the incidence of the catastrophe is fairly universal throughout the area, as in the case of drought, the figures may very nearly reflect normal conditions and any obvious deficiencies apply, not to the relief population alone, but to the general population. In short, poverty resulting in dependency is a relative concept only made meaningful when measured against the condition of the self-supporting overlying population.

If farm operators are included, one-half of the heads of the relief families surveyed were employed[1] in June 1934. The proportion employed was highest in the Appalachian-Ozark (72 percent), Spring Wheat (71 percent) and Winter Wheat (50 percent) areas, lowest in the Cotton Areas (Table XIV). For the 65 counties, all but 15 percent of the employed were operating or attempting to operate farms; of the 15 percent who were not farm operators, about 5 percent were farm laborers, the remaining 10

---

[1]Occupation, as used in this section of the report, refers to June 1934 employment and should not be confused with "usual occupation" discussed earlier. Farm operators were classified as employed if they were operating or attempting to operate a farm in June.

percent being engaged in varied types of non-agricultural employment. In the Lake States Cut-Over Area 10 percent, and in the Eastern Cotton Belt about 7 percent of the family heads were employed in non-agricultural occupations. In the latter area, 7 percent of the family heads (5 percent of the whites, 9 percent of the Negroes) receiving relief were employed as farm laborers in June 1934.

Of the families who were operating farms (42.4 percent of all families receiving relief) in June 1934, 43 percent owned all or part of the land they were farming, 55 percent were farming rented land as tenants or croppers, and about 2 percent were squatters or homesteaders (Table XX). Of the farm operators who owned their land, 55 percent reported real estate mortgages. About 37 percent of all families operating farms (about 50 percent of the tenants, 40 percent of the owners and 5 percent of the croppers) reported chattel mortgages. About 70 percent of the farm operators reported dairy cows, 60 percent work stock, 60 percent hogs, and 85 percent poultry.

Of families in which the head was unemployed in June 1934 (50 percent of those receiving relief), 22 percent owned their homes, 69 percent were renters and 9 percent were squatters. Of those who owned their homes, approximately one-fourth reported real estate mortgages. Only 4 percent of the unemployed reported chattel mortgages. The small number of these families reporting mortgage indebtedness is undoubtedly a result of the low value of the property they owned. Only about one-fifth owned dairy cows, less than 5 percent owned work stock, 13 percent owned hogs and only one-third owned poultry (Table XXI).

Families in which the head was employed in non-agricultural occupations in June 1934 owned their homes in more instances than families with unemployed heads, but other indices indicate that they were similar in economic status to the latter.

## A. The Appalachian-Ozark Area

Nearly 69 percent of the families receiving relief in the counties surveyed were operating farms, 3 percent of the heads of families were employed at non-agricultural occupations and 28 percent were unemployed. Because of cheap land and the proximity to the land of persons formerly employed in the industries of this area, large numbers of those who lost industrial jobs turned to subsistence farming. Thirty-two percent were owners,

12 percent tenants and 25 percent croppers. Of those who owned
their farms, but 23 percent reported mortgages. The farmers
receiving relief were living on smaller farms than the average
for the same counties in 1930. Nearly 38 percent were operating
farms of less than 20 acres, and almost 75 percent, farms of
less than 50 acres with the median farm 27 acres. In 1930 in
these same counties, 20 percent of the farms were under 20 acres,
and 47 percent of the farms under 50 acres with the median farm
56 acres. The farms in the counties surveyed were, in 1930,
slightly larger than in the Southern Appalachian Area as a whole
(15, p. 54). In this region only about one-third of the land
in farms was crop land in 1929. If the farmers receiving relief
had this ratio of crop land to total farm acreage, 75 percent
of them had less than 17 acres of crop land, about 50 percent
less than 10 acres and 38 percent less than 7 acres.

About 70 percent of the farm operators receiving relief reported dairy cows, 40 percent work stock, 60 percent hogs and a
little over 80 percent poultry. These percentages were only
slightly lower than for the Southern Appalachian Area as a whole:
about two-thirds of all farmers reported dairy cows and five-
sixths work stock in 1930 (15, pp. 67-69). The farm families
receiving relief lacked work stock, a reflection of the large
proportion of croppers. Only 6 percent of the farm operators
reported chattel mortgages, a smaller percentage than among
Negroes in the Cotton Areas.

The large proportion of families living on small farms and
the absence of real estate and chattel mortgages characterize
the self-sufficing agriculture of this area. These families
have never attained other than the simplest standards of living—standards not much above the subsistence level—and although those receiving relief probably had an income only slightly lower than the general population, the economic margin was so
narrow that a small loss in income particularly cash income,
forced them to accept relief. The farmers have depended upon
wages earned for work off the farm for a considerable part of
their cash income. During 1929 the value of the farm products
sold, traded or used on the farm was less than $400 on 30 per-
cent of the farms in the Southern Appalachians and under $600 on
50 percent of the farms. The annual income from the farm is
quite frequently under $100 after farm expenses are paid. Dur-
ing 1929 the average Southern Appalachian farmer worked 53 days

off his farm for wages (*15*, p. 54). This figure does not take
into account wages earned by other members of the family which
local studies indicate to be an important item (*17*). To a farmer whose total cash income was $400 or less, the loss of outside
employment which yielded as much as $100 annually meant at least
a 25 percent reduction in total cash income (Fig. VI).

Thus although the majority of the heads of families receiving
relief reported their usual occupation as "farmer" most of them
undoubtedly had had an alternate source of income. Since the
industrial depression shut off employment opportunities for many
who would normally have migrated from this area to northern cities and also curtailed employment in the mines and factories of
the area, the increasing population has had to depend upon agriculture for its subsistence. Among the reasons frequently given
for families receiving relief were "Farm too small", "Loss of
supplementary occupation", "Poor land", all reasons which indicate the poor economic circumstances of the farmers. The population has increased as natural resources have decreased so that
now the only hope of assuring these farmers a decent standard
of living lies in the development of some source of industrial
employment.

Families with unemployed heads made up 28 percent of those
receiving relief. Of this group about one-quarter owned their
homes, three-fifths were renters and one-sixth squatters. Only
12 percent of the owned homes were mortgaged, an indication in
most cases of the small value of property rather than the freedom from debt of the owner. Furthe evidence of the economic
status of this group was the near absence of chattel mortgages.
In this day of installment buying, families with any credit
standing would have reported more chattel mortgages than the 1.5
percent of this group.

Nearly 30 percent of the unemployed reported dairy cows, 24
percent reported hogs and 45 percent kept poultry, but less than
6 percent of the families owned any work stock. Yet the number
of unemployed family heads who reported dairy cows, hogs and
poultry was greater than that for the unemployed of any other
area. Only among whites in the Eastern Cotton Belt was the proportion of the unemployed reporting these types of livestock
anywhere near as large and many of the latter were migrants from
the Appalachian-Ozark Area who had carried their mode of living
with them into the cotton country.

### B.  The Lake States Cut-Over Area

Only 29 percent of the families receiving relief in this area
were farming in June 1934, most of them as owner-operators.
Almost three-fifths (59 percent) of the heads of families were
without employment, 10 percent were employed in non-agricultural
occupations and about 2 percent were farm laborers (Table XIV).

Of the farmers, 69 percent owned the land which they were
farming, 27 percent were renters, 3 percent homesteaders, and
two families were squatters.  Fifty-two percent of the farm
owners reported mortgages and twenty-one percent of the farm
operators reported chattel mortgages.  The make-shift nature of
the farming operations of the families receiving relief is evident from the fact that only one-half of them reported work
stock.  This is a higher percentage than in the Appalachian-
Ozark Area but in the latter area many of the farmers were croppers who depended upon the landlord for the necessary work ani-
mals, while most of the farmers in this area owned their own
land, and the majority had recently shifted to farming after
losing their usual jobs.  Eighty percent of the farm operators
owned dairy cows, 45 percent other cattle, 33 percent owned hogs
and 76 percent reported poultry (Table XXI).

About one-half of the farmers receiving relief operated farms
of less than 50 acres and 81 percent farms under 100 acres in
size.  Only 22 percent of the farms in these same counties in
1930 contained less than 50 acres and 54 percent less than 100
acres.  It does not follow from this that the size of the farm
was necessarily responsible for the families appearing on the
rolls for many industrial workers had been thrown on relief by
the loss of their usual job and had turned to the land for a
possible solution of their employment problem.  These "farms"
were small, poorly equipped and under-stocked because of the
financial straits in which the owner found himself upon losing
his job.  The relief situation in both is evidence of the precariousness of a part-time farming economy based almost solely
on exploitative industries (Table XXII).

The unemployed, who made up about three-fifths of the relief
load in this area, owned property or had chattel mortgages in
fewer instances than those who were farming.  About 39 percent
owned their homes, 53 percent were renters and 7 percent squatters.  Only 3 percent reported chattel mortgages and only 24
percent of those who owned their homes reported real estate

mortgages. These low mortgage figures probably reflect the small value of the property. About 17 percent had dairy cows, only 3 percent had work stock, 5 percent kept hogs and less than 20 percent reported poultry (Table XXI). The contrast between this group and the unemployed group in the Appalachian-Ozark Area illustrates some basic differences in the economy of the two areas. The latter is historically agricultural and the population indigenous to the area; this area only recently resorted to agriculture and many of the people are immigrants. In the Appalachian-Ozark Area, the unemployed group receiving relief was a relatively small part of the total relief load, and the relief benefit per family was low, as most of the families were able partially to support themselves on the land; in this area, although some had turned to farming, the number of unemployed was large and relief benefits were high as few of the families had either the training, experience or capital to enable them to attain the material standards of living to which they were accustomed.

## C.  The Wheat Areas

The families receiving relief in this region included more families, who, under ordinary conditions, were able to enjoy a satisfactory scale of living, than did either the families of the Appalachian-Ozark or of the Lake States Cut-Over Area. In the Spring Wheat Area 68 percent and in the Winter Wheat Area 46 percent of the heads of families receiving relief were farming in June 1934. In the former area about 50 percent of the farmers owned their land and in the latter area about 40 percent. Aside from those who were farming, few of the family heads in either area were employed: over 29 percent in the Spring Wheat and more than 50 percent in the Winter Wheat Area were unemployed in June 1934 (Table XIV).

Over 70 percent of the farmers receiving relief in the Spring Wheat Area were operating farms of 260 acres or larger (more than 80 percent of the farms in these same counties in 1930 were in this size group); 7 percent of the farmers receiving relief were operating farms of 1000 acres or more (18 percent of all farms in the counties surveyed in 1930 were in this size group) (Table XXII).

In the Winter Wheat Area approximately 55 percent of the farmers receiving relief were operating farms of 260 acres or

more (80 percent of all farms in 1930) and only 4 percent of the
farmers receiving relief were operating farms of 1000 acres or
more (but about 16 percent of all farms in 1930). In both areas
farm operators with less than a half-section of land (320 acres)
were on the relief rolls more frequently than those with larger
acreages, farmers with one section (640 acres) having about the
average relief rate for the group.

More than four-fifths of the farm owners receiving relief in
the Wheat Areas reported their farms mortgaged; of the farm operators 79 percent in the Spring Wheat and 61 percent in the
Winter Wheat Areas reported chattel mortgages. Of the farm
owners, 85 and 65 percent reported chattel mortgages, while for
the tenants the percentages were 73 and 58. These mortgage
data indicate something of the debt burden of these farmers.
The investigators reported that in one county in the Winter
Wheat Area, the chattel mortgage indebtedness alone was equal,
in 1934, to the value of a normal wheat crop at one dollar per
bushel. As this county had a complete crop failure in 1934, this
debt burden may never be entirely amortized. Only by some debt
adjustment and assistance in replacing their capital can many
of these farmers hope to cover their losses even with normal
crop conditions (Tables XX and XXI).

About 76 percent of the farm operators receiving relief in
the Spring Wheat Area and 83 percent of those in the Winter Wheat
Area reported dairy cows, 78 and 46 percent reported other cattle. In each of these areas about 66 percent reported hogs, and
90 percent reported poultry. Work stock was reported by 91 percent of the farm operators in the Spring Wheat Area and by 72
percent in the Winter Wheat Area. The relatively small proportion of the farmers receiving relief in the Winter Wheat Area
who reported no cattle other than dairy cows indicates something
of the change to wheat farming in this area in recent years. It
may, however, reflect the effects of the government cattle buying program in the drought areas.

Of the unemployed heads of families receiving relief in the
Wheat Areas, 22 percent owned their homes, 76 percent were renters, the remaining 2 percent were squatters. Only 39 percent
of the owned homes were mortgaged and 10 percent (16 percent in
the Spring and 7 percent in the Winter Wheat Area) of the unemployed heads reported chattel mortgages. About 12 percent owned
dairy cows in the Spring Wheat Area and 27 percent in the Winter

Wheat Area; 13 and 6 percent reported workstock, 5 and 11 percent reported hogs, and about 25 and 35 percent reported poultry. Except for workstock and cattle, the families with unemployed heads in the Winter Wheat Area owned more livestock than
the same group in the Spring Wheat Area. This difference was
probably due to the greater number of displaced farmers among
the unemployed in the Winter Wheat Area who were still trying
to produce some of their food supply (Table XXI).

### D.   The Western Cotton Area

Only 30 percent of the white and 28 percent of the Negro
heads of families receiving relief were employed in June 1934,
most of them as farm operators. Twenty-one percent of the white
and 25 percent of the Negro farm operators owned the land they
were farming and about 61 percent of all owners (73 percent of
the whites and 11 percent of the Negroes) reported mortgages.
Over 40 percent of the white and about 14 percent of the Negro
farm operators reported chattel mortgages.

Over 70 percent of the white and about 50 percent of the
Negro farmers receiving relief reported dairy cows and workstock, and over 90 percent of all farm operators kept poultry.
More than one-eighth of the farmers operated farms under 20
acres, over half of them farms under 58 acres, and two-thirds
of them farms smaller than 100 acres. As in the Wheat Areas,
those operating small farms had a higher relief rate than the
operators of the larger farms; one-half of the farms in the same
counties in 1930 were under 104 acres as compared with one-half
under 58 acres for the relief group.

A large proportion of the 70 percent of families receiving
relief in which the head of the family was unemployed in June
1934 were displaced farm tenants and unemployed farm laborers.
Only about 16 percent of this group owned their homes, 55 percent of the white and 60 percent of the Negroes were renters
and 29 percent and 23 percent were squatters. This squatter
group was without resources of any kind, unable to find work and
literally stranded in the area.

### E.   The Eastern Cotton Belt

In approximately one-third of the families receiving relief,
the head of the family was employed in June 1934. As a much

larger percentage of white than Negro families included gainful
workers the proportion of the employable Negroes actually employed in June 1934 was larger than for whites. About 5 percent
of the white and 9 percent of the Negro family heads were employed as farm laborers, and 5 and 9 percent, respectively,
in other occupations. The remaining 68 percent of the white
and 63 percent of the Negro heads of families were unemployed
in June 1934

Only 22 percent of the white and 16 percent of the Negro farm
operators owned their farms; the remainder were renting land.
Of those who owned land, 69 percent of the whites and 46 percent
of the Negroes reported real estate mortgages. Thirty-one percent of the white and 14 percent of the Negro farm operators
reported chattel mortgages. As more than three-fourths of the
farmers receiving relief were tenants or croppers in June 1934,
this low chattel mortgage indebtedness was to be expected, as
most of the capital and equipment of the farm is furnished by
the landlord under the share-cropper system.

Dairy cows were reported by 61 percent of the white and about
40 percent of the Negro farm operators. About 66 percent of the
white and 61 percent of the Negro farmers reported work stock
available and 65 and 54 percent, respectively, kept hogs.
Poultry was reported by about 80 percent of all farm operators.

The farmers receiving relief were operating farms smaller
than the average for the same counties in 1930: 20 percent had
farms of less than 10 acres, 42 percent farms of less than 20
acres. Only 5 percent of the farms in these same counties (in
1930) were smaller than 10 acres and but 22 percent smaller than
20 acres. From these and other data available it is evident
that most of the farmers receiving relief in this area were
those habitually near the economic margin.

There were fewer home owners among the unemployed heads of
families receiving relief in this than in any other area, less
than 12 percent reporting possession of real estate. Of the
owners, 29 percent reported real estate mortgages. Six percent
of the white and 3 percent of the Negro unemployed heads of families were squatters. Less than 2 percent of the unemployed
reported chattel mortgages. One-fourth of the whites and less
than one-tenth of the Negroes kept dairy cows, about one-sixth
of the whites and one-fifth of the Negroes reported hogs. Almost
as few reported work stock or other types of livestock.

The families of non-agricultural workers, a large proportion of which lived in villages and towns, reported livestock less frequently than did the families of unemployed persons. Farm laborer families reported dairy cows, hogs and chickens more frequently than the families of non-agricultural and unemployed persons.

## V.   PLANS AND PROSPECTS FOR REHABILITATION
## OF THE FAMILIES RECEIVING RELIEF

To rehabilitate, in the strictest sense of the word, means to
restore to a previously attained status, to make solvent again.
In this narrow sense of the term rehabilitation would mean to
many families receiving relief only a return to a socio-economic
status more insecure than the one they enjoy as recipients of
relief. Rehabilitation, if it is to be of maximum social value,
must therefore be conceived more broadly.   It will need to set
as its goals the helping of families to attain and maintain a
social and economic status commensurate with at least the minimum standards of health, wealth, security and social well-being
considered essential to national welfare. The effectiveness of
the rehabilitation program aimed to attain these ends will be
determined by the kind and extent of the human and material resources available and the facility with which they can be brought
together for the improvement of the status of the community.

The material resources of any community, present or potential,
will be of value in a rehabilitation program only to the extent
to which the families to be assisted are capable of utilizing
them and to the extent to which they are made available for use.
In some of the areas under discussion, human resources will be
much more of a limiting factor than the availability of material
resources.   This extremely obvious fact may be easily over-
looked.   The characteristics of the family and the community
of which it is a part may be such that the family, even if given
financial assistance, will shortly return to the relief rolls.
By human resources are meant all cultural factors such as the
training, experience and aptitudes of the family and its members,
the niche which the family occupies in the social structure of
the community, and the relationship of the types of families and
of community organization to the economic organization. A case
in point is that of the Eastern Cotton Belt cropper family.
Although it appears possible to improve the standards of living
of the cotton croppers through a system of diversified farming,
human inertia to such a change, both among the land-owners and
the croppers themselves, may delay it for a generation or more.
While it may be possible to provide an illiterate share-cropper

with a small farm of his own, the probability that the average cropper will be able to manage it successfully is slight. Likewise it may be a questionable policy to try to make a dairy farmer out of a coal miner who is used to an eight-hour day with Saturday afternoons and Sundays off, or even to try to train a dry-land farmer to operate an irrigated farm. More dubious still would be the relocation of families in a new community of which they would find it difficult to become a part because of their race, religion or prejudice on the part of the community, or the relocation upon an isolated farm of a village or town family if the wife and homemaker knew nothing about, or disliked, farm life. In areas where women seldom work in the fields, the rehabilitation of families on small farms which may require considerable farm labor on the part of the wife or daughter is not likely to be successful, because the family would lose caste if its women did farm work. Although rehabilitation by setting the family up on a small farm and furnishing outside work for the husband should be successful in the South and possibly in the Appalachian-Ozark Area, it will not be very successful in other areas unless the combination of farm and non-farm work is such that most of the work can be done by male members of the family. Farm units, outside the Cotton Areas, will need for the most part to be gauged to the labor of one male plus only incidental labor of other members of the family.

The prospect of rehabilitating families on relief in the communities in which they live reduces to an answer to the question, "To what extent and by what methods can they be assisted to utilize the available material resources so that they may become self-supporting, productive members of these communities?" The answer to be returned varies widely and depends upon the resources of the area, their availability, and the capacity of the families to use them. Families that cannot be rehabilitated in place because of lack of suitable resources will have to be assisted to resettle elsewhere.

## A.  Capacity of Families Receiving Relief to Become Self-Supporting

All of the foregoing information takes on relevance in this study only insofar as it enables one to estimate the prospects of rehabilitating the families studied. In the opinion of local relief workers, 20 percent of the families receiving relief in

the 65 counties were incapable of self-support, 15 percent capable but in need of supervision as well as temporary financial
aid, and 65 percent capable of self-support if given only temporary financial aid (Table 9). The majority of the families
classified as incapable were aged one-person cases, other families with aged heads, broken families consisting usually of a
woman with children under 16 years of age, and families containing but one gainful worker in which the number of dependents
(aged persons and children) per worker was too great to make
self-support possible. Of those families considered incapable
of self-support 54 percent included no gainful workers 16 years
of age and over, 15 percent included only one female gainful

TABLE 9. CAPACITY FOR SELF-SUPPORT OF FAMILIES RECEIVING RELIEF BY SEX OF HEAD OF FAMILY

| CAPACITY FOR SELF-SUPPORT BY SEX OF HEAD | TOTAL ALL AREAS | APPA- LACHIAN OZARK | LAKE STATES CUT- OVER | SHORT GRASS | | WESTERN COTTON | | EASTERN COTTON | |
|---|---|---|---|---|---|---|---|---|---|
| | | | | SPRING WHEAT | WINTER WHEAT | WHITE | NEGRO | WHITE | NEGRO |
| **ALL FAMILIES** | | | | | | | | | |
| NUMBER................. | 10,771 | 2,167 | 1,738 | 1,311 | 2,007 | 800 | 164 | 1,347 | 1,237 |
| PERCENT................. | 100 | 100 | 100 | 100 | 100 | 100 | 100 | 100 | 100 |
| INCAPABLE.............. | 20 | 15 | 22 | 16 | 14 | 15 | 23 | 20 | 39 |
| CAPABLE................ | 80 | 85 | 78 | 84 | 86 | 85 | 77 | 80 | 61 |
| WITH SUPERVISION.... | 15 | 29 | 7 | 9 | 8 | 10 | 23 | 17 | 22 |
| WITHOUT SUPERVISION. | 65 | 56 | 71 | 75 | 78 | 75 | 54 | 63 | 39 |
| **FAMILIES WITH MALE HEADS** | | | | | | | | | |
| NUMBER................. | 9,235 | 1,021 | 1,560 | 1,208 | 1,860 | 704 | 128 | 1,114 | 740 |
| PERCENT................. | 100 | 100 | 100 | 100 | 100 | 100 | 100 | 100 | 100 |
| INCAPABLE.............. | 15 | 12 | 19 | 13 | 11 | 13 | 20 | 16 | 27 |
| CAPABLE................ | 85 | 88 | 81 | 87 | 89 | 87 | 80 | 84 | 73 |
| WITH SUPERVISION.... | 15 | 29 | 7 | 10 | 8 | 10 | 24 | 18 | 24 |
| WITHOUT SUPERVISION. | 70 | 59 | 74 | 77 | 81 | 77 | 56 | 66 | 49 |
| **FAMILIES WITH FEMALE HEADS** | | | | | | | | | |
| NUMBER............. .... | 1,536 | 246 | 178 | 103 | 147 | 96 | 36 | 233 | 497 |
| PERCENT................. | 100 | 100 | 100 | 100 | 100 | 100 | 100 | 100 | 100 |
| INCAPABLE.. .......... | 47 | 44 | 50 | 49 | 48 | 27 | 36 | 35 | 56 |
| CAPABLE............... | 53 | 56 | 50 | 51 | 52 | 73 | 64 | 65 | 44 |
| WITH SUPERVISION.... | 14 | 27 | 2 | 5 | 8 | 8 | 17 | 12 | 19 |
| WITHOUT SUPERVISION. | 39 | 29 | 48 | 46 | 44 | 65 | 47 | 53 | 25 |

worker and another 2 percent included two or more female but no
male gainful workers—a total of 71 percent of the families
considered incapable of self-support by the local relief workers
included no male gainful workers. Of the 29 percent remaining,
21 percent included only one male gainful worker and many of the
latter were workers incapable of performing normal tasks, because
of age or other disability.

Only about 15 percent of the Appalachian-Ozark, Spring and
Winter Wheat, and Western Cotton Area white families were considered incapable of self-support (Table 9). In these four area
groups the proportion of normal families among those receiving
relief was highest, ranging from 77 to 89 percent. In the first
three the percentage of all families including gainful workers
was also highest.

As might be expected because of the composition of families with woman heads, about one-half were classified as incapable as compared with but 15 percent of families with male heads. The largest proportion of families with female heads classified as incapable was for Negro families in the Eastern Cotton Belt (56 percent), the smallest in the Western Cotton Area and for white families in the Eastern Cotton Belt (27 to 36 percent). Taking family type into consideration, it is obvious that the greatest proportions of families with female heads were classified as capable in the areas in which women are accustomed to working in the fields.

Of all families receiving relief in the 65 counties, 18 percent of the open country families, 24 percent of the village families and 21 percent of the town families were classified as incapable of self-support (Table XXIII). This variation between the open country and population centers was largely a result of the congregation of families with female heads in villages and towns. In the Eastern Cotton Belt where the proportion of Negro families with female heads in the open country was higher than in villages, the proportion of the open country Negro families considered incapable of self-support was also higher.

In conclusion, it is clearly apparent that the families considered impossible to rehabilitate (20 percent of all) are chiefly those which would be provided for by a comprehensive system of social legislation.

### B.    Indices of Standards of Living, and Education

Some indication of the differences in the material standards of living of the farmers in the counties surveyed are apparent in the following tabulation of the number having certain facilities and conveniences in their homes at the time of the 1930 Census (Table 10). The Spring and Winter Wheat and Lake States Cut-Over Areas exceed the United States average in number of radios, and the latter exceeds it in number of telephones, with the former two only slightly lower. All are below the United States average for proportion of homes with electric lights, the Lake States Cut-Over Area again being high with 8 percent. The Winter Wheat and Western Cotton Area counties were highest in percentage of farms with water piped to the dwelling and to the bathroom, with the Spring Wheat and Lake States Cut-Over Areas poor seconds.

At the bottom of the list for all these items stand the Eastern Cotton Belt counties with 2 percent or fewer farms reporting
radio, electric lights or water piped to the house and, fewer
than 5 percent of the farms with telephones. The Appalachian-
Ozark farmers reported almost as few conveniences, less than 8
percent having telephones and less than 4 percent reporting other

| TABLE 10. PERCENTAGE OF FARMS IN THE COUNTIES SURVEYED WITH SPECIFIED FACILITIES, 1930[a] | | | | | SHORT GRASS | | | |
|---|---|---|---|---|---|---|---|---|
| | U. S. TOTAL | TOTAL ALL AREAS | APPA- LACHIAN OZARK | LAKE STATES CUT-OVER | SPRING WHEAT | WINTER WHEAT | WESTERN COTTON | EASTERN COTTON |
| TELEPHONE.................... | 34.0 | 15.3 | 7.5 | 38.1 | 31.7 | 31.4 | 22.0 | 4.9 |
| RADIO........................ | 21.8 | 9.6 | 2.7 | 25.0 | 35.7 | 25.1 | 9.2 | 1.8 |
| ELECTRIC LIGHTS IN DWELLING. | 13.4 | 3.8 | 3.6 | 8.0 | 4.7 | 5.1 | 4.7 | 2.1 |
| WATER PIPED TO: | | | | | | | | |
| DWELLING.................. | 15.8 | 6.4 | 3.4 | 7.8 | 6.2 | 19.0 | 14.3 | 1.8 |
| BATHROOM.................. | 8.4 | 3.3 | 1.6 | 2.4 | 2.4 | 7.9 | 8.4 | 1.5 |
| [a]U. S. CENSUS OF AGRICULTURE, 1930. | | | | | | | | |

conveniences. The possession of the above conveniences indicates, roughly, the wide variation among these areas with respect
to social organization and standards of living. The average
amount of relief granted in June 1934 in the six areas was highest in the areas in which the percentage of farms reporting
radios (in 1930) was highest.

When it is considered that the farmers receiving relief in
such areas as the Appalachian-Ozark, Lake States Cut-Over and
the two Cotton Areas were on the smaller farms and were apparently families habitually near the economic margin, as contrasted
with the families receiving relief in the Wheat Areas who more
nearly represented an economic cross-section of the population,
the wide differences between families receiving relief in the
two groups of areas becomes more apparent.

Another index of the socio-economic levels of the various
areas is the education of the heads of families receiving relief
in June 1934 in the counties surveyed. It is also an indication
of the type of rehabilitation program possible in each area.
One-half of the Negro family heads and one-fifth of the whites
in the Eastern Cotton Belt reported no schooling, and four-fifths
of the Negroes and about one-half of the whites had less than
five years (Table 11). Although the percentage of family heads
with no schooling in the Appalachian-Ozark Area was less than
for whites in the Eastern Cotton Belt, the proportion that had
completed fewer than five grades (56 percent) was larger.

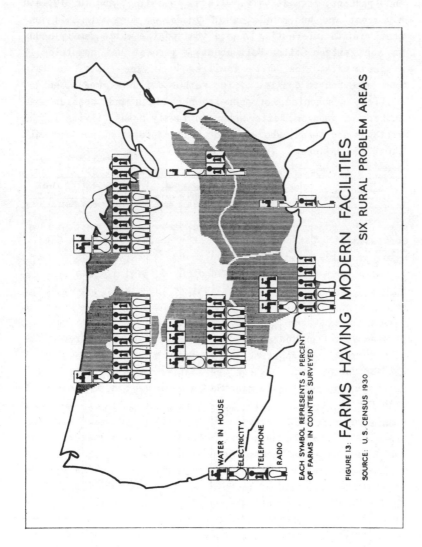

WATER IN HOUSE

ELECTRICITY

TELEPHONE

RADIO

EACH SYMBOL REPRESENTS 5 PERCENT OF FARMS IN COUNTIES SURVEYED

FIGURE 13: FARMS HAVING MODERN FACILITIES

SIX RURAL PROBLEM AREAS

SOURCE: U. S. CENSUS 1930

The heads of families receiving relief in the Spring and Winter Wheat and Lake States Cut-Over Areas included about 5.3, and 8 percent, respectively, with no schooling, and 10, 12, and 6 percent who had completed 11 grades or more. In this connection it is interesting to note that of the white family heads in the Eastern Cotton Belt about 9 percent had completed 11 grades or more. The white families receiving relief in this area appeared to consist of two rather definite groups, an unskilled, unschooled, cropper-laborer class and considerable numbers of younger, better schooled family heads, living in the villages and towns, who were formerly employed at non-agricultural occupations.

TABLE 11. GRADE IN SCHOOL FINISHED BY HEADS OF FAMILIES RECEIVING RELIEF

| GRADE IN SCHOOL FINISHED BY HEAD | TOTAL ALL AREAS | APPA-LACHIAN OZARK | LAKE STATES CUT-OVER | SHORT GRASS | | WESTERN COTTON | | EASTERN COTTON | |
|---|---|---|---|---|---|---|---|---|---|
| | | | | SPRING WHEAT | WINTER WHEAT | WHITE | NEGRO | WHITE | NEGRO |
| *Number* | | | | | | | | | |
| ALL FAMILIES............. | 10,771 | 2,167 | 1,738 | 1,311 | 2,007 | 800 | 164 | 1,347 | 1,237 |
| FAMILIES REPORTING SCHOOLING OF HEAD........ | 8,265 | 1,779 | 1,063 | 1,017 | 1,145 | 788 | 162 | 1,239 | 1,072 |
| NONE.................. | 1,325 | 260 | 80 | 54 | 29 | 71 | 38 | 251 | 542 |
| 1-4.................. | 2,263 | 738 | 282 | 150 | 131 | 223 | 59 | 337 | 343 |
| 5-7.................. | 2,081 | 508 | 280 | 231 | 270 | 249 | 46 | 357 | 140 |
| 8.................. | 1,609 | 189 | 282 | 417 | 458 | 115 | 11 | 117 | 20 |
| 9-10................. | 497 | 55 | 79 | 64 | 123 | 90 | 4 | 70 | 12 |
| 11-12................. | 351 | 19 | 49 | 77 | 103 | 30 | 3 | 63 | 7 |
| OVER 12.............. | 139 | 10 | 11 | 24 | 31 | 10 | 1 | 44 | 8 |
| UNKNOWN.............. | 2,506 | 388 | 675 | 294 | 862 | 12 | 2 | 108 | 165 |
| *Percent* | | | | | | | | | |
| FAMILIES REPORTING SCHOOLING OF HEAD........ | 100.0 | 100.0 | 100.0 | 100.0 | 100.0 | 100.0 | 100.0 | 100.0 | 100.0 |
| NONE.................. | 16.0 | 14.6 | 7.5 | 5.3 | 2.5 | 9.0 | 23.4 | 20.3 | 50.5 |
| 1-4.................. | 27.4 | 41.5 | 26.5 | 14.7 | 11.4 | 28.3 | 36.4 | 27.2 | 32.0 |
| 5-7.................. | 25.2 | 28.6 | 26.4 | 22.7 | 23.6 | 31.6 | 28.4 | 28.8 | 13.1 |
| 8.................. | 19.5 | 10.6 | 26.5 | 41.0 | 40.0 | 14.6 | 6.8 | 9.4 | 1.9 |
| 9-10................. | 6.0 | 3.1 | 7.5 | 6.3 | 10.8 | 11.4 | 2.5 | 5.6 | 1.1 |
| 11-12................. | 4.2 | 1.1 | 4.6 | 7.6 | 9.0 | 3.8 | 1.9 | 5.1 | 0.7 |
| OVER 12.............. | 1.7 | 0.5 | 1.0 | 2.4 | 2.7 | 1.3 | 0.6 | 3.6 | 0.7 |

Although the data on schooling presented above are probably not comparable from area to area because of variation in school standards, they do indicate area differences, as the poorest school systems from the standpoint of length of terms, equipment, and training of teachers, are in those areas in which the heads of families reported a minimum of schooling.

## C.  Occupational Experience and Rehabilitation

Nearly half of the families receiving relief who were judged
capable of self-support[1] had male heads reporting agricultural
experience.  Thirty-seven percent of all heads were operating
farms in June 1934 and 6 percent were unemployed farm operators,
making a total of 43 percent with experience as farm operators;
about 2 percent were employed farm laborers and 4 percent unemployed farm laborers. Of the remaining 50 percent of the families, 3 percent were capable families with male heads employed
in non-agricultural occupations and 22 percent of the families
had unemployed male heads whose usual occupations were non-
agricultural (Table XXIV).

Although families capable of self-support with male heads who
were farming or had been farm operators made up 43 percent of
the relief load in the 65 counties surveyed, only 33 percent of
all families were families with male heads considered capable
of being rehabilitated as farmers (the difference was largely
due to the Lake States Cut-Over Area, where many of those who
were farming in June 1934 had recently shifted to agriculture
because they had lost their industrial jobs); but another 28
percent were considered capable of operating small plots as a
means of partial support in conjunction with other employment
(Table XXV). The basis for the local relief workers' classification of each family by type of work for which it was qualified
thus appears to have been largely its past occupational experience.

According to a classification which presupposes rehabilitation on the type of farm prevalent in each area and at a standard of living near the average for the area, the proportion of
all families receiving relief who were classified as capable of
rehabilitation as full-time farmers varied from but 18 percent
in the Appalachian-Ozark and Lake States Cut-Over Area to 64
percent in the Spring Wheat Area.  Naturally, those classified
as capable of becoming farm operators in the Appalachian-Ozark
Area might not succeed as farm operators under another type of
farming and many entirely capable of self-support as cotton
tenants or croppers would not know how to operate a wheat farm
in the Great Plains region.

[1] The local relief workers were asked to classify each family which they considered
capable of self-support, according to its qualifications for operating a farm or
a garden plot (part-time farm) with other employment:  all capable families not
considered likely to be successful as full or part-time farmers are included under
the heading "other employment".

Thirty-one percent of all families were classified as capable of rehabilitation on the land if given supplementary employment of some kind. The percentage falling in this group was highest in the Appalachian-Ozark (65 percent) and Lake States Cut-Over (44 percent) Areas, lowest in the Eastern Cotton (11 to 12 percent) and Spring Wheat Areas (11 percent) (Table XXV).

The proportion of the families receiving relief who were considered unlikely prospects for successful rehabilitation as operators of full or part-time farms but capable of successful rehabilitation in some other occupation varied from less than 3 percent in the Appalachian-Ozark Area to 23 and 31 percent for white families in the Western and Eastern Cotton Areas, respectively. It is obvious from these classifications, even though they are based on subjective judgments, that the type of rehabilitation program which will be successful in one area would likely fail in another. Moreover, occupational experience is only one of the limiting factors. Age, family composition, socio-economic status and racial factors further complicate and differentiate the type of problem that must be solved in each area.

### D. Rehabilitation Prospects in Each Area.

*1. The Appalachian-Ozark Area.* The rehabilitation of this vast cultural area offers a greater task than does any of the five other areas as it will involve (1) the moving of families from submarginal lands, (2) the regulation of the commercial exploitation of the area's natural resources so as to insure their orderly development, (3) the development of forests and recreational areas, and (4) the extension of educational opportunities.

The average family receiving relief in June 1934 was a normal family, consisting of husband, wife, and three children. The husband was between 40 and 45 years of age, had received less than five years of schooling, and was a tenant (or cropper) farmer on a farm of about 37 acres, not more than 10 acres of which was tillable. The family owned a horse or mule, kept one or two cows, some hogs for its meat supply and a small flock of chickens. It had always lived in the same county, in a house without electric lights, running water or any other modern convenience, had no radio, telephone, or automobile. What limited personal property the family owned was free of mortgage. In normal times the husband secured a considerable portion of his *cash income* by work off his farm. Because of the drought in 1931, and the loss of his supplementary occupation, the family came onto the relief rolls in 1932 and has been receiving relief more or less regularly ever since.

The above characterization of the average family indicates rather clearly the type of family receiving relief. Nearly 60 percent of the families were the families of farm operators and another 14 percent the families of unskilled laborers. Nearly 83 percent were normal families and 66 percent included one or more children under 16 years of age. About three-fourths of all the families including children under 16 years and only one-sixth persons 65 years of age and older. Over 90 percent of the families included gainful workers 16 years of age or older and about 86 percent included male gainful workers. Almost two-thirds of all persons in the families receiving relief were under 25 years of age. Of those who were farming in June 1934, about 98 percent were operating farms of less than 20 acres or in other words, 3 to 6 acres of tillable land.

The resident population is already too large to permit an adequate standard of living and is increasing rapidly. The largest increases are among the young adults. As a result of heavy emigration of young men and women from this area to Northern cities during the 1920's, the number of persons 20 to 30 years of age in 1930 was much smaller than of those 10 to 20 years. Without migration the number of young adults between ages 20 and 30 years will have increased 25 to 30 percent by 1935. Recall that one-fourth of the male family heads receiving relief in June 1934 were under 32 years of age. The seriousness of the problem is indicated by the fact that large numbers of these young adults have been receiving relief for three or four years, most of them for more than two years. It can be expected, however, that with the development of a standard of living some-what above the subsistence level, the birth rate of this area will eventually decline.

It is difficult to see how, under any program of rehabilitation or reemployment, all the man power of this area can be absorbed in any industrial or agricultural employment possible at the moment. The coal and lumber industries, about which the present part-time farming economy has grown up, are the only important non-agricultural resources immediately available. Past experience with such exploitative industries indicates the

insecurity of an economy built around them. The agricultural
land available is very limited but some farm families who are
located on submarginal farms with their poor soils and vertical
fields should be relocated on more fertile lands which would
furnish an adequate income. Much of the land withdrawn from
farming should be set up as forest areas (18, p. 176) and developed to offer a certain amount of supplementary employment
to farm families located in the area and to establish a stable
forest industry. Dovetailed with the creation of forest lands
is the commercial opportunity for the development of recreational
activities. The area's scenery, climate and proximity to population centers are propitious to such a development (Fig. VII).

In the face of all the facts the prospects for rehabilitation
of families receiving relief appear none too good. Some form
of industrial employment must be found to supplement the income
from the farms if the present population is to remain in this
area without government subsidy in the form of relief. Some
families could be employed in a reforestation program which is
badly needed and some improvement could be brought about by
diversification of the agricultural practice which at present
centers too much on a few crops. Fruit can be grown successfully
in many parts if a market can be found.

In the opinion of the local relief workers only about one-
sixth of the families receiving relief were qualified to operate
full-time farms, about two-thirds to operate a part-time farm
in connection with other employment and less than 3 percent for
other employment (Table XXV). The prospects for rehabilitation
of these families rests, in two-thirds of the cases, upon the
possibility of securing a steady source of part-time employment
for families already living upon the land. Emigration must be
encouraged but it will be unwise to carry out any widespread
resettlement projects which will radically change the environment
under which these families live. The problems involved here can
only be solved by substituting for the present economy of this
area a planned economy which will insure orderly development of
the natural resources. The area's importance in the national
economy must be recognized and the agriculture and other industry
organized so as to benefit the population of the area rather
than to be left to the whim and caprice of individual farmers,
mining companies and timber operators. Without some rational
plan of future development this area will continue to present
a serious social problem.

Along with a planned development of the resources of the area must go an educational system which will assist youth better to assimilate the ideas and methods of modern industrial civilization. The public schools in a large part of this area are poorly equipped and the emigrants to regions of higher school standards are severely handicapped by their lack of training. Only in sections of the Eastern Cotton Belt are educational facilities poorer. Improvement is evident in North Carolina, and West Virginia where the financial responsibility for the school system has been taken over by the state. Through its financial support the state of West Virginia, for example, is able to supply communities with facilities beyond the economic means of the local community. The program is being geared to adult vocational problems as well as to the children of school age and to t h e more academic subjects, and will serve as an example for the entire area.

In a resettlement program for this area the simple standard of living of the population must be kept continually in mind. It will be difficult to obtain community support for a program which gives families on the relief rolls better homes, for instance, than those occupied by the average family not receiving relief. In this connection it will be well to bear in mind that fewer than 5 out of each 100 farmers in the Southern Appalachian region had electric lights or a bathroom (in 1930) and that almost as few had telephones. Before living standards of the relief group can be raised appreciably the standards of the majority of the families in this area must also be raised. Only through a long time program of education coupled with some means of increasing family income is such improvement possible.

If agencies such as the Tennessee Valley Authority, through making cheap power available over a large part of this area, can encourage the development of new industries and resources, they will contribute much to a solution of the problems of the area. From the standpoint of the social organization of the Appalachian-Ozark Area, it will be more desirable to bring the industries to the people than to have large numbers of them migrate to strange environments elsewhere.

2. *The Lake States Cut-Over Area.* The future of this area depends on a rehabilitation program which can be developed around a land zoning program and the dominant industries of this area: forestry, mining, agriculture and recreational projects. A large

area is suitable only for reforestation (Fig. 14), and the stranded farm families should be relocated on more arable land and other families provided with part - time work in a reforestation program which in the end will establish a stable forestry and woodworking industry.

The families receiving relief in this area were of two distinct types: one-person families, usually lone males too old to work or unable to find employment who were formerly employed in the forests or mines, and normal families consisting of a husband, wife and two or three children. The average family on the relief rolls was a family of four. The head of the family was between 45 and 50 years of age and had less than 7 years of schooling. He was without employment in June 1934, and was usually employed as an unskilled or semi-skilled worker in the lumbering or woodworking industries, or in the mines. He lived in the open country in a rented house but owned no livestock of any kind. His few chattels were not mortgaged.

The majority of the families receiving relief in the counties surveyed in this area were those of non-agricultural workers. Only one-fourth of the families were capable families with male heads (Table XXIV) and living on farms in June 1934. Few of the remaining families had any farming experience. Only about 18 percent of the families (about three-fourths of those with farming experience) were considered capable of becoming full-time farmers. Another 44 percent were considered capable of rehabilitation on the land if given supplementary employment, 16 percent were capable of non-farm work only, and 22 percent were incapable of being rehabilitated.

Nearly two-thirds of the incapable families were families without gainful workers and families consisting of lone males and one-third were families without male gainful workers. The majority of the incapables were aged lumbermen no longer able to earn enough to support themselves, most of whom were living alone. However, this latter group contained some gainful workers who, if given employment, could at least partially support themselves, and their families. The occupational experience of the head of the families receiving relief, coupled with the local relief workers' classification of their qualifications, indicates the necessity of proceeding cautiously in any further development of full or part-time farming in this area. Unless supplementary employment can be found for at least one-fourth of

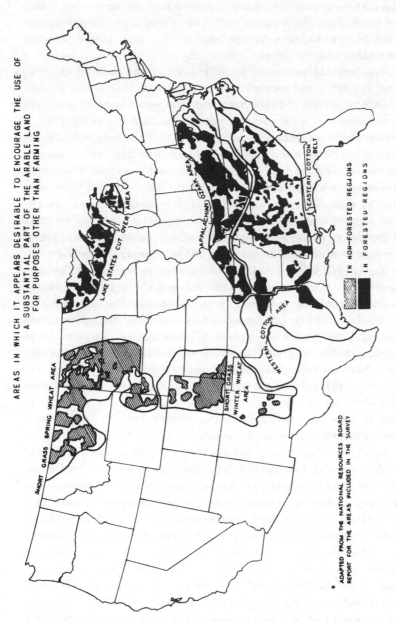

FIGURE 14

AREAS IN WHICH IT APPEARS DESIRABLE TO ENCOURAGE THE USE OF A SUBSTANTIAL PART OF THE ARABLE LAND FOR PURPOSES OTHER THAN FARMING

SHORT GRASS SPRING WHEAT AREA

LAKE STATES CUT OVER AREA

APPALACHIAN-OZARK AREA

EASTERN COTTON BELT

SHORT GRASS WINTER WHEAT AREA

WESTERN COTTON AREA

IN NON-FORESTED REGIONS

IN FORESTED REGIONS

ADAPTED FROM THE NATIONAL RESOURCES BOARD REPORT FOR THE AREAS INCLUDED IN THE SURVEY

the relief group now farming, they probably cannot attain complete self-support. Of the families not on farms, more than one-half might be set up as part-time farmers if additional employment can be assured to supplement their farm income. Unless some steady source of employment can be found, it will be futile to encourage these families to remain on the land by lending them equipment and capital.

Careful zoning of the land according to its best uses, the development of farm-forest communities, and the relocation on better land of capable farmers now on poor land seem to be indicated. Others should be assisted in clearing their land and increasing the size of their farms to make agriculture a more stable and profitable enterprise (Fig. 15). It should also be kept in mind that many of the families receiving relief are recent migrants who probably should be encouraged to emigrate elsewhere as employment picks up. The stranded communities of the copper mine, timber and woodworking areas are separate problems. It will be to the interests of this group, and of society in general to assist them either to leave the area or to locate on land suitable for farming. Under the present system (or lack of system) the families most poorly equipped for farming are finding their way onto the poorest lands. A well-planned rural rehabilitation program for this area should be gauged to the available resources, and not become just an instrument for setting up additional marginal farm units. Considerable population adjustments will be necessary to correct the ill-advised promotion of land settlement which has contributed to the economic insecurity engendered by the collapse of the lumbering and mining industries. The development of recreation as a source of income offers possibilities for a few families. Lakes, fishing and climatic conditions of the area are favorable (Fig. VII). The area is fortunately situated near population centers, and though recreational facilities are embryonic in their present development, they offer promising possibilities of becoming a permanent industry. If some of the energy and money spent in extolling the dubious virtues of "Cloverland" to uninformed buyers had been turned to developing what now is admitted to be "The Land of Hiawatha", some of the present troubles of this area could have been avoided. Only through a system of land zoning, such as that used in Wisconsin, can a repetition of wildly speculative land selling schemes be avoided.

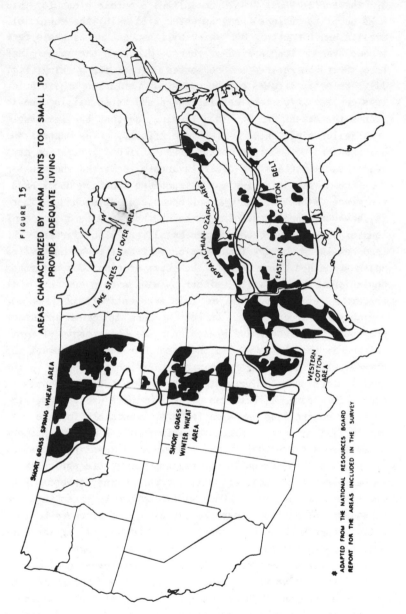

FIGURE 15

AREAS CHARACTERIZED BY FARM UNITS TOO SMALL TO PROVIDE ADEQUATE LIVING

SHORT GRASS SPRING WHEAT AREA

LAKE STATES CUT OVER AREA

APPALACHIAN-OZARK AREA

EASTERN COTTON BELT

SHORT GRASS WINTER WHEAT AREA

WESTERN COTTON AREA

* ADAPTED FROM THE NATIONAL RESOURCES BOARD REPORT FOR THE AREAS INCLUDED IN THE SURVEY

*3. The Spring Wheat Area.*  Social and economic plans for this
area ought to include a program which will bring the rapid soil
erosion under control  and which will assure  an  adequate farm
income over  a  long period of years.  Much  of  the submarginal
land should be  retired and replanted in grass for grazing (Fig.
14).  Selected farmers cán be assisted in enlarging their holdings  so  as  to  restore cattle, sheep and horse raising and to
reduce the extent  of  dry land farming, so that the inevitable
crop failures will have less severe effects.   The Montana and
Nebraska projects for the construction of flood irrigation dams
and dikes in coulees and other favorable locations where water
from the torrential rains may be impounded should be encouraged,
and where favorable, irrigation homesteads developed.   There
is, however, some scepticism as to whether a dry land farmer of
long experience can become a successful irrigation farmer.  The
land remaining  in  dry land farming will have to be cultivated
under  a  method which permits the least erosion, for a further
depletion of the top soils, either by wind or rain erosion, will
render  a  large proportion of  this area entirely useless for
agricultural production.   In what appears to be  a  necessary
program, there is a demand placed upon the Departments of Agriculture in the states within the area  for  the development and
dissemination of a long range production program geared to the
social needs  and  the natural resources  of  the area.  Only in
such a long range diversified program is there prospect of permanently controlling the major factors responsible for the present relief situation. All informants familiar with the history
of this area agree that such a program will involve relocation
of many families now on farms marginal for arable agriculture,
either because of  soil and climatic conditions, or because of
the size of their farms.  Care will need to be taken that the
necessary relocation is carried out as a part of the rehabilitation program.  The necessary reorganization of  agriculture
must be based on a land policy which will insure against a repetition of the present difficulties. A resettlement policy will
be of little value unless measures are  taken to  curb the un-
bridled expansion of wheat acreage in years of ample rainfall.
    The typical family receiving relief was a family of four or
five persons, consisting of husband, wife and two or three children.  The husband, past 50 years of age, had received 8 years
of schooling and had lived in the county in which he was receiv-

ing relief 10 years or more.  He was a farm operator renting a
farm of about 400 acres.  As a result of a succession of crop
failures due to drought, he had to apply for relief in order to
obtain food for his family and feed for his livestock. His farm
equipment and his livestock were mortgaged and in order to subsist he had been forced to use some of his capital. In many
cases he had been able to remain in the area only through a succession of loans.

Three-fourths of the families receiving relief were the families of farm owners and tenants, who were forced to accept relief because of the severe drought. Poor soil in some counties
and a low and variable rainfall throughout the area makes wheat-
growing a speculative enterprise.  Many small farms have been
cut out of what was originally good grazing land, and the extension of arable agriculture has resulted in trouble for both
the farmers and the ranchers. The majority of the farm families
receiving relief have achieved a standard of living which insures that they will present few social problems if given adequate income.

In the opinion of local relief workers, about two-thirds of
all families receiving relief were capable of operating farms
if assisted in recouping their capital losses of recent years:
11 percent (most of whom were young families who had not accumu-
lated enough capital to become farmers) were considered qualified for rehabilitation on farms if given supplementary employment (Table XXV).  Of the remaining 25 percent of the families
16 percent were classified as incapable of self-support, and 9
percent as fitted only for non-agricultural work, or work as
laborers on farms.

4.  *The Winter Wheat Area.*  The recent rapid expansion of dry-
land farming in this area without regard to the rainfall cycle
has led to the present relief situation.  Since 1920 there has
been a phenomenal increase in the acreage brought under the plow
and planted to wheat.  In the hope of quick profits, farmers
rushed into this area, bought tractors and combines, apparently
on the assumption that the good years would last forever.  The
boom was encouraged by good wheat prices and by a period of
years during which there were few serious crop failures.  The
successive crop failures of the past few years have bankrupted
many farmers and left them, and the farm laborers whom they formerly employed, stranded.  Here, as in the Spring Wheat Area,

it will be necessary to relocate some of the farmers and remodel the agricultural economy to insure more stability in good years and bad.

Wheat production in this area is a highly speculative venture and until more knowledge is gained of the periodicity of weather conditions, a specialized type of farming seems to lead to a questionable economy. Large areas of the region which have been destroyed by erosion will have to be withdrawn from cultivation and eventually returned to grazing (Fig 14). Likewise, other submarginal lands will sooner or later have to be retired. Many of the farms are at present too small to be operated in an extensive agricultural and grazing economy. An increase in farm size would permit a more diversified farming. In the southeastern section of the area the move away from wheat to other small grains and sorghums should be encouraged to reduce the social effects of periodically recurring crop failures inherent in the present one-crop system of agriculture. Unless measures are taken to prevent further wind erosion through the use of cover crops, or by listing, much of this area will be subjected to wind erosion to an extent which will eventually make farming impossible. Water resources of the area could be improved by a conservation program which would attempt to impound the waters of the torrential rains in coulees and other suitable places.

Although the general characteristics of the families receiving relief were similar to those of Spring Wheat families, more of those on relief rolls in this area were young families, and many of them had moved into the county in which they were receiving relief during the past five years. In the opinion of the local relief workers, about 46 percent of the families receiving relief could become self-supporting farmers and another 23 percent part-time farmers, if given help. Over 17 percent of the families were considered capable of self-support but not qualified to operate either full or part-time farms. Many of the displaced farmers will probably need to be assisted to locate under more favorable conditions if they are to remain off the relief rolls.

These two Wheat Areas are prime examples of the sort of economy which can develop under individual initiative with no thought of social and economic consequences either to the state, to the region, or to the nation. A constructive rehabilitation policy will face the need for some change in farm organization in these areas, and will not encourage farmers to plow up land which is submarginal for arable agriculture.

5. *The Western Cotton Area.* In this area the immediate relief problem is related to the following several factors: (1) an enormous and rapid expansion of a one-crop agricultural system, (2) depressed market prices, (3) adverse crop conditions, and (4) an unstable tenancy system coupled with a great demand for seasonal labor.

Since the western limits of this area have been pushed nearer the precipitation limits below which cotton cannot be grown, an abnormally dry year necessarily results in widespread crop failure. Moreover, increasing use of machinery has made small farms unprofitable and displaced a great many tenants and laborers. The stability of this area will depend upon the development of an adequate agricultural program which will make the best utilization of the available land for farm families of all classes. Lumbering and the petroleum industries will not play an important part in a rehabilitation program. The former is minor in importance to the agricultural industry in the area, and the latter is already too overcrowded to offer employment. When the cotton acreage was expanded many small farms were established where the acreage was too small to provide profitable management. The median size farm of farmers on relief was 58 acres. The need for consolidation of farms and for the diversification of crops is essential (*18,* p. 159) (Fig. 15).

The majority of the families receiving relief in this area were farmers and farm laborers, most of them white families. The average age of male heads of families was about 44 years and their average schooling about six grades for whites and four grades for Negroes. The average family head was renting the house in which he lived and owned no livestock and few chattels.

About 41 percent of all white and 27 percent of all Negro families were considered capable of rehabilitation as farm operators, 22 percent of the whites and 35 percent of the Negroes as part-time farmers. About 23 percent of the whites and 15 percent of the Negroes were classified as capable of self-support but not qualified for rehabilitation on the land. Of the Negro families 23 percent were considered incapable of attaining self-support. Fifty-eight percent of these families contained no gainful workers and an additional 16 percent contained no

male gainful workers. In other words, practically all of this
group consisted of families which included no adult males of
working age.

Almost one-fifth of the families receiving relief in this
area were unemployed squatters, marooned in the area. These
squatters were, for the most part, young families. Further immigration of this class of laborer into the area should be dis-
couraged and a considerable proportion of those now in the area
should be given assistance in moving elsewhere. Because of the
seasonal nature of labor needs, much could be accomplished by
setting up the unemployed farm laborers on small plots of land
under proper supervision so that they could produce part of
their food supply and derive some income from work which they
can do during the slack season in the cotton fields.

Adjustments must be made in the system of agriculture in the
western part of this area if the effects of recurring dry years
are to be avoided. As in the Wheat Areas, arable agriculture
based on a one-crop system makes for social and economic insecurity. These adjustments will require the resettlement of some
of the present population on better lands elsewhere.

In the eastern part of the area the problems are akin to those
of the Eastern Cotton Belt with its cropping system. Only through
a far-reaching and long-time rehabilitation program can the situation be remedied. Education and gradual induction of the
present share-croppers, or their posterity, into the status of
land-owning farmers appears to be indicated.

6.  *The Eastern Cotton Belt.* The socio-economic status of the
average family receiving relief in this area is such that only
through a long-time program of education can it learn to manage
its own affairs efficiently. The colonial system of agriculture
(9), based on the exploitation of both the laborer, and the
land on which he works, for the benefit of the mother country,
has left in its wake denuded, worn-out soils and a large population of illiterate, subservient workers, poorly equipped to guide
their own destinies.

The typical family receiving relief in the Eastern Cotton
Belt counties was an unemployed farm cropper, either white or
Negro. About one-fifth of the white families and more than
two-fifths of the Negro families included fewer than three persons; one-person families and broken families consisting of women and children made up about one-fifth of the white and two-

fifths of the Negro families receiving relief. The average age
of female heads of families receiving relief was about 46 years
for whites and 55 years for Negroes; for male heads of families
41 and 48 years, respectively. Over 25 percent of the male and
37 percent of the female heads of Negro families were 65 years
of age and older. The typical relief family lived in a shack
unfit for human habitation, owned little or no livestock and
its chattels were few and unmortgaged.

About 31 percent of the white families and 17 percent of the
Negro families were classified as unlikely prospects for rehabilitation on the land, about 20 and 39 percent, respectively,
as incapable of self-support. Of the white families considered
incapable of self-support, 46 percent included no gainful workers, 24 percent one female gainful worker only, and an additional
4 percent included no male gainful workers, making a total of
almost three-fourths without male gainful workers. Of the remaining 26 percent, the majority were families including male
workers who because of old age or other incapacities, or because
of their youthfulness, were unable to attain complete self-support. Most of the families with only one female gainful worker
were broken families consisting of a woman with children under
16 years of age. Of the Negro families 39 percent were considered incapable of attaining self-support. Sixty-four percent
of these families contained no gainful workers and an additional
25 percent contained no male gainful workers. In other words,
practically all of this group consisted of families which included no adult males of working age.

Much of the soil which has been depleted by over cultivation
is so submarginal in this area that it will find its best utilization as forest land (Fig. 14). On other marginal lands at-
tempts should be made to control erosion by terracing, contour
cultivation and cover crops and to restore the soil's fertility
by leguminous crops, and by a general program of diversified
farming. Not only will diversified farming assist in eliminat-
ing many of the defects of the cotton agricultural system as it
exists, but it will permit the farm families to produce more
subsistence crops. The pasturing of cattle from the drought
areas throughout the South may have a very marked and favorable
effect on the change towards diversification (6, p. 23). In
Alabama there has been a trend towards beef cattle, dairy, and
mixed type farming conducted mostly by the white operators.

Extension of land ownership is indicated as a partial solution
to problems of economic instability in this area. In the opinion of the local relief workers about 99 percent of the white
and 33 percent of the Negro families were capable of operating
farms, and about 11 percent of all families capable of rehabilitation on the land in connection with a supplementary job (Table
XXV). To attempt to set up many of these families on their own
farms and expect them to manage their own affairs will be  futile. A rural rehabilitation program for the majority of the
families receiving relief must furnish careful supervision over
a period of years if it is to succeed. The cropper who has always depended upon his landlord to keep his accounts and tell
him what to do, and when to do it, cannot be transformed over
night into a successful independent farmer.  An important factor limiting the prospects for rehabilitation in this area is
the resources of the families themselves.  Only the more re-
sourceful tenants and croppers can be expected to succeed as
independent farm owners; the remainder will require close supervision. Little will be accomplished toward the solution of present problems, however, by perpetuation of the "furnishing" system
under government auspices; the rural rehabilitation programs of
many states in this area have thus far done little more than
this.  These programs to date have been conceived as a form of
emergency work relief. Something more is needed:  the share-
cropper system and its one-crop agriculture must be fundamentally
changed if the cotton farmer is not to remain economically insecure.  A satisfactory rehabilitation program must assist in
the breaking up of this system of economic serfdom. The program
will need to be gauged to the abilities of the present generation
of farmers but it must also plan for the next generation so that
they will not be dependent share-croppers and farm laborers of
the present type.

The large number of white families classified for non-agricultural rehabilitation were unemployed workers in the mills of
the villages and towns, some of them former emigrants who had
returned from the cities.  For these the final hope appears to
be a revival of industrial employment.  Supplementing the seasonal wage by making land available on which to produce subsistence crops or garden produce would help to bring a stability
which has been unknown to a large number of families in this
area. But resettlement of these families on small plots of land

will be successful, in most instances, only if they are given some supervision. Without it, the average non-agricultural worker receiving relief in this area is not likely to improve his economic status even though he has land of his own.

# APPENDIX A

Tables

TABLE I. PROPORTION OF THE RURAL, TOWN AND CITY POPULATION OF THE UNITED STATES IN THE SIX PROBLEM AREAS[a]

| | UNITED STATES TOTAL | TOTAL ALL AREAS | APPA- LACHIAN OZARK | LAKE STATES CUT- OVER | SHORT GRASS | | WESTERN COTTON | EASTERN COTTON |
| | | | | | SPRING WHEAT | WINTER WHEAT | | |
|---|---|---|---|---|---|---|---|---|
| | *Number* | | | | | | | |
| TOTAL............ | 122,775,046 | 24,766,519 | 5,283,253 | 1,348,480 | 855,117 | 1,201,198 | 4,539,037 | 11,539,434 |
| CITY........... | 64,237,233 | 4,288,597 | 548,603 | 447,684 | 105,958 | 274,551 | 1,077,840 | 1,833,961 |
| RURAL AND TOWN. | 58,537,813 | 20,477,922 | 4,734,650 | 900,796 | 749,159 | 926,647 | 3,461,197 | 9,705,473 |
| TOWN......... | 4,717,590 | 1,228,204 | 199,596 | 112,790 | 27,427 | 59,266 | 258,988 | 570,137 |
| RURAL........ | 53,820,223 | 19,249,718 | 4,535,054 | 788,006 | 721,732 | 867,381 | 3,202,209 | 9,135,336 |
| | *Percent* | | | | | | | |
| TOTAL............ | 100.0 | 20.2 | 4.3 | 1.1 | 0.7 | 1.0 | 3.7 | 9.4 |
| CITY........... | 100.0 | 6.7 | 0.9 | 0.7 | 0.2 | 0.4 | 1.7 | 2.9 |
| RURAL AND TOWN. | 100.0 | 35.0 | 8.1 | 1.5 | 1.3 | 1.6 | 5.9 | 16.6 |
| TOWN......... | 100.0 | 26.0 | 4.2 | 2.4 | 0.6 | 1.3 | 5.5 | 12.1 |
| RURAL........ | 100.0 | 35.8 | 8.4 | 1.5 | 1.3 | 1.6 | 5.9 | 17.0 |

[a]U. S. CENSUS, 1930.

TABLE II. PROPORTION OF ALL FARMERS OF THE UNITED STATES IN THE SIX RURAL PROBLEM AREAS[a]

| FARMERS BY TENURE | UNITED STATES TOTAL | TOTAL ALL AREAS | APPA- LACHIAN OZARK | LAKE STATES CUT- OVER | SHORT GRASS | | WESTERN COTTON | EASTERN COTTON |
| | | | | | SPRING WHEAT | WINTER WHEAT | | |
|---|---|---|---|---|---|---|---|---|
| | *Number* | | | | | | | |
| ALL FARMERS........... | 6,288,648 | 2,679,085 | 493,083 | 94,180 | 106,521 | 112,349 | 487,997 | 1,384,955 |
| OWNER (AND MANAGER). | 3,624,283 | 1,178,424 | 354,244 | 83,872 | 75,477 | 67,323 | 168,778 | 428,730 |
| TENANT.............. | 1,888,087 | 865,141 | 103,855 | 10,308 | 31,044 | 45,026 | 212,464 | 462,444 |
| CROPPER............. | 776,278 | 635,520 | 34,984 | ----- | ----- | ----- | 106,755 | 493,781 |
| | *Percent* | | | | | | | |
| ALL FARMERS........... | 100.0 | 42.6 | 7.8 | 1.5 | 1.7 | 1.8 | 7.8 | 22.0 |
| OWNER (AND MANAGER). | 100.0 | 32.5 | 9.8 | 2.3 | 2.1 | 1.9 | 4.6 | 11.8 |
| TENANT.............. | 100.0 | 45.8 | 5.5 | 0.5 | 1.6 | 2.4 | 11.3 | 24.5 |
| CROPPER............. | 100.0 | 81.9 | 4.5 | ----- | ----- | ----- | 13.8 | 63.6 |

[a]U. S. CENSUS OF AGRICULTURE, 1930.

TABLE III.   PERCENTAGE OF THE NEGRO FARMERS OF THE UNITED STATES IN THE COTTON AREAS[a]

| FARMERS BY TENURE | UNITED STATES | THE COTTON AREAS | | |
|---|---|---|---|---|
| | | TOTAL | WESTERN | EASTERN |
| | | *Number* | | |
| ALL NEGRO FARMERS...................... | 916,070 | 704,798 | 95,837 | 608,961 |
| OWNERS(AND MANAGER).................. | 205,842 | 106,433 | 23,083 | 83,350 |
| TENANT.............................. | 317,331 | 255,185 | 34,232 | 220,953 |
| CROPPER............................. | 392,897 | 343,180 | 38,522 | 304,658 |
| | | *Percent* | | |
| ALL NEGRO FARMERS...................... | 100 | 76.9 | 10.5 | 66.4 |
| OWNER (AND MANAGER)................... | 100 | 51.7 | 11.2 | 40.5 |
| TENANT.............................. | 100 | 80.4 | 10.8 | 69.6 |
| CROPPER............................. | 100 | 87.3 | 9.8 | 77.5 |

[a]U. S. CENSUS, 1930.

TABLE IV.   AGRICULTURAL AND CLIMATIC DATA FROM THE KANSAS COUNTIES IN THE WINTER WHEAT AREA

| YEARS | PERCENT ACREAGE ABANDONED[a] | YIELD PER ACRE SOWN[a] | YIELD PER ACRE HARVESTED[a] | PRICE PER BUSHEL | ANNUAL AVERAGE TEMPERATURE (CROP YEAR) | ANNUAL AMOUNT RAINFALL (CROP YEAR) | POPULATION | PERCENT OF TOTAL ACREAGE IN WHEAT | TRACTOR PER 10,000 ACRES | COMBINES PER 10,000 ACRES |
|---|---|---|---|---|---|---|---|---|---|---|
| 1911 | 75.4 | 1.0 | 3.9 | .84 | 56.3 | 19.6 | 134,338 | 11.6 | -- | -- |
| 1912 | 33.7 | 6.3 | 9.6 | .75 | 51.2 | 21.4 | 124,616 | 10.3 | -- | -- |
| 1913 | 55.8 | 2.3 | 5.2 | .76 | 53.9 | 15.8 | 123,810 | 9.4 | -- | -- |
| 1914 | 0.0 | 17.1 | 17.1 | .83 | 55.7 | 20.1 | 119,848 | 11.7 | -- | -- |
| 1915 | 15.8 | 11.5 | 13.6 | .89 | 53.6 | 20.3 | 125,670 | 11.8 | 2 | -- |
| 1916 | 11.2 | 12.4 | 14.0 | 1.36 | 54.2 | 20.9 | 140,219 | 13.3 | 3 | -- |
| 1917 | 84.3 | 0.7 | 4.6 | 2.01 | 53.4 | 11.9 | 150,661 | 15.9 | 3 | -- |
| 1918 | 62.1 | 2.3 | 6.0 | 1.93 | 54.1 | 16.2 | 146,862 | 14.7 | 4 | -- |
| 1919 | 0.0 | 11.4 | 11.4 | 1.96 | 54.2 | 18.4 | 143,859 | 15.2 | 5 | -- |
| 1920 | 9.7 | 13.9 | 15.9 | 1.82 | 54.0 | 16.1 | 150,706 | 16.3 | 7 | -- |
| 1921 | 13.0 | 8.5 | 9.8 | .96 | 55.8 | 25.1 | 153,791 | 18.1 | 10 | -- |
| 1922 | 29.6 | 7.2 | 10.2 | .90 | 54.9 | 22.3 | 157,665 | 19.8 | 10 | -- |
| 1923 | 65.8 | 2.0 | 5.8 | .80 | 55.6 | 22.0 | 160,081 | 19.5 | 12 | 3 |
| 1924 | 6.6 | 14.3 | 15.3 | 1.07 | 53.1 | 20.3 | 160,123 | 17.4 | 14 | 3 |
| 1925 | 14.5 | 6.6 | 7.7 | 1.38 | 56.2 | 23.5 | 163,590 | 19.9 | 14 | 4 |
| 1926 | 20.0 | 9.9 | 12.4 | 1.17 | 54.1 | 24.1 | 164,045 | 22.4 | 19 | 5 |
| 1927 | 42.6 | 2.7 | 4.7 | 1.18 | 55.2 | 22.6 | 161,218 | 24.3 | 21 | 6 |
| 1928 | 31.4 | 12.1 | 17.7 | .91 | 54.1 | 26.7 | 163,188 | 23.7 | 24 | 8 |
| 1929 | 3.0 | 14.2 | 14.6 | 1.00 | 53.9 | 24.4 | 168,356 | 23.9 | 27 | 13 |
| 1930 | 6.3 | 11.8 | 12.6 | .60 | 54.8 | 16.9 | 177,845 | 27.7 | 24 | 15 |
| 1931 | 3.0 | 17.5 | 18.0 | .33 | 56.0 | 21.0 | 182,785 | 30.7 | 25 | 16 |
| 1932 | 34.0 | 6.3 | 9.5 | .30 | 56.7 | 16.2 | 184,378 | 24.8 | 31 | 21 |
| 1933 | | | | | 55.7 (54.2[b]) | 16.5 (20.7[b]) | | | | |

[a]LIMITED TO WINTER WHEAT ACREAGE.
[b]NORMAL.

TABLE V. RESIDENCE OF RURAL AND TOWN FAMILIES IN THE AREAS AND THE COUNTIES SURVEYED:
ALSO PROPORTION OF THE FAMILIES IN EACH AREA IN THE COUNTIES SURVEYED

| RESIDENCE | TOTAL ALL AREAS | APPA- LACHIAN OZARK | LAKE STATES CUT- OVER | SHORT GRASS | | | WESTERN COTTON | | EASTERN COTTON | |
|---|---|---|---|---|---|---|---|---|---|---|
| | | | | TOTAL | SPRING WHEAT | WINTER WHEAT | WHITE | NEGRO | WHITE | NEGRO |
| *Families in Area* | | | | | | | | | | |
| TOTAL NUMBER. | 4,484,257 | 1,001,672 | 198,256 | 389,780 | 171,072 | 218,708 | 779,866 | | 2,114,683 | |
| PERCENT...... | 100.0 | 100.0 | 100.0 | 100.0 | 100.0 | 100.0 | 100.0 | | 100.0 | |
| RURAL...... | 93.7 | 95.1 | 90.8 | 94.5 | 96.1 | 93.3 | 91.8 | | 93.9 | |
| TOWN....... | 6.3 | 4.9 | 9.2 | 5.5 | 3.9 | 6.7 | 8.2 | | 6.1 | |
| *Families in Counties Surveyed* | | | | | | | | | | |
| TOTAL NUMBER. | 238,523 | 48,437 | 29,024 | 38,794 | 15,030 | 23,764 | 37,827 | | 84,441 | |
| PERCENT...... | 100.0 | 100.0 | 100.0 | 100.0 | 100.0 | 100.0 | 100.0 | 100.0 | 100.0 | 100.0 |
| RURAL...... | 90.6 | 98.5 | 84.6 | 84.4 | 92.3 | 79.5 | 87.3 | 84.8 | 88.8 | 95.5 |
| TOWN....... | 9.4 | 1.5 | 15.4 | 15.6 | 7.7 | 20.5 | 12.7 | 15.2 | 11.2 | 4.5 |
| *Percent of Families in Area in Counties Surveyed* | | | | | | | | | | |
| TOTAL........ | 5.3 | 4.8 | 14.6 | 10.0 | 8.8 | 10.9 | 4.9 | | 4.0 | |
| RURAL...... | 5.1 | 5.0 | 13.6 | 8.9 | 8.4 | 9.3 | 4.6 | | 3.9 | |
| TOWN....... | 8.0 | 1.5 | 24.5 | 28.3 | 17.3 | 33.4 | 7.7 | | 4.9 | |

TABLE VI. PERCENTAGE OF FARM OPERATOR FAMILIES IN EACH TENURE GROUP IN SIX RURAL AREAS:
COMPARISON OF ALL RURAL AND TOWN FAMILIES IN THE AREA AND IN COUNTIES
SURVEYED, 1930, AND FAMILIES RECEIVING RELIEF IN JUNE 1934

| | TOTAL ALL AREAS | APPA- LACHIAN OZARK | LAKE STATES CUT- OVER | SHORT GRASS | | | WESTERN COTTON | | EASTERN COTTON | |
|---|---|---|---|---|---|---|---|---|---|---|
| | | | | TOTAL | SPRING WHEAT | WINTER WHEAT | WHITE | NEGRO | WHITE | NEGRO |
| *Total Area - 1930* | | | | | | | | | | |
| ALL FAMILIES........ | 100.0 | 100.0 | 100.0 | 100.0 | 100.0 | 100.0 | 100.0 | 100.0 | 100.0 | 100.0 |
| FARM OWNER........ | 26.3 | 35.3 | 42.3 | 36.6 | 44.1 | 30.8 | 22.4 | 17.8 | 27.6 | 9.7 |
| FARM TENANT....... | 20.1 | 10.4 | 5.2 | 19.5 | 18.2 | 20.6 | 27.4 | 26.3 | 19.3 | 25.6 |
| FARM CROPPER...... | 13.4 | 3.5 | ----- | ----- | ----- | ----- | 10.5 | 29.6 | 15.1 | 35.3 |
| ALL NON-FARM[a]..... | 40.2 | 50.8 | 52.5 | 43.9 | 37.7 | 48.6 | 39.7 | 26.3 | 38.0 | 29.4 |
| *Counties Surveyed - 1930* | | | | | | | | | | |
| ALL FAMILIES........ | 100.0 | 100.0 | 100.0 | 100.0 | 100.0 | 100.0 | 100.0 | 100.0 | 100.0 | 100.0 |
| FARM OWNER........ | 27.4 | 38.1 | 40.5 | 38.9 | 44.6 | 35.2 | 19.7 | 13.3 | 26.0 | 6.9 |
| FARM TENANT....... | 20.2 | 12.1 | 5.1 | 20.5 | 17.9 | 22.2 | 27.6 | 17.7 | 19.8 | 32.7 |
| FARM CROPPER...... | 12.2 | 3.3 | ----- | ----- | ----- | ----- | 8.8 | 20.1 | 18.8 | 35.1 |
| ALL NON-FARM[a]..... | 40.2 | 46.5 | 54.4 | 40.6 | 37.5 | 42.6 | 43.9 | 48.9 | 35.4 | 25.3 |
| *Rural and Town Families Receiving Relief -* *June 1934 Counties Surveyed* | | | | | | | | | | |
| ALL FAMILIES........ | 100.0 | 100.0 | 100.0 | 100.0 | 100.0 | 100.0 | 100.0 | 100.0 | 100.0 | 100.0 |
| FARM OWNER........ | 18.2 | 26.4 | 13.9 | 28.1 | 39.5 | 20.6 | 7.2 | 6.1 | 7.3 | 3.9 |
| FARM TENANT....... | 17.2 | 9.7 | 5.5 | 33.0 | 35.2 | 31.7 | 26.9 | 14.6 | 9.5 | 6.9 |
| FARM CROPPER...... | 11.3 | 23.3 | ----- | ----- | ----- | ----- | 7.2 | 7.3 | 24.7 | 25.3 |
| ALL NON-FARM[a]..... | 52.3 | 40.6 | 80.6 | 38.9 | 25.3 | 47.7 | 58.7 | 72.0 | 58.5 | 63.9 |

[a] INCLUDES FAMILIES OF AGRICULTURAL LABORERS.

TABLE VII.—PERCENTAGE OF FAMILIES IN COUNTIES SURVEYED RECEIVING DIRECT, WORK, OR BOTH DIRECT AND WORK RELIEF, BY SEX OF HEAD

| TYPE OF RELIEF | TOTAL ALL AREAS | APPA-LACHIAN OZARK | LAKE STATES CUT-OVER | SHORT GRASS | | WESTERN COTTON | | EASTERN COTTON | |
|---|---|---|---|---|---|---|---|---|---|
| | | | | SPRING WHEAT | WINTER WHEAT | WHITE | NEGRO | WHITE | NEGRO |
| *All Families* | | | | | | | | | |
| TOTAL.................... | 100 | 100 | 100 | 100 | 100 | 100 | 100 | 100 | 100 |
| DIRECT ONLY.............. | 55 | 67 | 65 | 46 | 21 | 69 | 87 | 56 | 75 |
| WORK ONLY............... | 33 | 28 | 17 | 46 | 62 | 11 | 1 | 35 | 18 |
| BOTH DIRECT AND WORK.... | 12 | 5 | 18 | 8 | 17 | 20 | 12 | 9 | 7 |
| *Families with Male Heads* | | | | | | | | | |
| TOTAL.................... | 100 | 100 | 100 | 100 | 100 | 100 | 100 | 100 | 100 |
| DIRECT ONLY.............. | 51 | 64 | 62 | 44 | 18 | 65 | 85 | 51 | 63 |
| WORK ONLY............... | 36 | 30 | 18 | 47 | 65 | 12 | 1 | 39 | 26 |
| BOTH DIRECT AND WORK.... | 13 | 6 | 20 | 9 | 17 | 23 | 14 | 10 | 11 |
| *Families with Female Heads* | | | | | | | | | |
| TOTAL.................... | 100 | 100 | 100 | 100 | 100 | 100 | 100 | 100 | 100 |
| DIRECT ONLY.............. | 85 | 88 | 90 | 64 | 67 | 93 | 94 | 78 | 92 |
| WORK ONLY............... | 11 | 9 | 5 | 30 | 27 | 2 | --- | 18 | 5 |
| BOTH DIRECT AND WORK.... | 4 | 3 | 5 | 6 | 6 | 5 | 6 | 4 | 3 |

TABLE VIII. AVERAGE VALUE PER FAMILY OF RELIEF RECEIVED DURING JUNE 1934 IN COUNTIES SURVEYED, BY TYPE OF RELIEF

| | TOTAL ALL AREAS | APPA-LACHIAN OZARK | LAKE STATES CUT-OVER | SHORT GRASS | | WESTERN COTTON | | EASTERN COTTON | |
|---|---|---|---|---|---|---|---|---|---|
| | | | | SPRING WHEAT | WINTER WHEAT | WHITE | NEGRO | WHITE | NEGRO |
| TOTAL.................... | $13 | $ 8 | $16 | $14 | $23 | $ 9 | $ 5 | $13 | $ 7 |
| DIRECT ONLY............ | 8 | 6 | 12 | 10 | 12 | 7 | 4 | 9 | 5 |
| WORK ONLY............ | 19 | 12 | 23 | 17 | 25 | 11 | 5 | 17 | 12 |
| BOTH DIRECT AND WORK.. | 21 | 12 | 27 | 14 | 28 | 16 | 13 | 19 | 12 |

TABLE IX. AVERAGE VALUE PER FAMILY OF RELIEF RECEIVED DURING JUNE 1934
IN SELECTED GROUPS OF STATES[a]

UNITED STATES TOTAL............................................................................. $23.30
    PRINCIPAL CITIES.......................................................................... 29.92
    REMAINDER OF COUNTRY...................................................................... 18.08

APPALACHIAN–OZARK AREA (WEST VIRGINIA, KENTUCKY AND TENNESSEE)..................................... 10.68

LAKE STATES CUT–OVER AREA (MICHIGAN, MINNESOTA AND WISCONSIN)...................................... 23.12

SPRING WHEAT AREA (NORTH AND SOUTH DAKOTA, MONTANA)............................................... 22.28

WINTER WHEAT AREA (KANSAS, OKLAHOMA AND NEW MEXICO).............................................. 12.22

WESTERN COTTON AREA (OKLAHOMA AND TEXAS)........................................................ 9.12

EASTERN COTTON BELT (ALABAMA, ARKANSAS, GEORGIA, MISSISSIPPI AND SOUTH CAROLINA)................. 11.75

[a]MONTHLY REPORT OF THE FEDERAL EMERGENCY RELIEF ADMINISTRATION, JULY 1 THROUGH JULY 31, 1934.

TABLE X. COMPARISON OF AVERAGE[a] SIZE OF FAMILY RECEIVING RELIEF AND OF
RURAL FARM AND NON–FARM FAMILIES, 1930

| AREA | FAMILIES RECEIVING RELIEF | TYPICAL STATE[b] IN AREA, 1930 | |
|---|---|---|---|
| | | RURAL FARM | RURAL NON–FARM |
| APPALACHIAN–OZARK.................. | 5.0 | 4.2 | 3.7 |
| LAKE STATES CUT–OVER............... | 3.7 | 4.1 | 3.1 |
| SHORT GRASS—SPRING WHEAT......... | 4.3 | 3.9 | 3.1 |
| SHORT GRASS—WINTER WHEAT......... | 4.0 | 4.1 | 3.4 |
| WESTERN COTTON | | | |
|   WHITE......................... | 4.5 | 4.1 | 3.4 |
|   NEGRO......................... | 3.5 | 3.9 | 2.7 |
| EASTERN COTTON | | | |
|   WHITE......................... | 4.2 | 4.5 | 3.8 |
|   NEGRO......................... | 3.1 | 4.1 | 2.9 |

[a]MEDIAN.
[b]MEDIAN STATE IN GROUP IN WHICH COUNTIES WERE SURVEYED.

TABLE XI. NORMALLY DEPENDENT PERSONS IN FAMILIES RECEIVING RELIEF[a]

| NUMBER OF PERSONS UNDER 16 YEARS AND 65 YEARS AND OLDER | TOTAL ALL AREAS | APPA- LACHIAN OZARK | LAKE STATES CUT- OVER | SHORT GRASS | | WESTERN COTTON | | EASTERN COTTON | |
|---|---|---|---|---|---|---|---|---|---|
| | | | | SPRING WHEAT | WINTER WHEAT | WHITE | NEGRO | WHITE | NEGRO |
| | | | | *Percent of Families* | | | | | |
| ALL FAMILIES.............. | 100.0 | 100.0 | 100.0 | 100.0 | 100.0 | 100.0 | 100.0 | 100.0 | 100.0 |
| 0..................... | 18.8 | 12.3 | 24.4 | 21.0 | 20.3 | 15.4 | 25.3 | 18.1 | 19.5 |
| 1..................... | 23.9 | 19.0 | 25.8 | 24.3 | 23.6 | 22.3 | 21.6 | 23.7 | 31.1 |
| 2..................... | 19.8 | 18.0 | 19.8 | 18.6 | 22.7 | 22.4 | 17.3 | 21.0 | 16.9 |
| 3..................... | 13.2 | 15.8 | 12.1 | 13.0 | 12.8 | 13.6 | 13.0 | 13.7 | 10.2 |
| 4..................... | 10.0 | 14.2 | 7.0 | 8.1 | 9.4 | 11.6 | 8.0 | 9.9 | 9.1 |
| 5..................... | 6.4 | 10.4 | 4.7 | 6.5 | 4.9 | 6.8 | 4.3 | 5.9 | 5.0 |
| 6..................... | 4.5 | 5.9 | 3.4 | 4.3 | 3.4 | 4.9 | 4.3 | 5.4 | 4.2 |
| 7 OR MORE............. | 3.4 | 4.4 | 2.8 | 4.2 | 2.9 | 3.0 | 6.2 | 2.3 | 4.0 |

[a]PERSONS UNDER 16 YEARS AND 65 YEARS OF AGE AND OVER.

TABLE XII. AVERAGE NUMBER OF NORMAL DEPENDENTS[a] PER FAMILY RECEIVING RELIEF

| | TOTAL ALL AREAS | APPA- LACHIAN OZARK | LAKE STATES CUT- OVER | SHORT GRASS | | WESTERN COTTON | | EASTERN COTTON | |
|---|---|---|---|---|---|---|---|---|---|
| | | | | SPRING WHEAT | WINTER WHEAT | WHITE | NEGRO | WHITE | NEGRO |
| | | | | *Per Family* | | | | | |
| TOTAL................... | 2.3 | 2.8 | 1.9 | 2.2 | 2.1 | 2.4 | 2.2 | 2.2 | 2.1 |
| PERSONS UNDER 16 YEARS.. | 2.3 | 2.6 | 1.8 | 2.0 | 1.9 | 2.2 | 1.9 | 2.0 | 1.7 |
| PERSONS 65 YEARS AND OVER | 0.2 | 0.2 | 0.3 | 0.1 | 0.2 | 0.2 | 0.2 | 0.2 | 0.4 |
| | | | | *Per Family with Dependents* | | | | | |
| TOTAL................... | 2.8 | 3.2 | 2.6 | 2.8 | 2.6 | 2.8 | 2.9 | 2.7 | 2.6 |
| PERSONS UNDER 16 YEARS.. | 2.8 | 3.2 | 2.9 | 3.0 | 2.7 | 3.0 | 3.1 | 2.9 | 3.0 |
| PERSONS 65 YEARS AND OVER | 1.2 | 1.3 | 1.2 | 1.2 | 1.3 | 1.2 | 1.4 | 1.3 | 1.2 |

[a]PERSONS UNDER 16 YEARS AND 65 YEARS OF AGE AND OVER.

TABLE XIII—A. USUAL OCCUPATIONS OF HEADS OF FAMILIES RECEIVING RELIEF IN THE COUNTIES SURVEYED

| Usual Occupation of Head of Family | Total All Areas | Appalachian Ozark | Lake States Cut-Over | Short Grass | | Western Cotton | | | Eastern Cotton | | |
|---|---|---|---|---|---|---|---|---|---|---|---|
| | | | | Spring Wheat | Winter Wheat | Total | White | Negro | Total | White | Negro |
| | | | | *Number* | | | | | | | |
| ALL FAMILIES............... | 10,771 | 2,167 | 1,758 | 1,311 | 2,007 | 964 | 800 | 164 | 2,584 | 1,347 | 1,237 |
| FARMER....................... | 5,036 | 1,288 | 337 | 979 | 1,049 | 377 | 331 | 46 | 1,006 | 559 | 447 |
| OWNER....................... | 1,960 | 572 | 242 | 518 | 414 | 68 | 58 | 10 | 146 | 98 | 48 |
| TENANT....................... | 1,854 | 211 | 95 | 461 | 635 | 239 | 215 | 24 | 213 | 128 | 85 |
| CROPPER..................... | 1,222 | 505 | --- | --- | --- | 70 | 58 | 12 | 647 | 333 | 314 |
| FARM LABORER................ | 929 | 43 | 61 | 22 | 172 | 167 | 128 | 39 | 464 | 157 | 307 |
| NON-AGRICULTURAL LABORER[a].. | 1,409 | 248 | 428 | 96 | 280 | 157 | 118 | 39 | 200 | 70 | 130 |
| SERVANT OR WAITER............ | 370 | 25 | 31 | 18 | 46 | 58 | 34 | 24 | 192 | 18 | 174 |
| MECHANIC..................... | 718 | 66 | 202 | 44 | 148 | 76 | 74 | 2 | 182 | 161 | 21 |
| MINER........................ | 327 | 126 | 187 | 6 | 3 | 1 | 1 | --- | 4 | 3 | 1 |
| LUMBERMAN, RAFTSMAN OR WOODCHOPPER | 233 | 107 | 105 | --- | --- | --- | --- | --- | 20 | 13 | 7 |
| FACTORY OR RAILROAD EMPLOYEE[a].... | 503 | 58 | 130 | 29 | 59 | 17 | 16 | 1 | 210 | 162 | 48 |
| PROFESSIONAL MAN, MERCHANT, BANKER OR OTHER PROPRIETOR........ | 200 | 22 | 35 | 18 | 45 | 19 | 13 | 6 | 61 | 45 | 16 |
| CLERICAL WORKER OR SALESMAN...... | 161 | 13 | 20 | 18 | 24 | 18 | 18 | --- | 68 | 65 | 3 |
| ALL OTHER OCCUPATIONS....... | 287 | 23 | 68 | 44 | 87 | 24 | 23 | 1 | 41 | 31 | 10 |
| NO USUAL OCCUPATION.......... | 410 | 104 | 103 | 17 | 44 | 29 | 28 | 1 | 113 | 53 | 60 |
| USUAL OCCUPATION UNKNOWN..... | 188 | 44 | 30 | 20 | 50 | 21 | 16 | 5 | 23 | 10 | 13 |

[a] NOT ELSEWHERE CLASSIFIED.

TABLE XIII-B. USUAL OCCUPATIONS OF HEADS OF FAMILIES RECEIVING RELIEF IN COUNTIES SURVEYED

| USUAL OCCUPATION OF HEAD OF FAMILY | TOTAL ALL AREAS | APPA-LACHIAN OZARK | LAKE STATES CUT-OVER | SHORT GRASS | | WESTERN COTTON | EASTERN COTTON |
|---|---|---|---|---|---|---|---|
| | | | | SPRING WHEAT | WINTER WHEAT | | |
| | | | Percent | | | | |
| ALL FAMILIES............................ | 100 | 100 | 100 | 100 | 100 | 100 | 100 |
| FARMER.............................. | 47 | 59 | 19 | 75 | 52 | 39 | 39 |
| OWNER.......................... | 18 | 26 | 14 | 40 | 20 | 7 | 6 |
| TENANT......................... | 17 | 10 | 5 | 35 | 32 | 25 | 8 |
| CROPPER........................ | 12 | 23 | --- | --- | --- | 7 | 25 |
| FARM LABORER........................ | 8 | 2 | 3 | 2 | 9 | 17 | 18 |
| NON-AGRICULTURAL LABORER[a]........... | 13 | 11 | 25 | 8 | 14 | 16 | 8 |
| SERVANT OR WAITER.................. | 3 | 1 | 2 | 1 | 2 | 6 | 7 |
| MECHANIC........................... | 7 | 3 | 12 | 3 | 8 | 8 | 7 |
| MINER.............................. | 3 | 6 | 11 | 1 | * | * | * |
| LUMBERMAN, RAFTSMAN OR WOODCHOPPER.. | 2 | 5 | 6 | --- | --- | --- | 1 |
| FACTORY OR RAILROAD EMPLOYEE[a]....... | 5 | 3 | 7 | 2 | 3 | 2 | 8 |
| PROFESSIONAL MAN, MERCHANT, BANKER OR OTHER PROPRIETOR............... | 2 | 1 | 2 | 1 | 2 | 2 | 2 |
| CLERICAL WORKER OR SALESMAN........ | 1 | 1 | 1 | 1 | 1 | 2 | 3 |
| ALL OTHER OCCUPATIONS.............. | 3 | 1 | 4 | 3 | 4 | 3 | 2 |
| NO USUAL OCCUPATION................ | 4 | 5 | 6 | 1 | 2 | 3 | 4 |
| USUAL OCCUPATION UNKNOWN........... | 2 | 2 | 2 | 2 | 3 | 2 | 1 |

[a] NOT ELSEWHERE CLASSIFIED.
* LESS THAN 0.5 PERCENT.

TABLE XIII–C. USUAL OCCUPATIONS OF HEADS OF WHITE AND NEGRO FAMILIES RECEIVING
RELIEF IN THE COUNTIES SURVEYED IN THE COTTON AREAS

| USUAL OCCUPATION OF HEAD OF FAMILY | PERCENT IN EACH OCCUPATION | | | | PERCENT OF WHITES AND NEGROES IN EACH OCCUPATION | | | | | |
|---|---|---|---|---|---|---|---|---|---|---|
| | WESTERN COTTON | | EASTERN COTTON | | WESTERN COTTON | | | EASTERN COTTON | | |
| | WHITE | NEGRO | WHITE | NEGRO | TOTAL | WHITE | NEGRO | TOTAL | WHITE | NEGRO |
| ALL FAMILIES..................... | 100 | 100 | 100 | 100 | 100 | 83 | 17 | 100 | 52 | 48 |
| FARMER....................... | 41 | 28 | 42 | 36 | 100 | 88 | 12 | 100 | 56 | 44 |
| OWNER.................. | 7 | 6 | 7 | 4 | 100 | 85 | 15 | 100 | 67 | 33 |
| TENANT................. | 27 | 15 | 10 | 7 | 100 | 90 | 10 | 100 | 60 | 40 |
| CROPPER................ | 7 | 7 | 25 | 25 | 100 | 83 | 17 | 100 | 51 | 49 |
| FARM LABORER................ | 16 | 24 | 12 | 25 | 100 | 77 | 23 | 100 | 34 | 66 |
| NON–AGRICULTURAL LABORER[a]... | 15 | 24 | 5 | 11 | 100 | 75 | 25 | 100 | 35 | 65 |
| SERVANT OR WAITER........... | 4 | 14 | 1 | 14 | 100 | 59 | 41 | 100 | 9 | 91 |
| MECHANIC.................... | 9 | 1 | 12 | 2 | 100 | 97 | 3 | 100 | 88 | 12 |
| MINER...................... | * | --- | * | * | 100 | 100 | --- | 100 | 75 | 25 |
| LUMBERMAN, RAFTSMAN OR WOOD–CHOPPER............... | --- | --- | 1 | * | --- | --- | --- | 100 | 65 | 35 |
| FACTORY OR RAILROAD EMPLOYEE[a] | 2 | 1 | 12 | 4 | 100 | 94 | 6 | 100 | 77 | 23 |
| PROFESSIONAL MAN, MERCHANT, BANKER, OR OTHER PROPRIE–TOR..................... | 2 | 4 | 3 | 1 | 100 | 68 | 32 | 100 | 74 | 26 |
| CLERICAL WORKER OR SALESMAN. | 2 | --- | 5 | * | 100 | 100 | --- | 100 | 96 | 4 |
| ALL OTHER OCCUPATIONS....... | 3 | 1 | 2 | 1 | 100 | 96 | 4 | 100 | 76 | 24 |
| NO USUAL OCCUPATION......... | 4 | 1 | 4 | 5 | 100 | 97 | 3 | 100 | 47 | 53 |
| USUAL OCCUPATION UNKNOWN.... | 2 | 3 | 1 | 1 | 100 | 76 | 24 | 100 | 43 | 57 |

[a] NOT ELSEWHERE CLASSIFIED.
* LESS THAN 0.5 PERCENT.

TABLE XIV—A. PRESENT OCCUPATION OF HEADS OF FAMILIES RECEIVING RELIEF

| Present Occupation | Total All Areas | Appa- lachian Ozark | Lake States Cut- Over | Short Grass | | Western Cotton | | Eastern Cotton | |
|---|---|---|---|---|---|---|---|---|---|
| | | | | Spring Wheat | Winter Wheat | White | Negro | White | Negro |
| *Number* | | | | | | | | | |
| ALL FAMILIES | 10,771 | 2,167 | 1,738 | 1,311 | 2,007 | 800 | 164 | 1,347 | 1,237 |
| FARMER | 4,571 | 1,487 | 509 | 895 | 919 | 194 | 35 | 291 | 241 |
| OWNER | 2,053 | 684 | 376 | 463 | 381 | 40 | 10 | 65 | 34 |
| TENANT | 1,684 | 257 | 133 | 432 | 538 | 126 | 20 | 108 | 70 |
| CROPPER | 834 | 546 | ---- | ---- | ---- | 28 | 5 | 118 | 137 |
| FARM LABORER | 254 | 12 | 31 | 2 | 11 | 17 | 4 | 63 | 114 |
| ALL OTHERS | 557 | 59 | 181 | 32 | 71 | 27 | 7 | 72 | 108 |
| UNEMPLOYED | 5,389 | 609 | 1,017 | 382 | 1,006 | 562 | 118 | 921 | 774 |
| *Percent* | | | | | | | | | |
| ALL FAMILIES | 100.0 | 100.0 | 100.0 | 100.0 | 100.0 | 100.0 | 100.0 | 100.0 | 100.0 |
| FARMER | 42.4 | 68.6 | 29.3 | 68.3 | 45.8 | 24.2 | 21.3 | 21.6 | 19.5 |
| OWNER | 19.1 | 31.5 | 21.6 | 35.3 | 19.0 | 5.0 | 6.1 | 4.8 | 2.7 |
| TENANT | 15.6 | 11.9 | 7.7 | 33.0 | 26.8 | 15.7 | 12.2 | 8.0 | 5.7 |
| CROPPER | 7.7 | 25.2 | ----- | ----- | ----- | 3.5 | 3.0 | 8.8 | 11.1 |
| FARM LABORER | 2.4 | 0.6 | 1.8 | 0.2 | 0.5 | 2.1 | 2.4 | 4.7 | 9.2 |
| ALL OTHERS | 5.2 | 2.7 | 10.4 | 2.4 | 3.5 | 3.4 | 4.3 | 5.3 | 8.7 |
| UNEMPLOYED | 50.0 | 28.1 | 58.5 | 29.1 | 50.2 | 70.3 | 72.0 | 68.4 | 62.6 |

TABLE XIV—B. PRESENT OCCUPATION OF MALE HEADS OF FAMILIES RECEIVING RELIEF

| Present Occupation | Total All Areas | Appa- lachian Ozark | Lake States Cut- Over | Short Grass | | Western Cotton | | Eastern Cotton | |
|---|---|---|---|---|---|---|---|---|---|
| | | | | Spring Wheat | Winter Wheat | White | Negro | White | Negro |
| *Number* | | | | | | | | | |
| ALL FAMILIES | 9,235 | 1,921 | 1,560 | 1,208 | 1,860 | 704 | 128 | 1,114 | 740 |
| FARMER | 4,266 | 1,391 | 473 | 866 | 892 | 173 | 30 | 262 | 179 |
| OWNER | 1,876 | 624 | 343 | 436 | 363 | 30 | 7 | 51 | 22 |
| TENANT | 1,631 | 250 | 130 | 430 | 529 | 116 | 18 | 102 | 56 |
| CROPPER | 759 | 517 | ---- | ---- | ---- | 27 | 5 | 109 | 101 |
| FARM LABORER | 197 | 12 | 30 | 2 | 11 | 17 | 4 | 54 | 67 |
| ALL OTHERS | 359 | 36 | 149 | 23 | 43 | 14 | 1 | 56 | 37 |
| UNEMPLOYED | 4,413 | 482 | 908 | 317 | 914 | 500 | 93 | 742 | 457 |
| *Percent* | | | | | | | | | |
| ALL FAMILIES | 100.0 | 100.0 | 100.0 | 100.0 | 100.0 | 100.0 | 100.0 | 100.0 | 100.0 |
| FARMER | 46.2 | 72.4 | 30.3 | 71.7 | 48.0 | 24.6 | 23.4 | 23.5 | 24.2 |
| OWNER | 20.3 | 32.5 | 22.0 | 36.1 | 19.6 | 4.3 | 5.5 | 4.6 | 3.0 |
| TENANT | 17.7 | 13.0 | 8.3 | 35.6 | 28.4 | 16.5 | 14.0 | 9.2 | 7.6 |
| CROPPER | 8.2 | 26.9 | ----- | ----- | ----- | 3.8 | 3.9 | 9.7 | 13.6 |
| FARM LABORER | 2.1 | 0.6 | 1.9 | 0.2 | 0.6 | 2.4 | 3.1 | 4.8 | 9.1 |
| ALL OTHERS | 3.9 | 1.9 | 9.6 | 1.9 | 2.3 | 2.0 | 0.8 | 5.0 | 5.0 |
| UNEMPLOYED | 47.8 | 25.1 | 58.2 | 26.2 | 49.1 | 71.0 | 72.7 | 66.7 | 61.7 |

TABLE XIV–C. PRESENT OCCUPATION OF FEMALE HEADS OF FAMILIES RECEIVING RELIEF

| PRESENT OCCUPATION | TOTAL ALL AREAS | APPA-LACHIAN OZARK | LAKE STATES CUT-OVER | SHORT GRASS | | WESTERN COTTON | | EASTERN COTTON | |
| | | | | SPRING WHEAT | WINTER WHEAT | WHITE | NEGRO | WHITE | NEGRO |
|---|---|---|---|---|---|---|---|---|---|
| | | | | *Number* | | | | | |
| ALL FAMILIES............ | 1,536 | 246 | 178 | 103 | 147 | 96 | 36 | 233 | 497 |
| FARMER.............. | 305 | 96 | 36 | 29 | 27 | 21 | 5 | 29 | 62 |
| OWNER.......... | 177 | 60 | 33 | 27 | 18 | 10 | 3 | 14 | 12 |
| TENANT........ | 53 | 7 | 3 | 2 | 9 | 10 | 2 | 6 | 14 |
| CROPPER....... | 75 | 29 | --- | --- | --- | 1 | -- | 9 | 36 |
| FARM LABORER....... | 57 | --- | 1 | --- | --- | -- | -- | 9 | 47 |
| ALL OTHERS......... | 198 | 23 | 32 | 9 | 28 | 13 | 6 | 16 | 71 |
| UNEMPLOYED......... | 976 | 127 | 109 | 65 | 92 | 62 | 25 | 179 | 317 |
| | | | | *Percent* | | | | | |
| ALL FAMILIES............ | 100.0 | 100.0 | 100.0 | 100.0 | 100.0 | 100.0 | 100.0 | 100.0 | 100.0 |
| FARMER.............. | 19.9 | 39.0 | 20.2 | 28.2 | 18.4 | 21.8 | 13.9 | 12.5 | 12.4 |
| OWNER.......... | 11.5 | 24.4 | 18.5 | 26.3 | 12.3 | 10.4 | 8.3 | 6.0 | 2.4 |
| TENANT........ | 3.5 | 2.8 | 1.7 | 1.9 | 6.1 | 10.4 | 5.6 | 2.6 | 2.8 |
| CROPPER....... | 4.9 | 11.8 | ----- | ----- | ----- | 1.0 | ----- | 3.9 | 7.2 |
| FARM LABORER....... | 3.7 | ----- | 0.6 | ----- | ----- | ----- | ----- | 3.9 | 9.4 |
| ALL OTHERS......... | 12.9 | 9.3 | 18.0 | 8.7 | 19.0 | 13.5 | 16.7 | 6.9 | 14.3 |
| UNEMPLOYED......... | 63.5 | 51.7 | 61.2 | 63.1 | 62.6 | 64.7 | 69.4 | 76.7 | 63.9 |

TABLE XV. PERCENTAGE OF FEMALES AMONG HEADS OF FAMILIES RECEIVING RELIEF, BY USUAL OCCUPATION

| Usual Occupation | Total All Areas | Appa- lachian Ozark | Lake States Cut- Over | Short Grass | | Western Cotton | | | Eastern Cotton | | |
|---|---|---|---|---|---|---|---|---|---|---|---|
| | | | | Spring Wheat | Winter Wheat | Total | White | Negro | Total | White | Negro |
| | | | | *Percent* | | | | | | | |
| ALL FAMILIES.............. | 14 | 11 | 10 | 8 | 7 | 14 | 12 | 22 | 28 | 17 | 40 |
| FARMER................ | 7 | 7 | 5 | 4 | 3 | 7 | 7 | 13 | 17 | 10 | 27 |
| OWNER............ | 9 | 10 | 5 | 6 | 5 | 19 | 17 | 30 | 30 | 19 | 50 |
| TENANT............ | 3 | 1 | 4 | 1 | 1 | 5 | 4 | 8 | 13 | 8 | 20 |
| CROPPER......... | 11 | 4 | -- | -- | -- | 6 | 5 | 8 | 16 | 7 | 25 |
| FARM LABORER......... | 20 | 2 | -- | -- | 1 | 2 | 1 | 5 | 38 | 22 | 47 |
| NON-AGRICULTURAL LA- BORER[a].......... | 3 | 2 | 1 | 7 | 1 | 3 | 1 | 8 | 9 | 4 | 12 |
| SERVANT OR WAITER.... | 84 | 92 | 68 | 78 | 78 | 90 | 88 | 92 | 86 | 94 | 85 |
| MECHANIC.............. | 3 | 5 | -- | 2 | 1 | 4 | 4 | -- | 6 | 6 | -- |
| MINER................. | -- | -- | -- | -- | -- | -- | -- | -- | -- | -- | -- |
| LUMBERMAN, RAFTSMAN OR WOODCHOPPER..... | -- | -- | -- | -- | -- | -- | -- | -- | -- | -- | -- |
| FACTORY OR RAILROAD EMPLOYEE[a]....... | 6 | 5 | 5 | -- | 2 | 12 | 13 | -- | 9 | 11 | 2 |
| PROFESSIONAL MAN, MER- CHANT, BANKER OR OTHER PROPRIETOR | 33 | 23 | 37 | 28 | 20 | 21 | 23 | 17 | 48 | 40 | 69 |
| CLERICAL WORKER OR SALESMAN........ | 25 | 31 | 20 | 28 | 29 | 11 | 11 | -- | 27 | 28 | -- |
| ALL OTHER OCCUPATIONS | 22 | 22 | 12 | 39 | 21 | 4 | 4 | -- | 32 | 29 | 40 |
| NO USUAL OCCUPATION.. | 94 | 96 | 95 | 94 | 91 | 97 | 96 | 100 | 91 | 96 | 87 |
| USUAL OCCUPATION UNKNOWN | 19 | 30 | 23 | 5 | 10 | 24 | 25 | 20 | 17 | 30 | 8 |

[a] NOT ELSEWHERE CLASSIFIED.

TABLE XVI. AVERAGE AGE[a] OF HEADS OF FAMILIES RECEIVING RELIEF BY USUAL OCCUPATION OF MALE HEADS IN SPECIFIED OCCUPATIONS

| SEX AND USUAL OCCUPATION | TOTAL ALL AREAS | APPALACHIAN OZARK | LAKE STATES CUTOVER | SHORT GRASS | | WESTERN COTTON | | EASTERN COTTON | |
|---|---|---|---|---|---|---|---|---|---|
| | | | | SPRING WHEAT | WINTER WHEAT | WHITE | NEGRO | WHITE | NEGRO |
| **TOTAL** | | | | | | | | | |
| FEMALE HEADS............. | 50.0 | 48.5 | 52.5 | 52.0 | 46.0 | 42.5 | 50.0 | 46.0 | 56.0 |
| MALE HEADS............... | 44.0 | 42.5 | 47.5 | 45.0 | 42.0 | 43.5 | 43.5 | 42.0 | 49.0 |
| FARMER................ | 45.0 | 42.5 | 53.0 | 45.5 | 42.5 | 44.0 | 49.5 | 44.0 | 55.0 |
| OWNER............... | 51.0 | 48.0 | 55.5 | 51.0 | 50.0 | 52.0 | 60.0 | 56.5 | 61.0 |
| TENANT.............. | 41.0 | 41.5 | 45.5 | 40.5 | 39.0 | 44.0 | 43.0 | 44.5 | 55.5 |
| CROPPER............. | 42.0 | 39.0 | ---- | ---- | ---- | 39.0 | 53.5 | 41.5 | 53.0 |
| FARM LABORER.......... | 40.0 | 38.5 | 36.0 | * | 38.0 | 42.5 | 37.0 | 38.0 | 47.0 |
| NON − AGRICULTURAL LABORER............ | 41.5 | 40.0 | 43.5 | 42.5 | 42.5 | 39.5 | 41.5 | 36.0 | 40.5 |
| MECHANIC.............. | 45.5 | 48.5 | 47.5 | 44.5 | 41.5 | 48.0 | * | 44.0 | * |
| MINER................. | 44.5 | 40.5 | 47.5 | * | * | * | * | * | * |
| LUMBERMAN, RAFTSMAN, OR WOODCHOPPER...... | 48.0 | 43.5 | 54.5 | * | * | * | * | * | * |
| FACTORY OR RAILROAD EMPLOYEE......... | 40.5 | 41.5 | 44.0 | 46.0 | 41.0 | * | * | 38.0 | 38.5 |

[a]MEDIAN AGE; 50 PERCENT WERE THIS AGE OR OLDER, 50 PERCENT YOUNGER. ALL FIGURES TO THE NEAREST 0.5 YEAR.
*NOT COMPUTED BECAUSE OF SMALL NUMBER OF CASES.

TABLE XVII. AGE DISTRIBUTION OF HEADS OF FAMILIES RECEIVING RELIEF

| AGE OF HEAD OF FAMILY | TOTAL ALL AREAS | APPALACHIAN OZARK | LAKE STATES CUTOVER | SHORT GRASS | | WESTERN COTTON | | EASTERN COTTON | |
|---|---|---|---|---|---|---|---|---|---|
| | | | | SPRING WHEAT | WINTER WHEAT | WHITE | NEGRO | WHITE | NEGRO |
| **ALL FAMILIES** | | | | | | | | | |
| NUMBER................ | 10,771 | 2,167 | 1,738 | 1,311 | 2,007 | 800 | 164 | 1,347 | 1,237 |
| PERCENT............... | 100.0 | 100.0 | 100.0 | 100.0 | 100.0 | 100.0 | 100.0 | 100.0 | 100.0 |
| UNDER 25 YEARS... | 6.9 | 6.9 | 4.5 | 3.9 | 8.7 | 9.3 | 9.8 | 8.5 | 6.6 |
| 25 − 44 YEARS.... | 44.2 | 48.2 | 39.9 | 44.5 | 47.5 | 44.6 | 40.5 | 48.1 | 33.7 |
| 45 − 64 YEARS.... | 34.8 | 33.4 | 38.4 | 41.0 | 33.7 | 36.0 | 30.7 | 32.8 | 29.3 |
| 65 YEARS AND OVER | 14.1 | 11.5 | 17.2 | 10.6 | 10.1 | 10.1 | 19.0 | 10.6 | 30.4 |
| **FAMILIES WITH MALE HEADS** | | | | | | | | | |
| NUMBER................ | 9,235 | 1,921 | 1,560 | 1,208 | 1,860 | 704 | 128 | 1,114 | 740 |
| PERCENT............... | 100.0 | 100.0 | 100.0 | 100.0 | 100.0 | 100.0 | 100.0 | 100.0 | 100.0 |
| UNDER 25 YEARS... | 7.1 | 7.3 | 4.9 | 3.7 | 8.5 | 9.8 | 10.2 | 8.7 | 7.6 |
| 25 − 44 YEARS.... | 45.7 | 49.4 | 40.7 | 46.2 | 48.3 | 43.7 | 43.3 | 49.5 | 36.1 |
| 45 − 64 YEARS.... | 34.5 | 32.2 | 38.0 | 40.0 | 33.2 | 36.1 | 26.8 | 32.2 | 30.9 |
| 65 YEARS AND OVER | 12.7 | 11.1 | 16.4 | 10.1 | 10.0 | 10.4 | 19.7 | 9.6 | 25.4 |
| **FAMILIES WITH FEMALE HEADS** | | | | | | | | | |
| NUMBER................ | 1,536 | 246 | 178 | 103 | 147 | 96 | 36 | 233 | 497 |
| PERCENT............... | 100.0 | 100.0 | 100.0 | 100.0 | 100.0 | 100.0 | 100.0 | 100.0 | 100.0 |
| UNDER 25 YEARS... | 5.4 | 3.7 | 1.7 | 5.8 | 10.2 | 5.2 | 8.3 | 7.4 | 5.1 |
| 25 − 44 YEARS.... | 35.2 | 38.9 | 32.6 | 25.2 | 37.4 | 51.0 | 30.6 | 41.6 | 30.1 |
| 45 − 64 YEARS.... | 36.7 | 43.0 | 42.1 | 53.4 | 40.1 | 35.4 | 44.4 | 35.9 | 27.1 |
| 65 YEARS AND OVER | 22.7 | 14.4 | 23.6 | 15.6 | 12.3 | 8.4 | 16.7 | 15.1 | 37.7 |

TABLE XVIII. SHIFTS IN OCCUPATION OR EMPLOYMENT STATUS MADE BY MALE FAMILY HEADS USUALLY EMPLOYED IN AGRICULTURAL AND NON-AGRICULTURAL OCCUPATIONS

| Employment Status in June 1934 by Usual Occupation | Total All Areas | Appalachian Ozark | Lake States Cut-Over | Short Grass | | Western Cotton | | Eastern Cotton | |
|---|---|---|---|---|---|---|---|---|---|
| | | | | Spring Wheat | Winter Wheat | White | Negro | White | Negro |
| | | | | *Percent* | | | | | |
| FARM OWNER | 100.0 | 100.0 | 100.0 | 100.0 | 100.0 | 100.0 | 100.0 | 100.0 | 100.0 |
| REMAINED FARM OWNER | 86.0 | 93.0 | 75.5 | 87.9 | 89.1 | 60.4 | 85.7 | 60.8 | 83.3 |
| CHANGED OCCUPATION | 3.6 | 0.8 | 5.7 | 3.5 | 4.8 | 6.3 | ----- | 10.1 | 4.2 |
| BECAME TENANT | 2.6 | 0.6 | 2.6 | 3.1 | 4.3 | 6.3 | ----- | 2.5 | 4.2 |
| BECAME CROPPER | 0.2 | 0.2 | ----- | ----- | ----- | ----- | ----- | 3.8 | ----- |
| BECAME FARM LABORER | 0.1 | ----- | 0.9 | ----- | ----- | ----- | ----- | ----- | ----- |
| BECAME NON-AGRICULTURAL WORKER | 0.7 | ----- | 2.2 | 0.4 | 0.5 | ----- | ----- | 3.8 | ----- |
| BECAME UNEMPLOYED | 10.4 | 6.2 | 18.8 | 8.6 | 6.1 | 33.3 | 14.3 | 29.1 | 12.5 |
| FARM TENANT | 100.0 | 100.0 | 100.0 | 100.0 | 100.0 | 100.0 | 100.0 | 100.0 | 100.0 |
| REMAINED FARM TENANT | 76.6 | 94.2 | 65.9 | 89.2 | 77.6 | 50.5 | 72.7 | 52.5 | 64.7 |
| CHANGED OCCUPATION | 3.4 | 4.3 | 13.2 | 1.3 | 1.4 | 4.4 | 4.6 | 10.2 | 5.8 |
| BECAME OWNER | 1.4 | 3.8 | 9.9 | 0.9 | 0.6 | ----- | 4.6 | ----- | ----- |
| BECAME CROPPER | 0.8 | 0.5 | ----- | ----- | ----- | 1.9 | ----- | 6.8 | 2.9 |
| BECAME FARM LABORER | 0.6 | ----- | 2.2 | ----- | 0.2 | 1.0 | ----- | 2.5 | 2.9 |
| BECAME NON-AGRICULTURAL WORKER | 0.6 | ----- | 1.1 | 0.4 | 0.6 | 1.5 | ----- | 0.9 | ----- |
| BECAME UNEMPLOYED | 20.0 | 1.5 | 20.9 | 9.5 | 21.0 | 45.1 | 22.7 | 37.3 | 29.5 |
| FARM CROPPER | 100.0 | 100.0 | ----- | ----- | ----- | 100.0 | 100.0 | 100.0 | 100.0 |
| REMAINED FARM CROPPER | 54.8 | 82.4 | ----- | ----- | ----- | 34.5 | 36.4 | 27.6 | 39.3 |
| CHANGED OCCUPATION | 10.1 | 6.2 | ----- | ----- | ----- | 9.1 | ----- | 15.3 | 12.0 |
| BECAME OWNER | 1.7 | 3.7 | ----- | ----- | ----- | ----- | ----- | ----- | ----- |
| BECAME TENANT | 3.4 | 1.7 | ----- | ----- | ----- | 1.8 | ----- | 6.5 | 3.4 |
| BECAME FARM LABORER | 3.3 | 0.4 | ----- | ----- | ----- | 5.5 | ----- | 5.9 | 5.6 |
| BECAME NON-AGRICULTURAL WORKER | 1.7 | 0.4 | ----- | ----- | ----- | 1.8 | ----- | 2.9 | 3.0 |
| BECAME UNEMPLOYED | 35.1 | 11.4 | ----- | ----- | ----- | 56.4 | 63.6 | 57.1 | 48.7 |
| FARM LABORER | 100.0 | 100.0 | 100.0 | 100.0 | 100.0 | 100.0 | 100.0 | 100.0 | 100.0 |
| REMAINED FARM LABORER | 10.8 | 19.0 | 26.2 | 9.1 | 5.3 | 7.9 | 10.8 | 23.8 | 28.8 |
| CHANGED OCCUPATION | 9.1 | 40.5 | 31.2 | 4.5 | 6.4 | 3.1 | 2.7 | 7.3 | 3.7 |
| BECAME OWNER | 2.1 | 16.7 | 13.1 | ----- | 0.6 | ----- | ----- | ----- | ----- |
| BECAME TENANT | 3.5 | 4.8 | 16.4 | 4.5 | 4.1 | 2.3 | ----- | 1.6 | 0.6 |
| BECAME CROPPER | 2.4 | 19.0 | ----- | ----- | ----- | 0.8 | ----- | 4.9 | 1.9 |
| BECAME NON-AGRICULTURAL WORKER | 1.1 | ----- | 1.7 | ----- | 1.7 | ----- | 2.7 | 0.8 | 1.2 |
| BECAME UNEMPLOYED | 74.1 | 40.5 | 42.6 | 86.4 | 88.3 | 89.0 | 86.5 | 68.9 | 67.5 |
| NON-AGRICULTURAL WORKER | 100.0 | 100.0 | 100.0 | 100.0 | 100.0 | 100.0 | 100.0 | 100.0 | 100.0 |
| REMAINED NON-AGRICULTURAL WORKER IN SAME OCCUPATION | 5.9 | 4.5 | 7.6 | 6.3 | 4.1 | 3.1 | ----- | 6.1 | 10.4 |
| CHANGED OCCUPATION | 17.6 | 42.1 | 22.4 | 6.3 | 4.4 | 4.7 | 6.4 | 8.6 | 6.9 |
| BECAME OWNER | 7.5 | 17.6 | 12.6 | 1.3 | 1.0 | 0.4 | ----- | 0.6 | 0.9 |
| BECAME TENANT | 3.7 | 6.4 | 4.2 | 3.2 | 2.1 | 1.9 | 4.3 | 3.4 | 0.9 |
| BECAME CROPPER | 3.4 | 17.0 | ----- | ----- | ----- | 0.8 | 2.1 | 1.5 | 1.7 |
| BECAME FARM LABORER | 0.7 | 0.3 | 0.9 | ----- | 0.2 | 0.8 | ----- | 0.8 | 2.1 |
| BECAME NON-AGRICULTURAL WORKER IN ANOTHER OCCUPATION | 2.3 | 0.8 | 4.7 | 1.3 | 1.1 | 0.8 | ----- | 2.3 | 1.3 |
| BECAME UNEMPLOYED | 76.5 | 53.4 | 70.0 | 87.4 | 91.5 | 92.2 | 93.6 | 85.3 | 82.7 |

NOTE: CROPPERS TABULATED SEPARATELY ONLY IN THE APPALACHIAN-OZARK AND COTTON AREAS.

TABLE XIX.  YEARS OF CONTINUOUS RESIDENCE IN THE COUNTY OF FAMILIES RECEIVING RELIEF

| YEARS OF CONTINUOUS RESIDENCE IN COUNTY | TOTAL ALL AREAS | APPA- LACHIAN OZARK | LAKE STATES CUT- OVER | SHORT GRASS | | | WESTERN COTTON | | EASTERN COTTON | |
|---|---|---|---|---|---|---|---|---|---|---|
| | | | | TOTAL | SPRING WHEAT | WINTER WHEAT | WHITE | NEGRO | WHITE | NEGRO |
| | | | | *Percent* | | | | | | |
| TOTAL.................. | 100.0 | 100.0 | 100.0 | 100.0 | 100.0 | 100.0 | 100.0 | 100.0 | 100.0 | 100.0 |
| LESS THAN 5 YEARS..... | 17.3 | 10.5 | 20.8 | 18.3 | 10.9 | 23.2 | 33.5 | 22.4 | 21.2 | 6.4 |
| LESS THAN 1 YEAR.... | 2.2 | 2.1 | 2.0 | 1.2 | 0.8 | 1.5 | 5.9 | 5.0 | 3.7 | 1.2 |
| 1 - 4 YEARS......... | 15.1 | 8.4 | 18.8 | 17.1 | 10.1 | 21.7 | 27.6 | 17.4 | 17.5 | 5.2 |
| 5 - 9 YEARS........... | 11.9 | 5.8 | 10.0 | 17.7 | 9.9 | 22.9 | 19.2 | 17.4 | 9.7 | 6.5 |
| 10 OR MORE YEARS...... | 70.8 | 83.7 | 69.2 | 64.0 | 79.2 | 53.9 | 47.3 | 60.2 | 69.1 | 87.1 |

TABLE XX-A.  FAMILIES CLASSIFIED BY PRESENT OCCUPATION OF HEAD OF HOUSEHOLD AND OWNERSHIP OF HOUSE OR FARM; ALSO OWNERS REPORTING MORTGAGES AND FAMILIES REPORTING GARDEN OR TRUCK PATCH

ALL OCCUPATIONS

| REAL ESTATE OWNERSHIP AND MORTGAGE CONDITION | TOTAL ALL AREAS | APPA- LACHIAN OZARK | LAKE STATES CUT- OVER | SHORT GRASS | | | WESTERN COTTON | | EASTERN COTTON | |
|---|---|---|---|---|---|---|---|---|---|---|
| | | | | TOTAL | SPRING WHEAT | WINTER WHEAT | WHITE | NEGRO | WHITE | NEGRO |
| | | | | *Number* | | | | | | |
| ALL FAMILIES................. | 10,771 | 2,167 | 1,738 | 3,318 | 1,311 | 2,007 | 800 | 164 | 1,346 | 1,238 |
| OWNER................... | 3,320 | 821 | 820 | 1,178 | 552 | 626 | 134 | 33 | 173 | 161 |
| RENTER.................. | 6,858 | 1,200 | 804 | 2,093 | 737 | 1,356 | 495 | 102 | 1,112 | 1,052 |
| SQUATTER................ | 548 | 138 | 91 | 34 | 15 | 19 | 171 | 29 | 60 | 25 |
| HOMESTEADER............. | 45 | 8 | 23 | 13 | 7 | 6 | --- | --- | 1 | ---- |
| OWNERS REPORTING MORTGAGES... | 1,462 | 172 | 306 | 806 | 403 | 403 | 44 | 4 | 89 | 41 |
| FAMILIES REPORTING GARDEN OR TRUCK PATCH............. | 7,816 | 2,041 | 1,511 | 1,725 | 1,064 | 661 | 398 | 108 | 1,052 | 981 |
| | | | | *Percent* | | | | | | |
| ALL FAMILIES................. | 100 | 100 | 100 | 100 | 100 | 100 | 100 | 100 | 100 | 100 |
| OWNER................... | 31 | 38 | 47 | 36 | 42 | 31 | 17 | 20 | 13 | 13 |
| RENTER.................. | 64 | 55 | 46 | 63 | 56 | 68 | 62 | 62 | 83 | 85 |
| SQUATTER................ | 5 | 6 | 5 | 1 | 1 | 1 | 21 | 18 | 4 | 2 |
| HOMESTEADER............. | * | * | 1 | * | 1 | * | --- | --- | * | --- |
| OWNERS REPORTING MORTGAGES... | 44 | 21 | 37 | 68 | 73 | 64 | 29 | | 39 | |
| FAMILIES REPORTING GARDEN OR TRUCK PATCH............. | 73 | 94 | 87 | 52 | 81 | 33 | 50 | 66 | 78 | 79 |

*LESS THAN 0.5 PERCENT.

TABLE XX-B. FAMILIES CLASSIFIED BY PRESENT OCCUPATION OF HEAD OF HOUSEHOLD AND OWNERSHIP OF HOUSE OR FARM; ALSO OWNERS REPORTING MORTGAGES AND FAMILIES REPORTING GARDEN OR TRUCK PATCH

FARM OPERATORS

| REAL ESTATE OWNERSHIP AND MORTGAGE CONDITION | TOTAL ALL AREAS | APPA-LACHIAN OZARK | LAKE STATES CUT-OVER | SHORT GRASS | | | WESTERN COTTON | | EASTERN COTTON | |
|---|---|---|---|---|---|---|---|---|---|---|
| | | | | TOTAL | SPRING WHEAT | WINTER WHEAT | WHITE | NEGRO | WHITE | NEGRO |
| *Number* | | | | | | | | | | |
| ALL FAMILIES.................. | 4,571 | 1,487 | 509 | 1,814 | 895 | 919 | 194 | 35 | 291 | 241 |
| OWNER.................... | 1,997 | 660 | 354 | 831 | 452 | 379 | 40 | 9 | 64 | 39 |
| RENTER................... | 2,499 | 785 | 138 | 970 | 436 | 534 | 153 | 25 | 226 | 202 |
| SQUATTER................. | 41 | 36 | 2 | 1 | 1 | --- | 1 | 1 | --- | --- |
| HOMESTEADER.............. | 34 | 6 | 15 | 12 | 6 | 6 | --- | --- | 1 | --- |
| OWNERS REPORTING MORTGAGES... | 1,098 | 151 | 185 | 670 | 364 | 306 | 29 | 1 | 44 | 18 |
| FAMILIES REPORTING GARDEN OR TRUCK PATCH............. | 3,810 | 1,471 | 504 | 1,129 | 825 | 304 | 152 | 34 | 282 | 238 |
| *Percent* | | | | | | | | | | |
| ALL FAMILIES.................. | 100 | 100 | 100 | 100 | 100 | 100 | 100 | 100 | 100 | 100 |
| OWNER.................... | 44 | 44 | 69 | 46 | 51 | 41 | 21 | --- | 22 | 16 |
| RENTER................... | 55 | 53 | 27 | 53 | 48 | 58 | 78 | --- | 78 | 84 |
| SQUATTER................. | 1 | 2 | * | * | * | --- | 1 | --- | --- | --- |
| HOMESTEADER.............. | * | * | 3 | 1 | 1 | 1 | --- | --- | * | --- |
| OWNERS REPORTING MORTGAGES... | 55 | 23 | 52 | 81 | 81 | 81 | --- | --- | 60 | |
| FAMILIES REPORTING GARDEN OR TRUCK PATCH............. | 83 | 99 | 99 | 62 | 92 | 33 | 78 | --- | 97 | 99 |

*LESS THAN 0.5 PERCENT.

TABLE XX-C. FAMILIES CLASSIFIED BY PRESENT OCCUPATION OF HEAD OF HOUSEHOLD AND OWNERSHIP OF HOUSE OR FARM; ALSO OWNERS REPORTING MORTGAGES AND FAMILIES REPORTING GARDEN OR TRUCK PATCH

NON-AGRICULTURAL WORKERS

| REAL ESTATE OWNERSHIP AND MORTGAGE CONDITION | TOTAL ALL AREAS | APPA-LACHIAN OZARK | LAKE STATES CUT-OVER | SHORT GRASS | | | WESTERN COTTON | | EASTERN COTTON | |
|---|---|---|---|---|---|---|---|---|---|---|
| | | | | TOTAL | SPRING WHEAT | WINTER WHEAT | WHITE | NEGRO | WHITE | NEGRO |
| *Number* | | | | | | | | | | |
| ALL FAMILIES.................. | 557 | 59 | 181 | 103 | 32 | 71 | 27 | 7 | 72 | 108 |
| OWNER.................... | 144 | 14 | 62 | 31 | 10 | 21 | 4 | 4 | 11 | 18 |
| RENTER................... | 383 | 42 | 102 | 70 | 21 | 49 | 17 | 3 | 59 | 90 |
| SQUATTER................. | 28 | 3 | 15 | 2 | 1 | 1 | 6 | - | 2 | --- |
| HOMESTEADER.............. | 2 | -- | 2 | --- | -- | -- | -- | - | -- | --- |
| OWNERS REPORTING MORTGAGES... | 54 | 3 | 26 | 13 | 4 | 9 | 2 | 1 | 6 | 3 |
| FAMILIES REPORTING GARDEN OR TRUCK PATCH............. | 378 | 53 | 149 | 37 | 21 | 16 | 11 | 5 | 46 | 77 |
| *Percent* | | | | | | | | | | |
| ALL FAMILIES.................. | 100 | 100 | 100 | 100 | 100 | 100 | 100 | 100 | 100 | 100 |
| OWNER.................... | 26 | 24 | 34 | 30 | --- | 30 | --- | --- | 15 | 17 |
| RENTER................... | 69 | 71 | 56 | 68 | --- | 69 | --- | --- | 82 | 83 |
| SQUATTER................. | 5 | 5 | 8 | 2 | --- | 1 | --- | --- | 3 | --- |
| HOMESTEADER.............. | * | --- | 1 | --- | --- | --- | --- | --- | --- | --- |
| OWNERS REPORTING MORTGAGES... | 38 | --- | 42 | --- | --- | --- | --- | --- | --- | --- |
| FAMILIES REPORTING GARDEN OR TRUCK PATCH............. | 68 | 90 | 82 | 36 | --- | 23 | --- | --- | 64 | 71 |

'LESS THAN 0.5 PERCENT.

TABLE XXI–A. FAMILIES REPORTING OWNERSHIP OF SPECIFIED CLASSES OF LIVESTOCK AND FAMILIES
REPORTING CHATTEL MORTGAGES BY PRESENT OCCUPATION OF HEAD OF FAMILY

ALL OCCUPATIONS

| CHATTELS AND CHATTEL MORTGAGES | TOTAL ALL AREAS | APPALACHIAN OZARK | LAKE STATES CUTOVER | SHORT GRASS | | | WESTERN COTTON | | EASTERN COTTON | |
|---|---|---|---|---|---|---|---|---|---|---|
| | | | | TOTAL | SPRING WHEAT | WINTER WHEAT | WHITE | NEGRO | WHITE | NEGRO |
| *Number* | | | | | | | | | | |
| ALL FAMILIES.................. | 10,771 | 2,167 | 1,738 | 3,318 | 1,311 | 2,007 | 800 | 164 | 1,346 | 1,239 |
| FAMILIES REPORTING | | | | | | | | | | |
| DAIRY COWS.............. | 4,589 | 1,223 | 640 | 1,780 | 733 | 1,047 | 294 | 29 | 442 | 181 |
| OTHER CATTLE........... | 1,966 | 395 | 303 | 1,179 | 734 | 445 | 30 | 3 | 35 | 21 |
| WORK STOCK............. | 3,082 | 604 | 299 | 1,595 | 867 | 728 | 161 | 23 | 228 | 172 |
| HOGS................... | 3,528 | 1,058 | 237 | 1,322 | 591 | 731 | 181 | 39 | 362 | 329 |
| SHEEP AND GOATS........ | 342 | 72 | 44 | 195 | 132 | 63 | 6 | 1 | 5 | 19 |
| POULTRY................ | 5,983 | 1,538 | 627 | 2,130 | 928 | 1,202 | 361 | 66 | 711 | 550 |
| FAMILIES REPORTING CHATTEL MORTGAGES.............. | 1,935 | 101 | 163 | 1,407 | 770 | 637 | 105 | 6 | 108 | 45 |
| *Percent* | | | | | | | | | | |
| ALL FAMILIES.................. | 100.0 | 100.0 | 100.0 | 100.0 | 100.0 | 100.0 | 100.0 | 100.0 | 100.0 | 100.0 |
| FAMILIES REPORTING | | | | | | | | | | |
| DAIRY COWS.............. | 42.6 | 56.4 | 36.8 | 53.6 | 55.9 | 52.2 | 36.8 | 17.7 | 32.8 | 14.6 |
| OTHER CATTLE........... | 18.3 | 18.2 | 17.4 | 35.5 | 56.0 | 22.2 | 3.8 | 1.8 | 2.6 | 1.7 |
| WORK STOCK............. | 28.6 | 27.9 | 17.2 | 48.1 | 66.1 | 36.3 | 20.1 | 14.0 | 16.9 | 13.9 |
| HOGS................... | 32.8 | 48.8 | 13.6 | 39.8 | 45.1 | 36.4 | 22.6 | 23.8 | 26.9 | 26.6 |
| SHEEP AND GOATS........ | 3.2 | 3.3 | 2.5 | 5.9 | 10.1 | 3.1 | 0.8 | 0.6 | 0.4 | 1.5 |
| POULTRY................ | 55.5 | 71.0 | 36.1 | 64.2 | 70.8 | 59.9 | 45.1 | 40.2 | 52.8 | 44.4 |
| FAMILIES REPORTING CHATTEL MORTGAGES.............. | 18.0 | 4.7 | 9.4 | 42.4 | 58.7 | 31.7 | 13.1 | 3.7 | 8.0 | 3.6 |

TABLE XXI–B. FAMILIES REPORTING OWNERSHIP OF SPECIFIED CLASSES OF LIVESTOCK AND FAMILIES
REPORTING CHATTEL MORTGAGES, BY PRESENT OCCUPATION OF HEAD OF FAMILY

FARM OPERATORS

| CHATTELS AND CHATTEL MORTGAGES | TOTAL ALL AREAS | APPALACHIAN OZARK | LAKE STATES CUTOVER | SHORT GRASS | | | WESTERN COTTON | | EASTERN COTTON | |
|---|---|---|---|---|---|---|---|---|---|---|
| | | | | TOTAL | SPRING WHEAT | WINTER WHEAT | WHITE | NEGRO | WHITE | NEGRO |
| *Number* | | | | | | | | | | |
| ALL FAMILIES................ | 4,571 | 1,487 | 509 | 1,814 | 895 | 919 | 194 | 35 | 291 | 241 |
| FAMILIES REPORTING | | | | | | | | | | |
| DAIRY COWS.............. | 3,304 | 1,018 | 418 | 1,444 | 684 | 760 | 139 | 17 | 176 | 92 |
| OTHER CATTLE........... | 1,733 | 339 | 230 | 1,125 | 701 | 424 | 16 | 3 | 10 | 10 |
| WORK STOCK............. | 2,786 | 562 | 259 | 1,470 | 811 | 659 | 136 | 18 | 193 | 148 |
| HOGS................... | 2,703 | 881 | 167 | 1,184 | 571 | 613 | 128 | 26 | 188 | 129 |
| SHEEP AND GOATS........ | 278 | 60 | 32 | 171 | 126 | 45 | --- | 1 | 1 | 13 |
| POULTRY................ | 3,897 | 1,223 | 387 | 1,651 | 824 | 827 | 177 | 30 | 239 | 190 |
| FAMILIES REPORTING CHATTEL MORTGAGES.............. | 1,675 | 90 | 108 | 1,265 | 705 | 560 | 84 | 5 | 89 | 34 |
| *Percent* | | | | | | | | | | |
| ALL FAMILIES................ | 100.0 | 100.0 | 100.0 | 100.0 | 100.0 | 100.0 | 100.0 | 100.0 | 100.0 | 100.0 |
| FAMILIES REPORTING | | | | | | | | | | |
| DAIRY COWS.............. | 72.3 | 68.5 | 82.1 | 79.6 | 76.4 | 82.7 | 71.6 | 48.6 | 60.5 | 38.2 |
| OTHER CATTLE........... | 37.9 | 22.8 | 45.2 | 62.0 | 78.3 | 46.1 | 8.2 | 8.6 | 3.4 | 4.1 |
| WORK STOCK............. | 60.9 | 37.8 | 50.9 | 81.0 | 90.6 | 71.7 | 70.1 | 51.4 | 66.3 | 61.4 |
| HOGS................... | 59.1 | 59.2 | 32.8 | 65.3 | 63.8 | 66.7 | 66.0 | 74.3 | 64.6 | 53.5 |
| SHEEP AND GOATS........ | 6.1 | 4.0 | 6.3 | 9.4 | 14.1 | 4.9 | ---- | 2.9 | 0.3 | 5.4 |
| POULTRY................ | 85.3 | 82.2 | 76.0 | 91.0 | 92.1 | 90.0 | 91.2 | 85.7 | 82.1 | 78.8 |
| FAMILIES REPORTING CHATTEL MORTGAGES.............. | 36.6 | 6.1 | 21.2 | 69.7 | 78.8 | 60.9 | 43.3 | 14.3 | 30.6 | 14.1 |

TABLE XXI-C. FAMILIES REPORTING OWNERSHIP OF SPECIFIED CLASSES OF LIVESTOCK AND FAMILIES REPORTING CHATTEL MORTGAGES, BY PRESENT OCCUPATION OF HEAD OF FAMILY

NON-AGRICULTURAL WORKERS

| CHATTELS AND CHATTEL MORTGAGES | TOTAL ALL AREAS | APPA-LACHIAN OZARK | LAKE STATES CUT-OVER | SHORT GRASS | | | WESTERN COTTON | | EASTERN COTTON | |
|---|---|---|---|---|---|---|---|---|---|---|
| | | | | TOTAL | SPRING WHEAT | WINTER WHEAT | WHITE | NEGRO | WHITE | NEGRO |
| *Number* | | | | | | | | | | |
| ALL FAMILIES | 557 | 59 | 181 | 103 | 32 | 71 | 27 | 7 | 72 | 108 |
| FAMILIES REPORTING | | | | | | | | | | |
| DAIRY COWS | 100 | 19 | 34 | 17 | 4 | 13 | 12 | 1 | 12 | 5 |
| OTHER CATTLE | 18 | 2 | 12 | 2 | 1 | 1 | 1 | - | -- | 1 |
| WORK STOCK | 28 | 6 | 8 | 9 | 4 | 5 | 1 | - | 1 | 3 |
| HOGS | 71 | 21 | 13 | 5 | 1 | 4 | 5 | - | 9 | 18 |
| SHEEP AND GOATS | 5 | -- | 3 | 1 | 1 | -- | 1 | - | -- | --- |
| POULTRY | 170 | 30 | 41 | 30 | 7 | 23 | 8 | 1 | 29 | 31 |
| FAMILIES REPORTING CHATTEL MORTGAGES | 32 | 2 | 18 | 9 | 5 | 4 | 1 | - | 2 | --- |
| *Percent* | | | | | | | | | | |
| ALL FAMILIES | 100.0 | 100.0 | 100.0 | 100.0 | 100.0 | 100.0 | 100.0 | 100.0 | 100.0 | 100.0 |
| FAMILIES REPORTING | | | | | | | | | | |
| DAIRY COWS | 18.0 | 32.2 | 18.8 | 16.5 | ----- | 18.3 | ----- | ----- | 16.7 | 4.6 |
| OTHER CATTLE | 3.2 | 3.4 | 6.6 | 1.9 | ----- | 1.4 | ----- | ----- | ----- | 0.9 |
| WORK STOCK | 5.0 | 10.2 | 4.4 | 8.7 | ----- | 7.0 | ----- | ----- | 1.4 | 2.8 |
| HOGS | 12.7 | 35.6 | 7.2 | 4.9 | ----- | 5.6 | ----- | ----- | 12.5 | 16.7 |
| SHEEP AND GOATS | 0.9 | ----- | 1.7 | 1.0 | ----- | ----- | ----- | ----- | ----- | ----- |
| POULTRY | 30.5 | 50.8 | 22.7 | 29.1 | ----- | 32.4 | ----- | ----- | 40.3 | 28.7 |
| FAMILIES REPORTING CHATTEL MORTGAGES | 5.7 | 3.4 | 9.9 | 8.7 | ----- | 5.6 | ----- | ----- | 2.8 | ----- |

TABLE XXI-D. FAMILIES REPORTING OWNERSHIP OF SPECIFIED CLASSES OF LIVESTOCK AND FAMILIES REPORTING CHATTEL MORTGAGES, BY PRESENT OCCUPATION OF HEAD OF FAMILY

UNEMPLOYED

| CHATTELS AND CHATTEL MORTGAGES | TOTAL ALL AREAS | APPA-LACHIAN OZARK | LAKE STATES CUT-OVER | SHORT GRASS | | | WESTERN COTTON | | EASTERN COTTON | |
|---|---|---|---|---|---|---|---|---|---|---|
| | | | | TOTAL | SPRING WHEAT | WINTER WHEAT | WHITE | NEGRO | WHITE | NEGRO |
| *Number* | | | | | | | | | | |
| ALL FAMILIES | 5,389 | 609 | 1,017 | 1,388 | 382 | 1,006 | 562 | 118 | 920 | 775 |
| FAMILIES REPORTING | | | | | | | | | | |
| DAIRY COWS | 1,130 | 181 | 178 | 316 | 44 | 272 | 138 | 11 | 237 | 69 |
| OTHER CATTLE | 207 | 52 | 56 | 51 | 32 | 19 | 13 | --- | 25 | 10 |
| WORK STOCK | 257 | 34 | 31 | 115 | 51 | 64 | 21 | 5 | 32 | 19 |
| HOGS | 688 | 148 | 54 | 132 | 19 | 113 | 45 | 13 | 148 | 148 |
| SHEEP AND GOATS | 56 | 12 | 6 | 23 | 5 | 18 | 5 | --- | 4 | 6 |
| POULTRY | 1,798 | 275 | 191 | 444 | 95 | 349 | 167 | 35 | 411 | 275 |
| FAMILIES REPORTING CHATTEL MORTGAGES | 224 | 9 | 33 | 133 | 60 | 73 | 20 | 1 | 17 | 11 |
| *Percent* | | | | | | | | | | |
| ALL FAMILIES | 100.0 | 100.0 | 100.0 | 100.0 | 100.0 | 100.0 | 100.0 | 100.0 | 100.0 | 100.0 |
| FAMILIES REPORTING | | | | | | | | | | |
| DAIRY COWS | 21.0 | 29.7 | 17.5 | 22.8 | 11.5 | 27.0 | 24.6 | 9.3 | 25.8 | 8.9 |
| OTHER CATTLE | 3.8 | 8.5 | 5.5 | 3.7 | 8.4 | 1.9 | 2.3 | ----- | 2.7 | 1.3 |
| WORK STOCK | 4.8 | 5.6 | 3.0 | 8.3 | 13.4 | 6.4 | 3.7 | 4.2 | 3.5 | 2.5 |
| HOGS | 12.8 | 24.3 | 5.3 | 9.5 | 5.0 | 11.2 | 8.0 | 11.0 | 16.1 | 19.1 |
| SHEEP AND GOATS | 1.0 | 2.0 | 0.6 | 1.7 | 1.3 | 1.8 | 0.9 | ----- | 0.4 | 0.8 |
| POULTRY | 33.4 | 45.2 | 18.8 | 32.0 | 24.9 | 34.7 | 29.7 | 29.7 | 44.7 | 35.5 |
| FAMILIES REPORTING CHATTEL MORTGAGES | 4.2 | 1.5 | 3.2 | 9.6 | 15.7 | 7.3 | 3.6 | 0.8 | 1.8 | 1.4 |

TABLE XXII. COMPARISON OF SIZE OF FARMS OPERATED BY FAMILIES RECEIVING RELIEF WHO WERE FARMING IN JUNE 1934 AND OF ALL FARMS IN SAME COUNTIES, 1930

| ACRES IN FARM | APPA- LACHIAN OZARK | LAKE STATES CUT- OVER | SHORT GRASS | | WESTERN COTTON | EASTERN COTTON |
|---|---|---|---|---|---|---|
| | | | SPRING WHEAT | WINTER WHEAT | | |
| *Farms of Families Receiving Relief* | | | | | | |
| TOTAL................................. | 100.0 | 100.0 | 100.0 | 100.0 | 100.0 | 100.0 |
| UNDER 10 ACRES..................... | 18.4 | 3.4 | | | 2.4 | 19.8 |
| 10—19 ACRES....................... | 19.2 | 1.8 | } 3.5 | } 10.2 | 11.2 | 22.4 |
| 20—49 ACRES....................... | 36.9 | 44.0 | | | 33.5 | 34.0 |
| 50—99 ACRES....................... | 14.7 | 31.6 | | | 19.4 | 15.2 |
| 100—174 ACRES..................... | 8.9 | 17.9 | 20.0 | 27.5 | 19.4 | 5.6 |
| 175—259 ACRES..................... | | | 4.9 | 6.8 | | |
| 260—499 ACRES..................... | } 1.8 | } 1.3 | 40.9 | 35.1 | } 14.1 | } 3.0 |
| 500—999 ACRES..................... | | | 23.5 | 16.7 | | |
| 1000 OR MORE ACRES................. | | | 7.2 | 3.7 | | |
| *All Farms[a] 1930* | | | | | | |
| TOTAL................................. | 100.0 | 100.0 | 100.0 | 100.0 | 100.0 | 100.0 |
| UNDER 10 ACRES..................... | 8.1 | 1.9 | | | 1.8 | 4.9 |
| 10—19 ACRES....................... | 11.8 | 2.0 | } 2.6 | } 6.1 | 4.9 | 17.5 |
| 20—49 ACRES....................... | 27.2 | 18.3 | | | 17.7 | 48.0 |
| 50—99 ACRES....................... | 25.9 | 31.3 | | | 24.1 | 17.6 |
| 100—174 ACRES..................... | 17.4 | 31.7 | 11.3 | 9.6 | 30.9 | 7.7 |
| 175—259 ACRES..................... | | | 5.0 | 4.8 | | |
| 260—499 ACRES..................... | } 9.5 | } 14.8 | 33.7 | 34.1 | } 20.4 | } 4.4 |
| 500—999 ACRES..................... | | | 29.2 | 28.7 | | |
| 1000 OR MORE ACRES................. | | | 18.3 | 16.5 | | |
| *Median Size of Farm* | | | | | | |
| FARMERS RECEIVING RELIEF.............. | 27 | 51 | 387 | 342 | 58 | 32 |
| ALL FARMS, 1930...................... | 56 | 94 | 481 | 465 | 104 | 37 |

[a]U. S. CENSUS OF AGRICULTURE, 1930

TABLE XXIII. CAPACITY FOR SELF-SUPPORT OF FAMILIES RECEIVING RELIEF, BY RESIDENCE IN OPEN COUNTRY, VILLAGE OR TOWN

| CAPACITY FOR SELF-SUPPORT BY RESIDENCE | TOTAL ALL AREAS | | APPA- LACHIAN OZARK | LAKE STATES CUT- OVER | SHORT GRASS | | WESTERN COTTON | | EASTERN COTTON | |
|---|---|---|---|---|---|---|---|---|---|---|
| | NUM- BER | PER- CENT | | | SPRING WHEAT | WINTER WHEAT | WHITE | NEGRO | WHITE | NEGRO |
| OPEN COUNTRY FAMILIES.. | 7,070 | 100 | 1,693 | 1,092 | 979 | 1,031 | 376 | 61 | 795 | 773 |
| INCAPABLE.......... | 1,261 | 18 | 297 | 241 | 106 | 73 | 32 | 10 | 167 | 335 |
| CAPABLE............ | 5,809 | 82 | 1,666 | 851 | 873 | 958 | 344 | 51 | 628 | 438 |
| WITH SUPER- VISION..... | 1,230 | 17 | 581 | 79 | 86 | 83 | 28 | 4 | 175 | 194 |
| WITHOUT SUPER- VISION..... | 4,579 | 65 | 1,085 | 772 | 787 | 875 | 316 | 47 | 453 | 244 |
| VILLAGE FAMILIES | 2,289 | 100 | 179 | 410 | 246 | 474 | 278 | 42 | 353 | 307 |
| INCAPABLE.......... | 546 | 24 | 25 | 89 | 78 | 123 | 62 | 11 | 54 | 104 |
| CAPABLE............ | 1,743 | 76 | 154 | 321 | 168 | 351 | 216 | 31 | 299 | 203 |
| WITH SUPER- VISION..... | 268 | 12 | 36 | 29 | 24 | 63 | 24 | 8 | 29 | 55 |
| WITHOUT SUPER- VISION..... | 1,475 | 64 | 118 | 292 | 144 | 288 | 192 | 23 | 270 | 148 |
| TOWN FAMILIES.......... | 1,412 | 100 | 25 | 236 | 86 | 502 | 146 | 61 | 199 | 157 |
| INCAPABLE.......... | 293 | 21 | 8 | 50 | 26 | 85 | 23 | 17 | 42 | 41 |
| CAPABLE............ | 1,119 | 79 | 17 | 186 | 60 | 416 | 123 | 44 | 157 | 116 |
| WITH SUPER- VISION..... | 143 | 10 | 3 | 7 | 13 | 20 | 27 | 25 | 27 | 21 |
| WITHOUT SUPER- VISION..... | 976 | 69 | 14 | 179 | 47 | 396 | 96 | 19 | 130 | 95 |

TABLE XXIV. SEX, EMPLOYMENT STATUS AND USUAL OCCUPATION OF UNEMPLOYED HEADS OF FAMILIES RECEIVING RELIEF AND CONSIDERED CAPABLE OF SELF-SUPPORT

| ITEM | TOTAL ALL AREAS | APPA- LACHIAN OZARK | LAKE STATES CUT- OVER | SHORT GRASS | | WESTERN COTTON | | EASTERN COTTON | |
|---|---|---|---|---|---|---|---|---|---|
| | | | | SPRING WHEAT | WINTER WHEAT | WHITE | NEGRO | WHITE | NEGRO |
| ALL FAMILIES............ | 100.0 | 100.0 | 100.0 | 100.0 | 100.0 | 100.0 | 100.0 | 100.0 | 100.0 |
| CAPABLE OF SELF-SUPPORT. | 80.5 | 84.8 | 78.1 | 84.0 | 86.0 | 85.4 | 76.8 | 80.5 | 61.2 |
| FAMILIES WITH FEMALE HEADS............... | 7.6 | 6.4 | 5.0 | 4.0 | 3.8 | 8.8 | 14.0 | 11.3 | 17.8 |
| FAMILIES WITH MALE HEADS............... | 72.9 | 78.4 | 73.1 | 80.0 | 82.2 | 76.6 | 62.8 | 69.2 | 43.4 |
| EMPLOYED MALE HEADS, JUNE 1934.......... | 41.8 | 62.4 | 34.4 | 63.8 | 44.8 | 24.2 | 20.7 | 25.3 | 20.4 |
| FARMER.............. | 37.2 | 60.5 | 25.0 | 62.3 | 42.5 | 20.9 | 17.7 | 18.0 | 12.8 |
| OWNER............. | 16.3 | 27.0 | 18.6 | 31.7 | 16.8 | 3.5 | 4.3 | 3.2 | 1.6 |
| TENANT AND CROPPER | 20.9 | 33.5 | 6.4 | 30.6 | 25.7 | 17.4 | 13.4 | 14.8 | 11.2 |
| FARM LABORER........ | 1.6 | 0.4 | 1.6 | 0.1 | 0.5 | 1.8 | 2.4 | 3.5 | 5.0 |
| OTHER OCCUPATIONS... | 3.0 | 1.5 | 7.8 | 1.4 | 1.8 | 1.5 | 0.6 | 3.8 | 2.6 |
| UNEMPLOYED MALE HEADS, JUNE 1934.......... | 31.1 | 16.0 | 38.7 | 16.2 | 37.4 | 52.4 | 42.1 | 42.9 | 23.0 |
| USUALLY FARMER...... | 5.6 | 1.8 | 1.5 | 3.4 | 6.4 | 13.9 | 5.5 | 12.7 | 5.4 |
| OWNER............. | 0.7 | 0.3 | 0.8 | 1.2 | 0.6 | 1.3 | 0.6 | 1.0 | 0.1 |
| TENANT AND CROPPER | 4.9 | 1.5 | 0.7 | 2.2 | 5.8 | 12.6 | 4.9 | 11.7 | 5.3 |
| USUALLY FARM LABORER | 4.0 | 0.5 | 1.0 | 1.2 | 6.4 | 12.8 | 14.6 | 5.1 | 5.4 |
| USUALLY NON-AGRICUL- TURAL WORKER...... | 21.5 | 13.7 | 36.2 | 11.6 | 24.6 | 25.7 | 21.9 | 26.1 | 12.2 |
| LABORER........... | 8.5 | 6.5 | 13.1 | 4.9 | 11.2 | 12.1 | 17.7 | 3.8 | 6.3 |
| MECHANIC.......... | 4.2 | 1.6 | 5.5 | 1.8 | 6.1 | 7.0 | 1.2 | 8.2 | 0.8 |
| FACTORY AND RAIL- ROAD EMPLOYEE... | 2.9 | 0.9 | 3.7 | 1.5 | 2.5 | 1.6 | 0.6 | 8.2 | 2.8 |
| ALL OTHERS........ | 5.9 | 4.7 | 13.9* | 3.4 | 4.8 | 5.0 | 2.4 | 5.9 | 2.3 |
| INCAPABLE OF SELF-SUPPORT | 19.5 | 15.2 | 21.9 | 16.0 | 14.0 | 14.6 | 23.2 | 19.5 | 38.8 |
| FAMILIES WITH FEMALE HEADS............... | 6.7 | 5.0 | 5.2 | 3.9 | 3.5 | 3.2 | 7.9 | 6.0 | 22.4 |
| FAMILIES WITH MALE HEADS............... | 12.8 | 10.2 | 16.7 | 12.1 | 10.5 | 11.4 | 15.3 | 13.5 | 16.4 |

*NEARLY 8 PERCENT WERE UNEMPLOYED MINERS, 2.5 PERCENT UNEMPLOYED LUMBERMEN.

TABLE XXV. KIND OF WORK FOR WHICH FAMILIES RECEIVING RELIEF WERE QUALIFIED,[a] BY SEX OF HEAD

| KIND OF WORK FOR WHICH FAMILY WAS QUALIFIED | TOTAL ALL AREAS | APPA- LACHIAN OZARK | LAKE STATES CUT- OVER | SHORT GRASS | | WESTERN COTTON | | EASTERN COTTON | |
|---|---|---|---|---|---|---|---|---|---|
| | | | | SPRING WHEAT | WINTER WHEAT | WHITE | NEGRO | WHITE | NEGRO |
| ALL FAMILIES...................... | 100.0 | 100.0 | 100.0 | 100.0 | 100.0 | 100.0 | 100.0 | 100.0 | 100.0 |
| CAPABLE OF SELF-SUPPORT........ | 80.5 | 84.8 | 78.1 | 84.0 | 86.0 | 85.4 | 76.8 | 80.5 | 61.2 |
| FARM OPERATOR................ | 34.9 | 17.5 | 18.4 | 64.2 | 45.9 | 40.8 | 27.4 | 38.7 | 32.5 |
| OPERATOR - GARDEN PLOT WITH OTHER EMPLOYMENT | 30.6 | 64.6 | 44.1 | 11.2 | 22.7 | 21.7 | 34.8 | 11.1 | 11.8 |
| OTHER EMPLOYMENT............. | 15.0 | 2.7 | 15.7 | 8.6 | 17.3 | 22.9 | 14.6 | 30.7 | 16.9 |
| INCAPABLE OF SELF-SUPPORT...... | 19.5 | 15.2 | 21.9 | 16.0 | 14.0 | 14.6 | 23.2 | 19.5 | 38.8 |
| FAMILIES WITH MALE HEADS......... | 85.7 | 98.6 | 89.8 | 92.1 | 92.7 | 88.0 | 78.0 | 82.7 | 59.8 |
| CAPABLE OF SELF-SUPPORT........ | 72.9 | 78.4 | 73.1 | 80.0 | 82.2 | 76.6 | 62.8 | 69.2 | 43.4 |
| FARM OPERATOR................ | 32.8 | 17.1 | 17.5 | 62.4 | 44.8 | 37.9 | 26.8 | 35.4 | 25.9 |
| OPERATOR - GARDEN PLOT WITH OTHER EMPLOYMENT | 28.4 | 59.7 | 42.4 | 11.0 | 21.8 | 21.1 | 31.1 | 9.7 | 7.7 |
| OTHER EMPLOYMENT............. | 11.7 | 1.6 | 13.2 | 6.6 | 15.6 | 17.6 | 4.9 | 24.1 | 9.8 |
| INCAPABLE OF SELF-SUPPORT...... | 12.8 | 10.2 | 16.7 | 12.1 | 10.5 | 11.4 | 15.2 | 13.5 | 16.4 |
| FAMILIES WITH FEMALE HEADS....... | 14.3 | 11.4 | 10.2 | 7.9 | 7.3 | 12.0 | 22.0 | 17.3 | 40.2 |
| CAPABLE OF SELF-SUPPORT........ | 7.6 | 6.4 | 5.0 | 4.0 | 3.8 | 8.8 | 14.0 | 11.3 | 17.8 |
| FARM OPERATOR................ | 2.0 | 0.4 | 0.9 | 1.8 | 1.2 | 2.9 | 0.6 | 3.3 | 6.6 |
| OPERATOR - GARDEN PLOT WITH OTHER EMPLOYMENT | 2.2 | 4.9 | 1.7 | 0.2 | 0.9 | 0.6 | 3.6 | 1.3 | 4.1 |
| OTHER EMPLOYMENT............. | 3.4 | 1.1 | 2.5 | 2.0 | 1.7 | 5.3 | 9.8 | 6.7 | 7.1 |
| INCAPABLE OF SELF-SUPPORT...... | 6.7 | 5.0 | 5.2 | 3.9 | 3.5 | 3.2 | 7.9 | 6.0 | 22.4 |

[a] IN THE OPINION OF LOCAL RELIEF WORKERS.

# APPENDIX B

## Figures

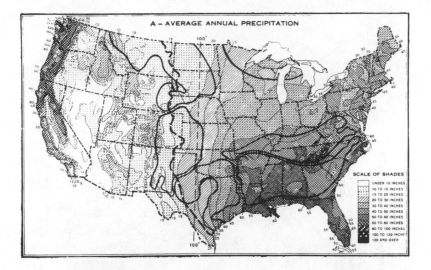

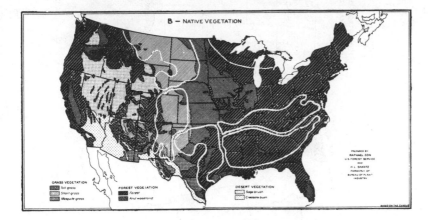

FIGURE I    Average Annual Precipitation and Native Vegetation  —  Native vegetation reflects the
            potential capacity of the virgin soil for agricultural and for forest production.  Note
            that the eastern boundry of the Short Grass region does not follow a line of equal
            precipitation, but crosses two precipitation zones:  It advances from about the 18 inch
            line in North Dakota to the 24 inch line in Texas, where, because evaporation is much
            greater and the rainfall more torrential, more rainfall is required to insure the same
            amount of available moisture.

SOURCE:     Baker, Oliver E., A Graphic Summary of American Agriculture, U. S. Department of
            Agriculture, Miscellaneous Publication Number 105 (Washington, Government Printing
            Office, May, 1931).

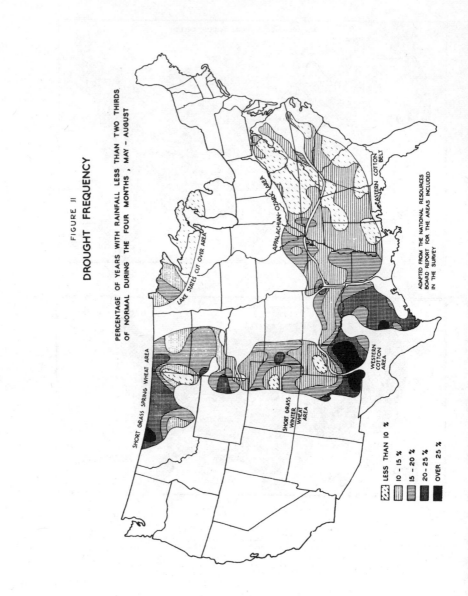

FIGURE II

DROUGHT FREQUENCY

PERCENTAGE OF YEARS WITH RAINFALL LESS THAN TWO THIRDS
OF NORMAL DURING THE FOUR MONTHS , MAY – AUGUST

ADAPTED FROM THE NATIONAL RESOURCES
BOARD REPORT FOR THE AREAS INCLUDED
IN THE SURVEY

LESS THAN 10 %
10 - 15 %
15 - 20 %
20 - 25 %
OVER 25 %

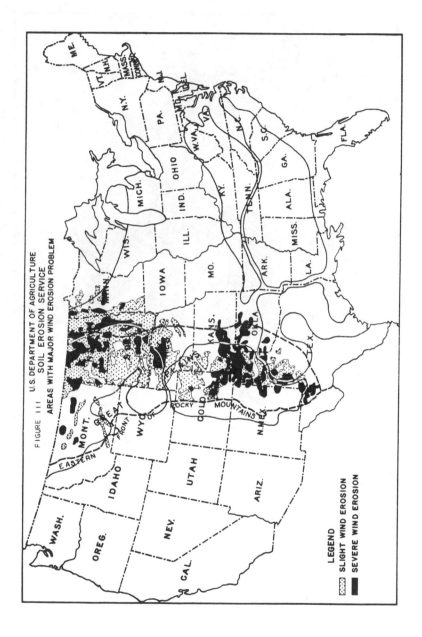

FIGURE III U.S. DEPARTMENT OF AGRICULTURE
SOIL EROSION SERVICE
AREAS WITH MAJOR WIND EROSION PROBLEM

LEGEND
SLIGHT WIND EROSION
SEVERE WIND EROSION

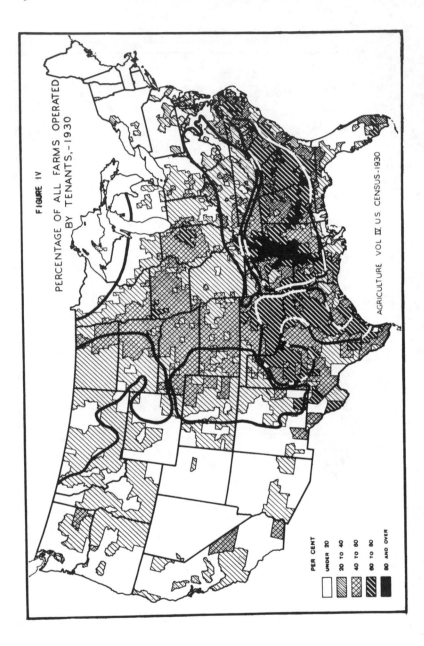

FIGURE IV

PERCENTAGE OF ALL FARMS OPERATED
BY TENANTS,-1930

AGRICULTURE VOL II. US CENSUS-1930

PER CENT

UNDER 20
20 TO 40
40 TO 60
60 TO 80
80 AND OVER

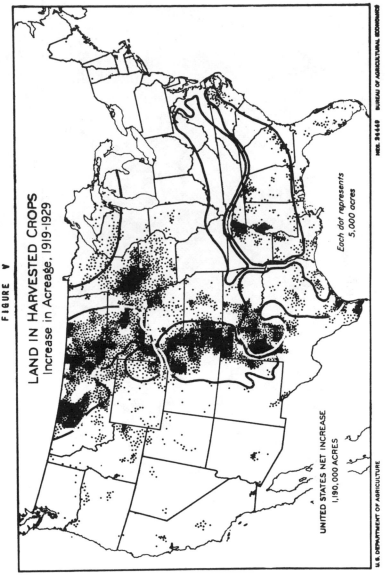

FIGURE V

LAND IN HARVESTED CROPS
Increase in Acreage, 1919-1929

Each dot represents
5,000 acres

UNITED STATES NET INCREASE
1,190,000 ACRES

U.S. DEPARTMENT OF AGRICULTURE

NEG. 24440 BUREAU OF AGRICULTURAL ECONOMICS

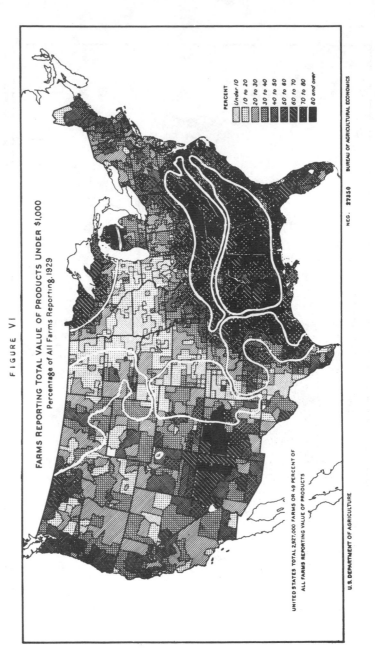

FIGURE VI

FARMS REPORTING TOTAL VALUE OF PRODUCTS UNDER $1,000
Percentage of All Farms Reporting,1929

PERCENT

Under 10
10 to 20
20 to 30
30 to 40
40 to 50
50 to 60
60 to 70
70 to 80
80 and over

UNITED STATES TOTAL 2,927,000 FARMS OR 49 PERCENT OF
ALL FARMS REPORTING VALUE OF PRODUCTS

U. S. DEPARTMENT OF AGRICULTURE

NEG.   27350      BUREAU OF AGRICULTURAL ECONOMICS

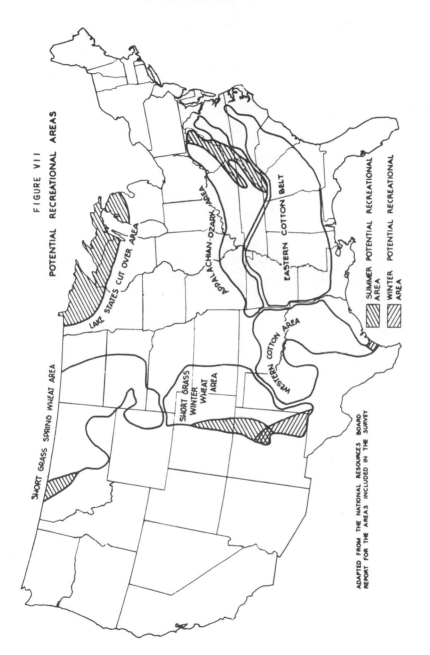

FIGURE VII

POTENTIAL RECREATIONAL AREAS

SHORT GRASS SPRING WHEAT AREA

LAKE STATES CUT OVER AREA

APPALACHIAN-OZARK AREA

EASTERN COTTON BELT

SHORT GRASS WINTER WHEAT AREA

WESTERN COTTON AREA

SUMMER POTENTIAL RECREATIONAL AREA

WINTER POTENTIAL RECREATIONAL AREA

ADAPTED FROM THE NATIONAL RESOURCES BOARD REPORT FOR THE AREAS INCLUDED IN THE SURVEY

# APPENDIX C

List of Sample Counties

List of Counties Included in Each of the Six Areas

## COUNTIES SURVEYED IN THE RURAL PROBLEM AREAS

**Appalachian-Ozark Area**

| | |
|---|---|
| Arkansas | Madison |
| | Searcy |
| Kentucky | Jackson |
| | Knox |
| | Pike |
| Tennessee | Bledsoe |
| | Fentress |
| | Grainger |
| North Carolina | Avery |
| | Jackson |
| Virginia | Russell |
| West Virginia | Webster |
| | Wyoming |

**Lake States Cut-Over Area**

| | |
|---|---|
| Michigan | Alcona |
| | Alger |
| | Iron |
| | Kalkaska |
| Minnesota | Aitkin |
| | Beltrami |
| | Crow Wing |
| Wisconsin | Oconto |
| | Oneida |
| | Washburn |

**Short Grass Spring Wheat Area**

| | |
|---|---|
| Montana | Phillips |
| | Prairie |
| Nebraska | Dawes |
| North Dakota | Burke |
| | Grant |
| South Dakota | Haakon |
| | Harding |
| | Tripp |

**Short Grass Winter Wheat Area**

| | |
|---|---|
| Colorado | Baca |
| | Cheyenne |
| | Yuma |
| Kansas | Hodgeman |
| | Meade |
| | Sherman |
| Nebraska | Cheyenne |
| New Mexico | Roosevelt |
| | Union |
| Oklahoma | Cimarron |
| Texas | Dallam |
| | Randall |
| | Roberts |

**Western Cotton Area**

| | |
|---|---|
| Oklahoma | Choctaw |
| | Tillman |
| Texas | Dawson |
| | Jones |
| | San Patricio |
| | Williamson |
| | Wood |

**Eastern Cotton Belt**

| | |
|---|---|
| Alabama | Dallas |
| | Limestone |
| Arkansas | Calhoun |
| Georgia | Meriwether |
| | Morgan |
| | Tift |
| Louisiana | Richland |
| | Union |
| Mississippi | Leflore |
| | Monroe |
| North Carolina | Anson |
| | Franklin |
| South Carolina | Sumter |
| | Marlboro |

## LIST OF COUNTIES IN THE SIX RURAL PROBLEM AREAS

### Appalachian-Ozark Area

Arkansas
  Boone
  Carroll
  Crawford
  Franklin
  Johnson
  Madison
  Marion
  Newton
  Searcy
  Stone
  Washington

Georgia
  Dade
  Fannin
  Gilmer
  Habersham
  Lumpkin
  Rabun
  Towns
  Union
  White

Illinois
  Franklin
  Hardin
  Hamilton
  Johnson
  Pope
  Saline
  Williamson

Kentucky
  Adair
  Allen
  Bell
  Breathitt
  Butler
  Caldwell
  Carter
  Casey
  Clay
  Clinton
  Crittenden
  Cumberland
  Edmonson
  Elliott
  Estill
  Floyd
  Grayson
  Greenup
  Harlan
  Hopkins
  Jackson
  Johnson
  Knott
  Knox
  Larue
  Laurel
  Lawrence
  Lee
  Leslie
  Letcher
  Lincoln
  Livingston
  McCreary
  Magoffin
  Martin
  Meade
  Menifee

  Metcalfe
  Monroe
  Morgan
  Muhlenberg
  Ohio
  Owsley
  Perry
  Pike
  Powell
  Pulaski
  Rockcastle
  Rowan
  Russell
  Wayne
  Whitley
  Wolfe

Missouri
  Bollinger
  Camden
  Carter
  Crawford
  Dent
  Douglas
  Iron
  Madison
  Oregon
  Reynolds
  St. Francois
  Ste. Genevieve
  Shannon
  Taney
  Washington
  Wayne

North Carolina
  Alexander
  Alleghany
  Ashe
  Avery
  Buncombe
  Burke
  Caldwell
  Chatham
  Cherokee
  Clay
  Graham
  Haywood
  Henderson
  Jackson
  McDowell
  Macon
  Madison
  Mitchell
  Moore
  Randolph
  Swain
  Transylvania
  Watauga
  Wilkes
  Yancey

Oklahoma
  Adair
  Cherokee
  Delaware
  Latimer
  Pushmataha

Tennessee
  Anderson

  Benton
  Bledsoe
  Blount
  Bradley
  Campbell
  Cannon
  Carter
  Claiborne
  Clay
  Cocke
  Coffee
  Cumberland
  Decatur
  De Kalb
  Fentress
  Franklin
  Grainger
  Grundy
  Hamblen
  Hancock
  Hawkins
  Hickman
  Houston
  Humphreys
  Jackson
  Jefferson
  Johnson
  Lewis
  McMinn
  Macon
  Marion
  Marshall
  Maury
  Monroe
  Morgan
  Overton
  Perry
  Pickett
  Polk
  Putnam
  Rhea
  Roane
  Sequatchie
  Sevier
  Scott
  Smith
  Stewart
  Sullivan
  Unicoi
  Union
  Van Buren
  Warren
  Washington
  Wayne
  White
  Williamson

Virginia
  Albemarle
  Alleghany
  Amherst
  Appomattox
  Bedford
  Botetourt
  Buchanan
  Campbell
  Carroll
  Craig
  Culpeper
  Floyd
  Franklin

  Giles
  Grayson
  Greene
  Henry
  Lee
  Madison
  Montgomery
  Nelson
  Orange
  Page
  Patrick
  Rappahannock
  Rockbridge
  Russell
  Scott
  Smyth
  Spotsylvania
  Stafford
  Tazewell
  Wise

West Virginia
  Barbour
  Boone
  Braxton
  Calhoun
  Clay
  Doddridge
  Fayette
  Gilmer
  Grant
  Greenbrier
  Hampshire
  Hancock
  Hardy
  Harrison
  Jackson
  Kanawha
  Lewis
  Lincoln
  Logan
  McDowell
  Marion
  Mason
  Mercer
  Mineral
  Mingo
  Monongalia
  Monroe
  Morgan
  Nicholas
  Pendleton
  Pleasants
  Pocahontas
  Preston
  Putnam
  Raleigh
  Randolph
  Ritchie
  Roane
  Summers
  Taylor
  Tucker
  Tyler
  Upshur
  Wayne
  Webster
  Wetzel
  Wirt
  Wood
  Wyoming

## Lake States Cut-Over

| | | | |
|---|---|---|---|
| Michigan | Iron | Roscommon | Wisconsin |
| Antrim | Kalkaska | Schoolcraft | Ashland |
| Alcona | Keweenaw | Wexford | Bayfield |
| Alger | Lake | | Burnett |
| Alpena | Luce | Minnesota | Douglas |
| Baraga | Leelanau | Aitkin | Florence |
| Benzie | Mackinac | Beltrami | Forest |
| Charlevoix | Manistee | Carlton | Iron |
| Cheboygan | Marquette | Cass | Langlade |
| Chippewa | Mason | Clearwater | Lincoln |
| Clare | Menominee | Cook | Marinette |
| Crawford | Midland | Crow Wing | Oconto |
| Delta | Missaukee | Hubbard | Oneida |
| Dickinson | Montmorency | Itasca | Price |
| Emmet | Newaygo | Koochiching | Rusk |
| Gladwin | Ogemaw | Lake | Sawyer |
| Gogebic | Ontonagon | Lake of the Woods | Taylor |
| Grand Traverse | Oscoda | Pine | Vilas |
| Houghton | Otsego | Roseau | Washburn |
| Iosco | Presque Isle | St. Louis | |

## Spring Wheat Area

| | | | |
|---|---|---|---|
| Montana | Wibaux | McKenzie | Fall River |
| Blaine | Yellowstone | Mercer | Faulk |
| Carbon | | Morton | Gregory |
| Carter | Nebraska | Mountrail | Haakon |
| Cascade | Box Butte | Nelson | Harding |
| Chouteau | Dawes | Oliver | Hughes |
| Daniels | Sioux | Pierce | Hyde |
| Dawson | | Ramsey | Jackson |
| Fallon | North Dakota | Renville | Jones |
| Fergus | Adams | Rolette | Lyman |
| Garfield | Barnes | Sheridan | McPherson |
| Glacier | Benson | Sioux | Meade |
| Golden Valley | Billings | Slope | Mellette |
| Hill | Bottineau | Stark | Perkins |
| Judith Basin | Bowman | Stutsman | Potter |
| Liberty | Burke | Towner | Shannon |
| McCone | Burleigh | Walsh | Spink |
| Musselshell | Cavalier | Ward | Stanley |
| Petroleum | Dickey | Wells | Sully |
| Phillips | Divide | Williams | Todd |
| Pondera | Dunn | | Tripp |
| Prairie | Eddy | South Dakota | Walworth |
| Richland | Emmons | Armstrong | Washabaugh |
| Roosevelt | Foster | Bennett | Washington |
| Sheridan | Golden Valley | Brown | Ziebach |
| Stillwater | Grant | Brule | |
| Sweet Grass | Hettinger | Buffalo | Wyoming |
| Teton | Kidder | Butte | Converse |
| Toole | Logan | Campbell | Goshen |
| Treasure | McHenry | Corson | Niobrara |
| Valley | McIntosh | Dewey | Platte |
| Wheatland | McLean | Edmunds | Weston |

## Winter Wheat Area

| | | | |
|---|---|---|---|
| Colorado | Huerfano | Pueblo | Clark |
| Adams | Kiowa | Sedgwick | Comanche |
| Arapahoe | Kit Carson | Washington | Decatur |
| Baca | Las Animas | Weld | Dickinson |
| Bent | Lincoln | Yuma | Edwards |
| Cheyenne | Logan | | Ellis |
| Crowley | Morgan | Kansas | Ellsworth |
| Douglas | Otero | Barber | Finney |
| Elbert | Phillips | Barton | Ford |
| El Paso | Prowers | Cheyenne | Gove |

### Winter Wheat Area

**Kansas (Cont.)**
Graham
Grant
Gray
Greeley
Hamilton
Harper
Harvey
Haskell
Hodgeman
Kearny
Kingman
Kiowa
Lane
Lincoln
Logan
McPherson
Marion
Meade
Mitchell
Morton
Ness
Norton
Osborne
Ottawa
Pawnee
Pratt
Rawlins
Reno
Rice
Rooks
Rush
Russell
Saline
Sedgwick
Seward
Scott
Sheridan
Sherman
Stafford
Stanton
Stevens
Sumner
Thomas
Trego
Wallace
Wichita

**Nebraska**
Banner
Chase
Cheyenne
Dawson
Deuel
Dundy
Frontier
Furnas
Gosper
Hayes
Hitchcock
Howard
Keith
Kimball
Morrill
Perkins
Redwillow
Sherman

**New Mexico**
Chaves
Colfax
Curry
De Baca
Eddy
Guadalupe
Harding
Lea
Mora
Quay
Roosevelt
San Miguel
Torrance
Union

**Oklahoma**
Alfalfa
Beaver
Blaine
Canadian
Cimarron
Custer
Dewey
Ellis
Garfield
Grant
Harper
Kay
Kingfisher
Major
Noble
Texas
Wood
Woodward

**Texas**
Andrews
Armstrong
Bailey
Carson
Castro
Cochran
Dallam
Deaf Smith
Donley
Ector
Gaines
Gray
Hansford
Hartley
Hemphill
Hutchinson
Lipscomb
Moore
Ochiltree
Oldham
Parmer
Potter
Randall
Roberts
Sherman
Yoakum

**Wyoming**
Laramie

### Western Cotton Area

**Texas**
Anderson
Angelina
Austin
Bastrop
Bee
Bell
Bosque
Bowie
Brazos
Burleson
Caldwell
Cameron
Camp
Cass
Cherokee
Childress
Coleman
Collin
Collingsworth
Colorado
Coryell
Cottle
Crosby
Dallas
Dawson
Delta
Denton
De Witt
Ellis
Erath
Falls
Fannin
Fayette
Fisher
Foard
Fort Bend
Franklin
Freestone
Gonzales
Grayson
Gregg
Grimes
Guadalupe
Hall
Hamilton
Hardeman
Harrison
Haskell
Henderson
Hidalgo
Hill
Hockley
Hopkins
Houston
Howard
Hunt
Johnson
Jones
Karnes
Kaufman
Knox
Lamar
Lamb
Lavaca
Lee
Leon
Limestone
Live Oak
Lubbock
Lynn
McLennan
Madison
Marion
Martin
Milam
Mitchell
Montgomery
Morris
Nacogdoches
Navarro
Nolan
Nueces
Panola
Polk
Rains
Red River
Robertson
Rockwall
Runnels
Rusk
Sabine
San Augustine
San Jacinto
San Patricio
Scurry
Shelby
Smith
Somervell
Starr
Stonewall
Taylor
Terry
Titus
Travis
Trinity
Upshur
Van Zandt
Walker
Waller
Washington
Wharton
Wheeler
Wichita
Wilbarger
Williamson
Wilson
Wood

**Oklahoma**
Beckham
Bryan
Caddo
Choctaw
Comanche
Cotton
Creek
Garvin

## Western Cotton Area

| | | | |
|---|---|---|---|
| Oklahoma (Cont.) | Jefferson | Muskogee | Stephens |
| Grady | Le Flore | Okfuskee | Tillman |
| Greer | Love | Okmulgee | Wagoner |
| Harmon | McClain | Pottawatomie | Washita |
| Haskell | McCurtain | Roger Mills | Kiowa |
| Hughes | McIntosh | Seminole | Lincoln |
| Jackson | Marshall | Sequoyah | |

## Eastern Cotton Area

| | | | |
|---|---|---|---|
| Alabama | Tallapoosa | Union | Irwin |
| Autauga | Tuscaloosa | Van Buren | Jackson |
| Barbour | Walker | White | Jasper |
| Bibb | Washington | Woodruff | Jefferson |
| Blount | Wilcox | Yell | Jenkins |
| Bullock | Winston | | Johnson |
| Butler | | Georgia | Lamar |
| Calhoun | Arkansas | Baker | Laurens |
| Chambers | Ashley | Baldwin | Lee |
| Cherokee | Bradley | Banks | Lincoln |
| Chilton | Calhoun | Barrow | McDuffie |
| Choctaw | Chicot | Bartow | Macon |
| Clarke | Clark | Ben Hill | Madison |
| Clay | Clay | Bleckley | Marion |
| Cleburne | Cleburne | Bulloch | Meriwether |
| Coffee | Cleveland | Burke | Miller |
| Colbert | Columbia | Butts | Mitchell |
| Conecuh | Conway | Calhoun | Monroe |
| Coosa | Craighead | Campbell | Montgomery |
| Covington | Crittenden | Candler | Morgan |
| Crenshaw | Cross | Carroll | Murray |
| Cullman | Dallas | Catoosa | Newton |
| Dale | Desha | Chatooga | Oconee |
| Dallas | Drew | Chattahoochee | Ogelthorpe |
| De Kalb | Faulkner | Cherokee | Paulding |
| Elmore | Garland | Clarke | Peach |
| Escambia | Grant | Clay | Pickens |
| Etowah | Greene | Clayton | Pike |
| Fayette | Hempstead | Cobb | Polk |
| Franklin | Hot Spring | Colquitt | Pulaski |
| Geneva | Howard | Columbia | Putnam |
| Greene | Independence | Coweta | Quitman |
| Hale | Izard | Crawford | Randolph |
| Henry | Jackson | Crisp | Richmond |
| Houston | Jefferson | Dawson | Rockdale |
| Jackson | Lafayette | De Kalb | Schley |
| Lamar | Lawrence | Dodge | Screven |
| Lawrence | Lee | Dooly | Spalding |
| Lee | Lincoln | Douglas | Stephens |
| Limestone | Little River | Early | Stewart |
| Lowndes | Logan | Elbert | Sumter |
| Macon | Lonoke | Emanuel | Talbot |
| Madison | Miller | Evans | Taliaferro |
| Marengo | Mississippi | Fayette | Taylor |
| Marion | Monroe | Floyd | Telfair |
| Marshall | Montgomery | Forsyth | Terrell |
| Monroe | Nevada | Franklin | Tift |
| Montgomery | Ouachita | Glascock | Toombs |
| Morgan | Perry | Gordon | Treutlen |
| Perry | Phillips | Greene | Troup |
| Pickens | Pike | Gwinnett | Turner |
| Pike | Poinsett | Hall | Twiggs |
| Lauderdale | Pope | Hancock | Upson |
| Randolph | Pulaski | Haralson | Walker |
| Russell | Randolph | Harris | Walton |
| St. Clair | St. Francis | Hart | Warren |
| Shelby | Saline | Heard | Washington |
| Sumter | Scott | Henry | Webster |
| Talladega | Sharp | Houston | Wheeler |

### Eastern Cotton Area

| | | | |
|---|---|---|---|
| **Georgia (Cont.)** | Clarke | Union | Calhoun |
| Whitfield | Clay | Walthall | Cherokee |
| Wilcox | Coahoma | Warren | Chesterfield |
| Wilkes | Covington | Washington | Clarendon |
| Wilkinson | De Soto | Wayne | Colleton |
| Worth | Franklin | Webster | Darlington |
| | George | Wilkinson | Dillon |
| **Louisiana** | Grenada | Winston | Dorchester |
| Avoyelles | Hinds | Yalobsisha | Edgefield |
| Bienville | Holmes | Yazoo | Fairfield |
| Bossier | Humphreys | | Greenville |
| Caddo | Issaquena | **Missouri** | Greenwood |
| Caldwell | Itawamba | Dunklin | Hampton |
| Catahaula | Jasper | New Madrid | Kershaw |
| Claiborne | Jefferson | Pemiscot | Lancaster |
| Concordia | Jefferson Davis | | Laurens |
| De Soto | Jones | **North Carolina** | Lee |
| East Carroll | Kemper | Anson | Lexington |
| Evangeline | Lafayette | Cabarrus | McCormick |
| Franklin | Lamar | Catawba | Marlboro |
| Grant | Lauderdale | Cleveland | Newberry |
| Jackson | Lawrence | Cumberland | Oconee |
| Lincoln | Leake | Franklin | Orangeburg |
| Madison | Lee | Gaston | Pickins |
| Morehouse | Laflore | Halifax | Richland |
| Natchitoches | Lincoln | Harnett | Saluda |
| Pointe Coupee | Lowndes | Hoke | Spartanburg |
| Ouachita | Madison | Iredell | Sumter |
| Rapides | Marion | Johnston | Union |
| Red River | Marshall | Lee | York |
| Richland | Monroe | Lincoln | |
| Sabine | Montgomery | Mecklenburg | **Tennessee** |
| St. Landry | Neshoba | Montgomery | Carroll |
| Tensas | Newton | Northampton | Chester |
| Union | Noxubee | Polk | Crockett |
| Vernon | Oktibbeha | Richmond | Dyer |
| Washington | Panola | Robeson | Fayette |
| Webster | Pike | Rowan | Gibson |
| West Carroll | Pontotoc | Rutherford | Hardeman |
| Winn | Prentiss | Sampson | Hardin |
| | Quitman | Scotland | Haywood |
| **Mississippi** | Rankin | Stanly | Henderson |
| Adams | Scott | Union | Lake |
| Alcorn | Sharkey | Warren | Lauderdale |
| Amite | Simpson | | Lawrence |
| Attala | Smith | **South Carolina** | McNairy |
| Benton | Sunflower | Abbeville | Madison |
| Bolivar | Tallahatchie | Aiken | Shelby |
| Calhoun | Tate | Allendale | Tipton |
| Carroll | Tippah | Anderson | |
| Chickasaw | Tishomingo | Bamberg | |
| Choctaw | Tunica | Barnwell | |
| Claiborne | | | |

# APPENDIX D

## Methodological Note

## METHODOLOGICAL NOTE

### Identification of the Areas

The "Problem Areas" which are the subject of this report were brought to the attention of the Federal Emergency Relief Administration by the monthly recurrence of high relief rates. Preliminary study of these and neighboring areas indicated that certain permanent combinations of factors were associated with the large proportion of families receiving relief in certain rural areas. Six such areas were identified and studied. The areas and the criteria, other than high relief rates, by which they were delimited were:

1. The Lake States Cut-Over
   a. Poor soil
   b. Short growing season
   c. Relatively small percentage of land in farms
   d. Decadent lumbering, woodworking and copper mining industries
   e. Unemployment in iron mines and in industry generally owing to technological improvements
2. The Appalachian—Ozark Area
   a. Mountainous terrain
   b. Little arable land—soil generally poor
   c. Large proportion of farms of self-sufficing or part-time type
   d. Decadent lumbering and woodworking industries—also abandoned coal mines in many counties
   e. A dense population—rapidly increasing due to a high rate of natural increase and lack of employment opportunities elsewhere
   f. A distinctive culture based on agriculture plus other employment, now in a period of change owing to loss of non-farm employment
3. The Short Grass—Spring Wheat Area
   a. Wheat-growing in a region of low and variable precipitation

    b.  Area roughly coincident with that in which the natural vegetation was "short grass"

4.  The Short Grass—Winter Wheat Area

    a.  Wheat-growing and other arable agriculture on an extensive scale, with large investments in power machinery, in a region of light and variable rainfall

    b.  Area delineated by natural vegetation "short-grass" line—an indication of rainfall, evaporation and soil type

5.  The Western Cotton Area

    a.  Cotton farming

    b.  Over-expansion of cotton farming and surplus of population due to immigration

    c.  Crop failure due to drought in western part of area

6.  The Eastern Cotton Belt

    a.  Cotton farming

    b.  A system of farming which grew out of the plantation system based on Negro slavery

    c.  Disruption of traditional system of agriculture due to loss of foreign markets and low prices of cotton

### Selection of the Sample Counties

The counties selected for intensive study were picked to represent insofar as possible in a limited sample the range of conditions prevalent in each area. Census tabulations and county relief data were utilized and the final selections verified by informed persons in State Agricultural Colleges and State Emergency Relief Administrations. The factors, in addition to relief rates, considered in selecting samples in each area were, briefly, as follows:

1.  Lake States Cut-Over Area

    a.  Percentage of land in farms

    b.  Percentage of gainful workers employed in agriculture, lumbering and woodworking industries, and mining

    c.  Geographic location

    d.  Percentage of population rural

2.  The Appalachian–Ozark Area
    a.  Percentage of farms—self-sufficing
    b.  Percentage of gainful workers employed in
        mining and in manufacturing
    c.  Geographic location
    d.  Percentage of population rural
3.  The Short Grass—Spring Wheat Area
    a.  Percentage of farm land in wheat
    b.  Average annual precipitation
    c.  Geographic location
    d.  Percentage of population rural
4.  The Short Grass—Winter Wheat
        Same as for Spring Wheat
5.  The Western Cotton Area
    a.  Percentage of farm land in cotton
    b.  Percentage of population rural
    c.  Percentage of farm tenancy
    d.  Percentage of rural population Negro
    e.  Geographic location
6.  The Eastern Cotton Belt
    a.  Percentage of farm land in cotton
    b.  Percentage of population rural
    c.  Percentage of farm tenancy
    d.  Percentage of rural population Negro
    e.  Average value of farm land per acre
    f.  Geographic location

## Sampling Procedure in the Counties

A random sample was taken of all resident families receiving unemployment relief and living in the county in June 1934. Each county was sampled so as to include approximately 150 cases. This was accomplished by taking every case, every other case, or every third case, etc., depending upon the number of families receiving relief. This method of sampling is based on the theory of a relatively homogeneous universe in each area.

# APPENDIX E

Household Schedule

F.E.R.A. Form DRS 60

- 240 -

## FEDERAL EMERGENCY RELIEF ADMINISTRATION
### HARRY L. HOPKINS, ADMINISTRATOR
### DIVISION OF RESEARCH AND STATISTICS
#### CORRINGTON GILL, DIRECTOR

## SURVEY OF RURAL PROBLEM AREAS
(JUNE 1934)
### HOUSEHOLD SCHEDULE

SCHEDULE No. ...................................................

COUNTY ...........................................................

STATE ..............................................................

NAME OF RELIEF AGENCY ...........................................

NAME OF HEAD OF HOUSEHOLD .....................................

ADDRESS ...........................................................

DATE OF LAST VISIT BY CASE WORKER ............................

I. Residence:

| | (a) | (b) |
|---|---|---|
| | *Present* | *April 1, 1930* |
| 1. | (......) | (......) Open country. |
| 2. | (......) | (......) Village (under 2,500). |
| 3. | (......) | (......) City (2,500–4,999). |
| 4. | (......) | (......) City (5,000 and over). |
| | | (......) Unknown. |

II. Years lived in county: Under 1, 1–4, 5–9, 10 or more, unknown (circle appropriate number).

III. Grade in school finished by head of household: None, 1–4, 5–7, 8, 9–10, 11–12, more than 12 (circle appropriate number).

IV. Color and nativity of head of household:
1. (......) Native white.
2. (......) Foreign white.
3. (......) Negro.
4. (......) Other (specify) ..............................

V. Nationality of head of household (specify):
1. ......................................................

VI. Marital status of head of household:
1. (......) Single.
2. (......) Married.
3. (......) Widowed.
4. (......) Divorced.
5. (......) Separated.
6. (......) Not ascertainable.

VII. Sex of head of household:
1. (......) Male.
2. (......) Female.

VIII. Age of head of household:
1. (......) Under 25 years.
2. (......) 25–44 years.
3. (......) 45–64 years.
4. (......) 65 years and over.
5. (......) Not ascertainable.

IX. Age and sex composition of household: (enter number of persons in each column).

| AGE | MALE | FEMALE |
|---|---|---|
| Under 10 years | | |
| 10–15 years | | |
| 16–24 years | | |
| 25–44 years | | |
| 45–64 years | | |
| 65 years and over | | |
| Unknown | | |

X. Number of persons in household:
1, 2, 3, 4, 5, 6, 7, 8, 9, 10, 11, 12, 13, 14, 15 or more (circle appropriate number).

XI. Composition of household:
1. (......) Single person.
2. (......) Husband, wife only.
3. (......) Husband, wife with others.
4. (......) Husband, wife, children under 16 years only.
5. (......) Husband, wife, children under 16 years with others.
6. (......) Husband, wife, children 16 years and over only.
7. (......) Husband, wife, children 16 years and over with others.
8. (......) Husband, wife, children both under and over 16 years only.
9. (......) Husband, wife, children both under and over 16 years with others.
10. (......) Woman, children under 16 years only.
11. (......) Woman, children under 16 years with others.
12. (......) Woman, children 16 years and over only.
13. (......) Woman, children 16 years and over with others.
14. (......) Woman, children both over and under 16 years only.
15. (......) Woman, children both over and under 16 years with others.
16. (......) Man, children under 16 years only.
17. (......) Man, children under 16 years with others.
18. (......) Man, children 16 years and over only.
19. (......) Man, children 16 years and over with others.
20. (......) Man, children both over and under 16 years only.
21. (......) Man, children both over and under 16 years with others.
22. (......) All other combinations.
23. Does this household include a "doubled-up" family which has combined since Jan. 1, 1930?

Yes (......); no (......); unknown (......).

**XII.** Number of workers in household (enter number of workers):

|  | TOTAL | MALE | FEMALE |
|---|---|---|---|
| (a) Gainful workers: | | | |
|     1. 10 and under 16 years......... | | | |
|     2. 16 years and over............... | | | |
| (b) Potential gainful workers: | | | |
|     1. 10 and under 16 years......... | | | |
|     2. 16 years and over............... | | | |

**XIII.** Occupation of head of household (see Instructions):

| *Usual* | *Present* | | *Usual* | *Present* | |
|---|---|---|---|---|---|
| 1. (......) | (......) Farm owner (and managers). | | 10. (......) | (......) Railroad employee not elsewhere classified (including employees in round house) | |
| 2. (......) | (......) Farm tenant. | | | | |
| 3. (......) | (......) Farm cropper. | | 11. (......) | (......) Professional man. | |
| 4. (......) | (......) Farm laborer. | | 12. (......) | (......) Merchant, banker, or other proprietor. | |
| 5. (......) | (......) Fisherman or hunter. | | | | |
| 6. (......) | (......) Lumberman, raftsman, or woodchopper. | | 13. (......) | (......) Clerical worker or salesman. | |
| 7. (......) | (......) Miner (including laborers, inspectors, and foremen in mines). | | 14. (......) | (......) Servant or waiter. | |
| | | | 15. (......) | (......) Laborer (not elsewhere classified). | |
| 8. (......) | (......) Mechanic (including building and all other mechanics). | | 16. (......) | (......) All other occupations. | |
| | | | 17. (......) | (......) Unemployed. | |
| 9. (......) | (......) Factory employee (including foremen, operatives, and laborers). | | 18. (......) | (......) Not ascertainable. | |

**XIV.** Are any members of the household skilled in some handicraft?

Yes (......).     No (......).       *Member*                *Craft*

..............................................     ..............................................

..............................................     ..............................................

**XV.** Land, livestock, and farm implements:

    1. Is household—

        (a) (......) Owner of farm or house?

        (b) (......) Renter of farm or house?

        (c) (......) Squatter?

        (d) (......) Homesteader?

    2. If house or farm owned, is it mortgaged? Yes (......). No (......). Not ascertainable (......).

    3. Does household have—

        (a) Dairy cows?.......... Yes......(......); number......(................); no......(..... ); not ascertainable......(......).

        (b) Other cattle?.......... Yes......(......); number......(................); no......(..... ); not ascertainable..... (......).

        (c) Work stock?.......... Yes......(......); number......(................); no......(......); not ascertainable......(......).

        (d) Hogs?.................. Yes......(......); number......(................); no......(......); not ascertainable......(......).

        (e) Sheep and goats?... Yes......(......); number......(................); no......(..... ); not ascertainable......(......).

        (f) Poultry?................ Yes......(......); number......(................); no......(......); not ascertainable......(......).

    4. Does household have access to or use of implements necessary for operation of present land holdings? Yes......(......); no......(......); not ascertainable......(......).

    5. Does household have home garden, or truck patch? Yes......(......); no......(......); not ascertainable......(......).

    6. Does household have chattels mortgaged? Yes......(......); no......(......); not ascertainable......(......).

    7. (a) Size of farm .......................... acres. Not ascertainable......(......).

        (b) Crop land ............................ acres. Not ascertainable......(......).

        (c) Pasture land .......................... acres. Not ascertainable......(......).

        (d) Acres in principal crops: ......................................... (..................) ....................................... (..................)

        ......................... (..................) ........................... (..................) ......................... (..................)

        Designate year reported for (a), (b), (c), (d) .........................................................................................

XVI. Household received relief (from any agency or organization):
    1. Before 1930: Yes......(......); no......(......); not ascertainable......(......).
    2. During 1930: Yes......(......); no......(......); not ascertainable......(......).
    3. During 1931: Yes......(......); no......(......); not ascertainable......(......).
    4. During 1932: Yes......(......); no......(......); not ascertainable......(......).
    5. During 1933: Yes......(......); no......(......).
    6. Value of relief received during June 1934:
            Direct relief... $............................
            Work relief.... $............................
    7. If relief is paid by an agency outside this county, specify agency..............................................................

XVII. Reasons for household receiving relief:
    1. (......) Head of household unable to work.
    2. (......) Head of household able to work but unable to find work.
    3. (......) Head of household able to work but unwilling to work.
    4. (......) Head of household working for wages but income insufficient.
    5. (......) Head of household lost supplementary occupation.
    6. (......) Loss of job by member of household other than head.
    7. (......) Crop failure.
    8. (......) Farming on poor land.
    9. (......) Farm too small.
    10. (......) Poor management of farm or business.
    11. (......) Poor management of household.
    12. (......) Losses or unusual expenses (exclusive of 15)
    13. (......) Tenant or cropper household displaced from agricultural employment due to reduction in crop acreage under A.A.A.
    14. (......) Tenant or cropper household displaced for other reasons than under 13.
    15. (......) Emergency expense for medical and dental services.
    16. (......) Other (specify) ..............................................................

XVIII. Classification of household according to prospects for rehabilitation:
    1. (......) Household will need continued financial assistance and some supervision because of:
        (a) 1. (......) Permanent disability. 2. (......) Old age. 3. (......) Widowhood. 4. (......) Other incapacity (specify)..............................................................
        (b) 5. (......) Incapable. 6. (......) Irresponsible of family support (specify nature of incapacity or irresponsibility) ..............................................................
    2. (......) Household will need constant supervision and temporary financial assistance.
    3. (......) Household will need temporary aid and temporary supervision.
    4. (......) Household will need only temporary relief.
    5. (......) Household will need temporary relief but chiefly replenishment of capital.

XIX. Is household qualified to operate:
    1. (......) Commercial farm (from which most products are sold).
    2. (......) Subsistence farm (most of products consumed at home).
    3. (......) Small plot as partial subsistence only, supplemented by other employment.
    4. (......) Forest workers and small plot as partial subsistence.
    5. (......) If none of the above apply, specify what household is best qualified to do ..............................................................
    ..............................................................
    6. (......) Not capable of rehabilitation. Reason ..............................................................
    ..............................................................

XX. Source of information:

| ITEM NUMBER | CASE RECORD | CASE WORKER | COUNTY RELIEF OFFICIAL | INTERVIEW WITH CASE | OTHER SOURCES (SPECIFY) |
|---|---|---|---|---|---|
| I. (a) Present residence | | | | | |
| (b) Residence 1930 | | | | | |
| II. Years in county | | | | | |
| III. Schooling | | | | | |
| IV. Color and nativity | | | | | |
| V. Nationality | | | | | |
| VI. Marital status | | | | | |
| VII. Sex of head | | | | | |
| VIII. Age of head | | | | | |
| IX. Age and sex | | | | | |
| X. Size of household | | | | | |
| XI. Composition of household | | | | | |
| XII. Workers | | | | | |
| XIII. Occupation | | | | | |
| XIV. Handicrafts | | | | | |
| XV. Land, livestock, etc | | | | | |
| XVI. Relief history | | | | | |
| XVII. Reasons for relief | | | | | |
| XVIII. Rehabilitation | | | | | |
| XIX. Qualifications | | | | | |

REMARKS: ........................................................................

(Signed) ........................ (Investigator)    Date, ........................, 1934.

APPENDIX F


List of References

## LIST OF REFERENCES

1. Anderson, Wm. and Zon, Raphael, "Social and Economic Effects of Past Land Developement", *Land Utilization in Minnesota*, pp. 56 - 73, Minneapolis: University of Minnesota
   Press, 1934.

2. Campbell, John C., *The Southern Highlander and His Homeland*,
   New York: Russell Sage Foundation, 1921, 405 pp., illus.

3. Clayton, C. F. and Nicholls, W. D., *Land Utilization in Laurel County, Kentucky*, U. S. Dept. of Agriculture, Tech.
   Bul. No. 289, 1932, 100 pp.

4. Coffman, L. D. Chm., *Land Utilization in Minnesota*, Minneapolis: University of Minnesota Press, 1934, 289 pp., illus.

5. Dodd, Wm. E., *The Cotton Kingdom*, New Haven, Connecticut:
   Yale University Press, 1919, 161 pp., illus.

6. Hoffsommer, Harold C., *Rural Problem Areas Survey*, Dallas
   County, Alabama, (Typewritten on file, Research Section,
   FERA, Washington, D. C.)

7. Kirkpatrick, E. L., *Rural Problem Areas Survey*, Regional
   Report on the Lake States Cut-Over Area, (Typewritten on
   file, Research Section, FERA, Washington, D. C.)

8. Vance, Rupert B., *Human Geography of the South, A Study in
   Regional Resources and Human Adequacy*, Chapel Hill, N. C.:
   University of North Carolina Press, 1932, 596 pp., illus.

9. Vance, Rupert B., *Regional Reconstruction: A Way Out for
   the South*, New York: Foreign Policy Association, and Chapel
   Hill, N. C.: University of North Carolina Press, 1935, 31 pp.

10. Wehrwein, George S., "A Social and Economic Program for
    Sub-marginal Areas of the Lake States", *Journal of Forestry*,
    XXIX (1931), 915-924.

11. Wehrwein, George S., and Parsons, Kenneth H., *Recreation as a Land Use*, Agricultural Experiment Station, University of Wisconsin, Bul. 422, 1933, 32 pp.

12. Zon, Raphael, *Timber Growing and Logging Practice in the Lake States*, U. S. Dept. of Agriculture, Bul. No. 1496, 1928, 64 pp., illus.

13. Zon, Raphael, and Garver, R. D., *Selective Logging in the Northern Hardwoods of the Lake States*, U. S. Dept. of Agriculture, Tech. Bul. No. 164, 1930, 46 pp.

14. United States Department of Commerce, Bureau of the Census, *Fifteenth Census of the United States: 1930. Population*, Government Printing Office, Washington, D. C., 1932.

15. *Economic and Social Problems and Conditions of the Southern Appalachians* by the Bureau of Agricultural Economics, Bureau of Home Economics and Forest Service, Miscellaneous Publication 205, Government Printing Office, Washington, D. C., 1935, 184 pp.

16. *Progress Report Kansas State Planning Board*, Topeka, Kansas, 1934, 188 pp., illus.

17. Nicholls, W. D. and Hawthorne, H. W., *Farm Management and Income of Farm Families in Laurel County, Kentucky*, Kentucky Agricultural Experiment Station, Bul. 305, 1930, pp. 223-283, illus.

18. *National Resources Board Report*, Government Printing Office, Washington, D. C., 1934, 455 pp., illus.

19. *Regional Problems in Agricultural Adjustment*, U. S. Dept. of Agriculture, A.A.A., G-31, Government Printing Office, Washington, D. C., 1935, 101 pp.

20. *Report of the Committee on the Upper Monongahela Valley*, West Virginia, U. S. Dept. of Interior, 1934, 136 pp.

21.  Hoffsommer, Harold C., *Rural Problem Areas Survey*, Morgan
     County, Georgia, (Typewritten on file, Research Section,
     FERA, Washington, D. C.)

22.  United States Department of Commerce, Bureau of the Census,
     *Farm Census*, Preliminary Report, 1935.

23.  United States Department of Commerce, Bureau of the Census,
     *Fifteenth Census of the United States: 1930. Agriculture*,
     Government Printing Office, Washington, D. C., 1932.

24.  Hoffsommer, Harold, *Education and Rehabilitation in Alabama
     Farm Households Receiving Relief*, Alabama Polytechnic In-
     stitute, Auburn, Alabama, Bul. No. 7, XXX, July 1935.